MOI /371.9046 /COO

From Inclusion to Engagement

D1388357

MOIBHI
RESOURCE CENTRE
SPECIAL NEEDS

CICE

M04396J0174

From Inclusion to Engagement

Helping Students Engage with Schooling through Policy and Practice

Paul Cooper and Barbara Jacobs

WILEY-BLACKWELL

A John Wiley & Sons, Ltd., Publication

This edition first published 2011
© 2011 John Wiley & Sons Ltd.

Wiley-Blackwell is an imprint of John Wiley & Sons, formed by the merger of Wiley's global Scientific, Technical, and Medical business with Blackwell Publishing.

Registered Office
John Wiley & Sons Ltd, The Atrium, Southern Gate, Chichester, West Sussex, PO19 8SQ, UK

Editorial Offices
The Atrium, Southern Gate, Chichester, West Sussex, PO19 8SQ, UK
9600 Garsington Road, Oxford, OX4 2DQ, UK
350 Main Street, Malden, MA 02148-5020, USA

For details of our global editorial offices, for customer services, and for information about how to apply for permission to reuse the copyright material in this book please see our website at www.wiley.com/wiley-blackwell.

The right of Paul Cooper and Barbara Jacobs to be identified as the author of this work has been asserted in accordance with the UK Copyright, Designs and Patents Act 1988.

All rights reserved. No part of this publication may be reproduced, stored in a retrieval system, or transmitted, in any form or by any means, electronic, mechanical, photocopying, recording or otherwise, except as permitted by the UK Copyright, Designs and Patents Act 1988, without the prior permission of the publisher.

Wiley also publishes its books in a variety of electronic formats. Some content that appears in print may not be available in electronic books.

Designations used by companies to distinguish their products are often claimed as trademarks. All brand names and product names used in this book are trade names, service marks, trademarks or registered trademarks of their respective owners. The publisher is not associated with any product or vendor mentioned in this book. This publication is designed to provide accurate and authoritative information in regard to the subject matter covered. It is sold on the understanding that the publisher is not engaged in rendering professional services. If professional advice or other expert assistance is required, the services of a competent professional should be sought.

Library of Congress Cataloging-in-Publication Data

Cooper, Paul, 1955-
  From inclusion to engagement : helping students engage with schooling through policy and practice / Paul Cooper and Barbara Jacobs.
    p. cm.
  Includes bibliographical references and index.
  ISBN 978-0-470-66484-1 (cloth) – ISBN 978-0-470-01946-7 (pbk.)
1. Inclusive education. 2.   Students with disabilities–Education. I. Jacobs, Barbara, 1945- II. Title.
  LC1200.C665 2011
  371.9'046–dc22

                                                                                    2010035695

A catalogue record for this book is available from the British Library.

Typeset in 10.5/12pt Minion by Aptara Inc., New Delhi, India.
Printed in Singapore by Ho Printing Singapore Pte Ltd

1   2011

Contents

List of Figures and Tables

Figures

Tables

About the Authors

Paul Cooper is Professor of Education at the University of Leicester. He has an international reputation for his work in the field of social, emotional and behavioural difficulties in schools. He has published widely in this area. He was editor of the international quarterly journal *Emotional and Behavioural Difficulties* for 14 years, until 2009. He is currently Co-Chair of the European Network for Social and Emotional Competence in Children, and Co-Editor of *The International Journal of Emotional Education*. In 2001 he was cowinner of the TES/NASEN Special Educational Needs Academic Book Award.

Barbara Jacobs is a professional writer, lecturer, broadcaster and researcher, who has recently completed a late-life PhD on autistic intelligence at the School of Education, University of Leicester.

Preface

Politics, Ideology and Education: Valuing Human Lives

There are arguments in favour of inclusive education which pitch themselves against ideas of labelling and special education (see Clarke *et al.*, 1998). Human beings, it is claimed, are disrespected and humiliated when disability labels are applied to them. Furthermore, it is argued that such disability labels provide a rationale for the creation of educational facilities which are separate from and are inferior to 'mainstream' education. It has been argued that in order to combat these exclusionary effects, the construct of special education should be dismantled along with the categorical thinking that goes with it; to be replaced with a pedagogy for inclusion which emphasizes a functional approach to dealing with barriers to learning that can be applied to all students in mainstream schools (Florian, 2008). Fundamental to this book is the view that such arguments are untenable, misguided and potentially harmful.

The logical inadequacy of such arguments has been demonstrated by Cigman (2007). She describes this type of inclusion argument as 'universalist' on the basis that it assumes that all mainstream neighbourhood schools have the capacity to cater for all students regardless of their needs or characteristics. It should be stated at this point that were there evidence to support the practical feasibility of the universalist view then the authors of this book would subscribe to it, because we share a commitment to the social justice and equity ethics that underpin it. However, as Cigman shows, the universalist argument rests on the unsteady ground of flawed dichotomous thinking and a tendency to ignore or attempt to bypass the need for empirical evidence. It also has the effect of disrespecting views and identities of some of the very people it purports to support. In short the universalist position not only promotes but seeks to impose a view of reality which has little more to sustain it than its proponents' commitment to it.

It is difficult to disagree with Cigman's analysis, which reveals that the universalist arguments are underpinned by the following assumptions:

- that 'special schools, and other non mainstream educational facilities in the late-20th/early-21st century are in principle the same as post-1944 special schools' (Cigman, 2007, p. 778);

- disability labels are 'humiliating in the same sense that in which special schools are institutionally humiliating' *per se* (Cigman, 2007, p. 779);
- disability labels are socially constructed and, therefore, objectively not 'real'; and
- mainstream schools are capable of providing effective education to all students.

It is difficult in a short preface to do justice to the subtlety and rigour of Cigman's argument, but put simply, she draws on recent evidence to suggest that:

- on the basis of first-hand experience, many students and parents find special school and other special provision preferable to mainstream schools (see also Cooper, 1993; Cooper and Tiknaz, 2007);
- disability labels are by no means always *experienced* as stigmatizing by their bearers, some of whom embrace and celebrate such labels as important aspects of their identities, while others use them to as a route to advantages of one kind or another (see also Susman, 1994);
- the objective reality of disability labels is less important to the bearers of the labels than aspects of their lived experience that they believe to be reflected in the label (see also Cooper and Shea, 1998); and
- there can never be a valid and reliable evidence base to the claim that all mainstream schools are capable of providing effective education to all students.

Evidence is the key, and an appraisal of evidence is at the heart of this book. We are particularly concerned with the needs of young people who are deemed to present with what we are calling 'Social, Emotional and Behavioural Difficulties' (SEBD). This is a label. It is neither a precise nor even universally recognized label. However, we see it as having a significant explanatory power when understood in certain ways. A key point here is that whether or not SEBD are 'real' in an objective sense, SEBD are defined by the behavioural and other characteristics of individuals who often find themselves marginalized, stigmatized and rejected in relation to perceptions held about the acceptability of their demeanour. The theoretical understandings which underpin and justify this label, which are explored in this book, give way to a wide range of interventions which we examine and evaluate on the basis of published research evidence.

The issue of labelling is a matter of particular importance in relation to SEBD. People for whom the SEBD label is appropriate will not miraculously cease to be perceived as problematic if the SEBD label is abandoned. On the contrary, they will most often be subject to blame, rejection and, in many cases social exclusion, on the basis of one of two beliefs: (1) that such treatment will encourage the individual to 'mend their ways'; or (2) the idea that bad behaviour equates with being a bad person and bad people should be shunned. Such primitive responses are still common in our schools and the society at large. A central message of this book is that an understanding of SEBD helps to demystify a major source of fear and disquiet, and points the way to effective intervention.

The authors of this book are committed to supporting the rights of all young people to an educational experience which makes available the best opportunities for enhancing their social, emotional and cognitive development. We acknowledge and regret that the presence of a more generously funded private education sector alongside the state funded one reflects inequalities which are endemic in many economically advanced societies. However, we also believe that the absence of economic capital should not restrict the educational choices available to parents and their children.

Ours is not a simply ideological position, it is pragmatic. It is a view based on available research evidence. As this book shows there are many different approaches to meeting the educational needs of students who may experience or be at risk of SEBD, many of these are within the realm of the mainstream school and mainstream teachers. Some of these approaches, however, involve specialist interventions of various kinds, some of which are located in mainstream school settings others of which are not. We take the perspective of the parent and/or student, whose main and immediate concern is to find an educational setting which offers the best opportunities for educational engagement.[1]

Our young people have a short period in which to benefit from the educational opportunities that are made available to them. Although lifelong learning opportunities are perhaps more readily available today than ever before, it is the educational experiences we have between the ages of 4 and 18 which are the most significant for most of us, in terms of their impact on our social and economic life chances. This makes it essential that educational policies and practices in general, and those directed at our most vulnerable students in particular, should be rooted as far as possible in rigorous empirical evidence.

Finally, we need to make reference to what some will see as an ideological element to this book. We subscribe to a bio-psycho-social approach, which we explain in Chapter 1. The bio-psycho-social approach, as we present it, is an attempt to make sense of the reality that we all inhabit today, based on the best available understandings of how human beings develop as social, psychological and biological beings. When there is evidence to support the universalist inclusion position, we will take it seriously. Until then we will continue to seek solutions to the problems faced by rejected and/or disaffected students which are based on a firm evidence base.

Paul Cooper and Barbara Jacobs
The University of Leicester
June 2010

---

[1] We expand on what we mean by 'educational engagement' in Chapter 1.

Acknowledgements

A significant proportion of this book is based on a literature review conducted by the authors for the National Council for Special Education (NCSE) Ireland. The authors were supported in this work by research staff at the NCSE, in particular Dr Jennifer Doran, and Dr Clare Farrell. We also received useful feedback from Dr Mary Byrne, also of NCSE.

In relation to the literature review we received invaluable additional support and critical feedback from a wide range of colleagues. Dr Carmel Cefai (University of Malta) contributed material that formed the basis for the section of 'resilience', as well as critical feedback on successive drafts. Mr Edwin Tanner, a doctoral student at the University of Leicester, provided material that was used as the basis for the section dealing with the management of the physical environment of the classroom. The following people provided critical feedback on successive drafts of the literature review and suggestions for items to be included: Professor Lyndal Bullock (University of North Texas, United States); Professor Helen Cowie (University of Surrey, United Kingdom); Mr Brian De Lord (Pupil and Parent Partnership, United Kingdom); Dr Lesley Hughes, (University of Hull, United Kingdom); Dr Ton Mooij, (Radboud University, The Netherlands); Professor Egide Royer (Laval University, Canada); Dr Ed Smeets (Radboud University, The Netherlands); Dr John Visser (University of Birmingham, United Kingdom); and Mr Martyn Weeds (Pupil and Parent Partnership, United Kingdom). Additional support was provided by Mr Wasyl Cajkler (University of Leicester, United Kingdom).

It should be stressed that these colleagues provided invaluable support for the literature review, but did not contribute to or comment on the arguments concerning the nature of inclusive education and the topic of 'educational engagement'. These aspects, of the book, were not part of the NCSE literature review.

Professor Richard Rose (University of Northampton, United Kingdom) read an early draft of the book, and offered insightful commentary which the authors found extremely helpful.

Acknowledgements

We are extremely grateful to all of these colleagues for their support, without which the book would lack the benefit of such a wide-ranging literature review. However, they cannot be held in any way responsible for any opinions or inaccuracies that the text may contain. These are the sole responsibility of the authors.

Paul Cooper
Barbara Jacobs
University of Leicester
Autumn, 2010

1

Introduction

From Inclusive Education to Educational Engagement – Putting Reality before Rhetoric and Finding the Elephant in the Living Room

Overview

This chapter examines the problematic construct of 'inclusive education' and draws attention to limitations in terms of its ability to offer practical and meaningful insights into how schools should operate in relation to our most vulnerable pupils, and particularly those who are seen to present with social, emotional and behavioural difficulties (SEBD).

The authors go on to establish the concept of 'educational engagement', which is defined in social, emotional and cognitive terms.

It is argued that 'attachment to schooling' is an essential feature of educational engagement and that this can be achieved through the development of teachers' skills and developments in school organization within the context of broader multi-disciplinary initiatives that are devoted to this end.

There is Something Rotten in the State of Inclusive Education

This book starts from the premise that there is something wrong with the current state of inclusive education many other countries of the world. This is noted by Shevlin *et al.* (2008, p. 143), who, with reference to UK OFSTED reports, find that 'despite certain progress (towards inclusion) certain seemingly intractable difficulties remain as barriers to the realization of the inclusion strategy'.

From Inclusion to Engagement: Helping Students Engage with Schooling through Policy and Practice
By Paul Cooper and Barbara Jacobs © 2011 John Wiley & Sons, Ltd

They highlight the point that students with Social, Emotional and Behavioural Difficulties (SEBD) are the most difficult to accommodate in mainstream schools because of the impact of such students on the wider community of students. More generally Barton (2005, p. 5) states, with reference to current United Kingdom context:

'Advocates of inclusion are very aware of the contradictory and competing policy context in which inclusion is located. This has led to the lack of political will on the part of government to unreservedly support inclusion'.

Curcic (2009) provides evidence from a review of inclusive practice in 18 countries that adds to this bleak picture, prefacing the article with the following statement:

In spite of a number of legislative moves, inclusive education has been surrounded by debates for various reasons. First, what is declared in legislation is not necessarily adequately implemented in practice, . . . or evenly within the borders of one country . . . . Second, some debates centre on the very nature of inclusion . . . . Researchers do not uniformly agree on what, in fact, constitutes inclusive practices (Curcic, 2009, p. 517).

To a rational mind this state of affairs beggars belief. How can it be possible for government policies to be made in the name of a concept for which there is no agreed definition? In these circumstances what is the basis for believing that such policies will be successful? Of course, in its most stripped down form, the central principle of inclusive education is the importance of social justice in and equality of access to education. This is entirely in tune with the founding principles of all liberal democratic societies. Serious problems arise, however, when attempts are made to operationalize these principles in a practical educational philosophy and an education system. As we will show in this chapter, current attempts to do this have often been unsuccessful, sometimes to a disastrous degree. We argue that a certain ideological rigidity has made a significant contribution to this failure. Having said this, we also note that educational policy is not made by the proponents of this inclusive ideology. We will also argue, however, that government policies serve powerful interests within any society and that well intentioned but simplistic ideological arguments serve as distractions from the real life problems experienced by pupils, families and staff in schools, and, at their worst, reinforce rather than challenge the status quo.

One of the problems here is that the inadequacies of the policy of so called inclusive education are felt relatively briefly by the promoters and architects of the policy. If a government is perceived to have failed in its management of the economy, that government falls, because even the relatively prosperous see the value of their capital either in decline or under threat of decline. If a government fails in its management of the education system the effects are not immediately obvious to the powerful sections of society whose economic, cultural and political capital, to varying degrees, insulate them from this failure. In fact, it is clear that educational inequality serves the interests of the more prosperous (Sutton Trust, 2010). Furthermore, it is easy to divert attention away from policy issues by appealing to popular prejudices about the competence and motivation of some teachers and the inadequacy of parental contributions to the educational experience of their offspring. Spurious comparisons between high and low performing schools are sometimes used to support these arguments.

The genuinely tragic consequences are, of course, visited on the people who are in greatest need of what it is that inclusive education claims to deliver. These are the vulnerable children and adolescents who depend on the effectiveness of the policy of inclusive education for their educational development. They may experience physical, sensory, cognitive, social, emotional or behavioural difficulties, sometimes in complex combinations. This is, of course, a widely diverse group, expressing different educational needs. The single thing that individuals in this group have in common is that they are perceived to present significant challenges which go beyond those that 'mainstream' teachers and schools are usually equipped to meet. They require accommodations and specific additional resources in order to engage effectively with formal educational experiences. These accommodations and resources are central to policies of inclusive education. When they are applied effectively, they enable. When their application is ineffective, they disable. Educational failure follows, often coupled with negative emotional and, sometimes, social consequences. The legacy of educational failure in the school years can be devastating in terms of the wastage of human talent and a lifetime of unfulfilled potential.

This sense of deep concern is reflected in the perceptions of another very important group of people who are directly affected by the policy of inclusive education – teachers:

> It is no surprise that teachers, whatever their beliefs about inclusive education, find coping with special needs in mainstream classrooms difficult without additional training and classroom support . . . Growing numbers of special needs are behaviour-related. At the same time, teachers feel under increasing pressure to achieve academic results at all costs in a curriculum which makes few concessions to what one current television programme calls 'the unteachables' (T.E.S., 2005).

The central point here is a challenge to the viability of inclusive education as it is currently practiced. The image created portrays the mainstream classroom teacher struggling to accommodate the needs of vulnerable students whose behaviour, as a consequence of their teachers' ill-preparedness, deteriorates, adding to the teachers' difficulties. In turn, the teachers are called to account not only for their failure to prevent misbehaviour from occurring, but for the concomitant impact that students with learning difficulties of various kinds (some of whom are disengaged from and antagonistic towards education) have on overall performance outcomes in national tests and public examinations. The tone of the quotation is one of righteous indignation at this situation, which is seen as being unjust for teachers, students with special needs and, ultimately, all students in such settings.

The theme of the injustices of inclusive education is taken up by another journalist in the same paper who declares 'Children with special needs are 24 times more likely to be segregated at school if they live in parts of North East England than they are in London's East End' (Lepkowska, 2005).

The article is based on statistics collected by the Centre for Inclusive Education (CSIE) and bears a quotation from its director, who describes these inequalities in the system as 'unfair and unjust'. This time the indignation is directed at continued use of segregated forms of provision (e.g., special schools and other non-mainstream placements) in certain parts of the country. The implication being that students who are placed in such settings are necessarily disadvantaged compared to their peers in mainstream schools. This assumption seems to be at odds with the findings from an empirical study carried out Macbeath *et al.* (2006), which is discussed in detail below.

Although these two positions are very different, they have two things in common. The first of which is a deep concern about the *state* of inclusive education in the United Kingdom. The second commonality is that they see students suffering as a result of a failure to implement inclusive practice effectively. Where they differ is in what they appear to mean by 'effective implementation'. The viewpoint of the second article is the most straightforward, in that it suggests that the effectiveness of the inclusive education project can be measured by the *location* of the student with SEN. It is implied that those who are in mainstream schools are, by definition, included, while those in segregated provision are not included. The first writer, on the other hand, is much more preoccupied with the quality of what is going in the mainstream setting. The claim made by this writer is that there are serious problems being created in mainstream school classrooms as a result of inadequate training of teachers, under-resourcing and, perhaps most worrying of all, an inadequate conceptual basis for the notion of 'inclusive education' which contributes to incoherence in government education policy. This, in turn, forces some teachers into a situation of confusion borne out of the dissonance they experience on a daily basis between the blatant inequalities of market driven education systems and an espoused social justice agenda associated with inclusive education.

This situation is illustrated well by a study of 21 English schools (10 first, middle and primary; 9 secondary and 2 special) where staff were committed to an inclusive education agenda (MacBeath *et al.*, 2006). They found a disastrous confection of 'good intentions' (p. 81), inadequate staff training and resources, competing agendas that, they argue, contribute to a rising tide of social, emotional and behavioural difficulties which, in turn, create additional demands that school teaching and support staff are ill-equipped to meet. The result is an unsatisfactory educational experience for staff and pupils in general. However, the remarkable claim that well intentioned efforts to promote inclusive education lead to an increase in social, emotional and behavioural difficulties has to be scrutinized. Because, if this is so, it suggests that the ill-defined notion of inclusive education may, in some respects, be responsible for more harm than good.

Why is Inclusive Education Going Wrong?

Before considering the findings of this study in more detail, it is important to stress that MacBeath *et al.* (2006) did not select their schools at random, rather they focused on schools which showed evidence of commitment to inclusive education practice:

> we deliberately set out to select schools that had made a commitment to implementing a policy of inclusion rather than selecting some schools that were not so involved. Our aim was to review current practice in favourable circumstances and not attempt to portray what was happening across the entire range. Where our research identifies problems and difficulties for children with learning difficulties, these issues are likely to be exacerbated elsewhere within the education system in schools where inclusion is given a lower priority (MacBeath *et al.*, 2006, p. 10).

These initial observations are borne out in the findings of the study which indicate that:

> In general teachers are positive towards the principle of inclusion.
>
> Teachers saw potential benefits in terms of widening all pupils' understandings of diversity and developing improved tolerance levels. However, deep concerns were aired about the challenges posed by students with 'complex emotional and behavioural needs' (p. 60) and how such difficulties affected the ability of staff to provide 'a suitable education' (p. 60) for these pupils. Furthermore, concerns were expressed about the capacity of mainstream schools to meet the social, emotional and educational needs of 'children with [other] complex needs' (p. 60).

The researchers note the tendency of pupils with SEN to be located in schools with high levels of social disadvantage, particularly those located in urban (as opposed to rural) areas, where 'parental choice' is made a realistic option owing to the availability of more than one school within reasonable travelling distance. The general point being made here can be verified by the reader through a brief perusal of league table figures for GCSE results in England, which show that, year on year, schools in deprived urban areas tend to have much higher levels of SEN and poorer outcomes at GSCE than those at the top of the league tables.

The central problem identified by MacBeath *et al.* (2006) is a lack of training and expertise in mainstream schools. In this study mainstream teachers were often found, by their own accounts, to lack necessary specialist skills for dealing with complex needs. This has to be seen in the context of limited opportunities for training in these areas, both in Initial Teacher Training and in Continual Professional Development. This problem was seen as being so significant that respondents described parents as sometimes knowing more than teachers about certain learning needs and being called on to 'train' school staff. It is important, of course, to commend school staff for being open to parents and consultative in seeking insights into students' learning needs. Teacher–parent collaboration is an important and neglected resource that is likely to benefit all students (Jones, 1995). However, the idea that parenthood is a sufficient qualification to be a teacher trainer is alarming for both teachers and parents. This begs the obvious question: can it be defensible for teachers and vulnerable students to be placed in circumstances where access to important pedagogical knowledge and skills is not routinely available from valid and reliable sources? Macbeath and colleagues' (2006) answer to this question is a resounding no.

In their study the consequences for students who experience such poor provision is a tendency to be involved in multiple school moves, a situation that was found to be all the more likely when social, emotional and or behavioural problems were implicated. This point bears comparison with research which has shown a relationship between frequent school moves, SEBD and exclusion (Hayden, 1997). It draws attention to the fact that while SEBD may sometimes, or even often, have their origins in social and other problems that occur outside of classrooms and schools, they can be (and often are) exacerbated and magnified by what takes place within classrooms and schools. Exclusion from school, be it formal or informal, is always an admission of a school's failure to meet the needs of the excluded. After all, the minimum purpose of schooling must be to promote positive social and educational engagement within a particular setting, meaning that the students have to be at the very least present in that setting. Clearly, such failure is not always the *fault* of the school, which, in the absence of appropriate expertise and/or resources, may opt for exclusion as a last resort in the interests of the wider school population. From the excludee's point of view, however, he or she has been failed, socially and educationally. This experience repeated time and again can only engender or exacerbate existing feelings of alienation from schools and schooling.

It is important to stress at this point that schools cannot avoid the admission of failure simply by keeping students on their premises whose social and educational needs they lack the resources to meet. Ironically, the promotion of the delusion that being present in a school equates with being socially and educationally included, is one of the most dishonest and insidious form of exclusion. Schools should never *pretend* to be able to cater for a student's needs, regardless of their falling rolls or other market force imperatives. Social justice and market forces are not compatible.

Ideals and ideology

There is a longstanding educational truism that 'education cannot compensate for society' (Bernstein, 1966). This observation has several penetrating and complex meanings, one of which is that, regardless of the rhetoric espoused by governments of whatever persuasion, education systems tend to reflect the inequalities and injustices that favour the most powerful and (by definition) privileged interest groups within the societies they serve. An education system is one of the tools employed by a society to sustain and reproduce itself. Commentators (and governments) claiming to be committed to social justice in education cannot be taken seriously if they fail to address the broader context of inequality in society. Yet, the political myopia of some proponents of inclusive education, who advocate the enrolment of students with special educational needs in local schools which may or may not be successful or effective, is staggering.

There are always competing value systems within cultures and societies. In contemporary Western cultures there is a continual struggle between a form of idealistic liberalism, which emphasizes the importance of collectivist values, equality among people and social justice, and an individualistic conservatism which portrays social inequality as a natural consequence of economic and social progress. The historically espoused role of the education systems in liberal democracies has been to serve the workforce needs of the society and to reinforce and cultivate what are perceived to be the best qualities within the prevailing culture. In the United Kingdom, for example, the expansion of educational provision has often been portrayed in terms of increasing equality of opportunity. Additionally, it has to be said, the accumulated evidence from 130 years of state funded education in the United Kingdom reveals the clear positive relationship between levels of educational achievement, good health, life expectancy and economic well-being.

However, recent evidence (Sutton Trust, 2008) points to a general slow-down in upward social mobility in both the United States and United Kingdom at the beginning of the twenty-first century. This has to be seen in the context of the strong association between social class and educational attainment as one of the few truly dependable findings to come out of social scientific research time and time again over the past 100 years or so. Children who come from socially deprived backgrounds are at much greater risk of educational failure than children who come from privileged backgrounds. In the United States, for example, one study found that in 1979 individuals from families in the top 25% of earners were four times more likely to successfully complete a four-year college degree programme than individuals from the bottom 25%. Disturbingly, they found that by 1994 the disparity had increased from 4 times, to 10 times (Educational Testing Service, 2005). In the United Kingdom similar concerns have been noted by the DfES (2004). There is a further association between educational failure and social, emotional and behavioural difficulties, as well as an association between social, emotional and behavioural problems and social disadvantage (Shneiders *et al.*, 2003). Of particular concern in the United Kingdom is the widening social gap between those who gain access to the most prestigious and well remunerated professions and those who do not. Research carried out by the Centre for Market and Public Organisation (Macmillan, 2009) shows that net family income is a far stronger predictor of gaining entry into the top professions (such as medicine, the law, banking and journalism) for people who were born in 1970 than it was for those who were born in 1958. This finding is contrasted with a general decline in the difference between the assessed IQ levels of professionals and those of the general population between these two birth cohorts. These outcomes point to the inevitable conclusion that family background plays a far greater role in occupational success than merit alone. The point is strengthened further when the link between progression to the highest levels within the top professions and attendance at prestigious universities is related to the fact that approximately 50% of the undergraduate places at Oxford and Cambridge Universities are taken up by students from the 7% of the general population who have attended fee paying schools. Furthermore it is depressing to note that in the twenty-first century one in three members of the UK's House of Commons benefited from a privately funded education (Macmillan, 2009).

In an unequal and competitive society it is not surprising that, in spite of some of the rhetoric surrounding inclusive education, there is an impulse among many members of our society to be less concerned with the extension of equality of opportunity than there is with the quest for personal advantage. This is reflected in the perennial concerns that have been expressed on BBC news reports in the United Kingdom about the fraudulent lengths that some parents will go to in order to gain a place for their child at their preferred school. This point has been underlined by a MORI poll (Cassidy, 2008) which identified the increasing popularity of independent schools among parents. In 2008 54% of adults thought independent schools offered higher educational standards than state schools; 57% stated that they would select independent education if they could afford it, and of those who would select an independent school 66% said it was because they believed them to offer better educational standards and 30% thought they demonstrated better behavioural standards.

This situation is problematic in itself, not least because it appears to intensify the plight of the most vulnerable families and students, who are at ever increasing risk of being left behind as the culture becomes ever more competitive and individualistic. This is already happening to those students who attend neighbourhood schools which are deemed to be 'failing', where parents with the most cultural and economic capital migrate, by one means or another, to schools occupying places higher up the league tables (Sutton Trust, 2010). Meanwhile, for reasons already discussed, the most vulnerable are left in large concentrations in schools lacking the expertise and resources to meet their needs.

An even more distressing feature here is the lack of connection between the recognition of this picture of growing social inequality, and measures which are being taken to cater for the most extremely disadvantaged students in our schools. This is not simply an issue affecting inclusion in the United Kingdom. A recent international literature review (Curcic, 2009) referred to above, found a pattern of muddled thinking, ill-informed practice and some situations in which the most vulnerable students were clearly disadvantaged by the failings of ill-judged and poorly implemented policies.

A central problem appears to the role of ideology in the inclusive education agenda. Although there are sometimes wide variations in the ways in which inclusion is operationally defined – from the insistence that all students should be educated in mainstream classes to the idea that specialist provision can form part of an inclusive continuum – there is a common attachment to the broad principle that inclusive education is concerned with the identification and removal of barriers to participation in mainstream educational settings. For many commentators this endeavour is a matter of human and civil rights; a challenge to 'discrimination and exclusion' (Barton, 2005, p. 6) that equates with some of the great emancipatory movements of history, such as those concerned with the abolition of slavery and the women's suffrage movement (Thomas and Vaughan, 2006).

There is clearly an historical basis for this position reflected in the discriminatory practices directed at individuals who were deemed 'handicapped'. The worst of these practices saw the forcible sterilization of the so called 'mentally subnormal' in some US states in the early twentieth century. The eugenics movement, which sought to justify such practices, promoted spurious theories claiming genetically based differences in cognitive abilities that rendered certain racial groups cognitively superior to others (Karier, 1976). Such arguments were used to justify social and economic inequalities between racial groups (Jensen, 1969). Sadly, such primitive thinking is not entirely a thing of the distant past. These views were reiterated in the 1990s in a widely read book by American academics Herrnstein and Murray (1994). It should be stressed that this book was widely dismissed on scientific grounds by informed readers. However, the case serves to illustrate the continued presence of discriminatory attitudes in Western cultures, vividly illustrated in the United Kingdom by the election to the European parliament of a candidate standing for the British National Party, an organization which openly promotes racial discrimination and eugenicist theories of racial purity.

These are important cultural trends which we ignore at our peril and which education systems in liberal democracies must challenge. It has been noted for example, that the United Kingdom 1945 health and handicapped pupils' regulations (Ministry of Health, 1945) effectively created a system for educating the minority of pupils who were deemed 'handicapped' which was separate from the system which was intended for the majority of 'non-handicapped' pupils. This special system was established under the auspices of the Ministry of Health as opposed to Ministry of Education which took care of the education of the latter group. It is also important to note that while the right to free education for 'all children' up to the age of 14 (later 15) was established in the 1944 Education Act, children who were classified as 'uneducable', under the 1945 regulations, were excluded from this entitlement. It was not until the Education Act of 1971 that this group (comprising of some 30 000 children) was finally permitted this entitlement, under the designation of 'Severe Learning Difficulties'.

Portrayed in this way, this is a shameful history that amounts to systematic discrimination against 'handicapped' pupils, whereby they were, to differing degrees, excluded from educational provision that was deemed to be the birthright of the non-handicapped. It would be a mistake, however, to read into this history a malignant political ideology, such as that which sustained the eugenics movement and continues to give rise to racist and other discriminatory impulses in human societies. As Tomlinson (1982) has argued, the historical origins of special education in Britain cannot be divorced from a 'powerful ideology of benevolent humanitarianism' (p. 26) which is reflected in the motivations of Victorian philanthropists, such as Dr Barnardo. This is not to say that special education can be understood entirely through this lens. As we have noted already, education cannot compensate for society; it can only serve it. Tomlinson (1982) seems to concur with this view when she observes that:

> education systems and their parts do not develop spontaneously . . . and they do not develop out of purely humanitarian motives. They develop because it is in the interests of particular groups in society that they should develop, and that they should develop in certain ways (p. 27).

She persuasively argues that chief among the social motivators behind the development of special education were economic interests, illustrated by the fact that the earliest schools for children with physical and sensory disabilities were focused on the development of trade skills (Tomlinson, 1982). Social control is another political motivator, most evident in the origins of schools for the socially 'maladjusted' (a precursor of what we now often referred to a Social, Emotional and Behavioural Difficulties) which have been linked with widespread concerns about the disruptive behaviour of inner city children who, during World War II, had been evacuated to quiet, rural communities (Bridgeland, 1971).

This argument suggests that the 'ideology of benevolent humanitarianism', referred to by Tomlinson, was exploited in the interests of political expediency. There is clearly some merit to this point of view. However, this ignores the unanticipated consequences of creating an often state funded alternative education system which, in some cases, attracted educators who were dissatisfied with the constraints of the main state funded system and exploited their marginal status as an opportunity to pioneer radical and progressive educational approaches. Some of the most striking examples of this are provided by twentieth century educators who ran residential schools and communities for 'maladjusted, pupils' the most unwelcome and maligned group of students (Bridgeland, 1971). We will return to the work of these 'pioneers' in the next chapter. For the purposes of the current discussion it is only necessary to state that from early in the twentieth century some of these schools were experimenting with what we would now call student centred approaches, including democratic organizational structures (e.g., Shaw, 1965; Wills, 1960). The distinctive features of these approaches was a respect for students as persons and a commitment to developing social and emotional competencies through the provision of caring and supportive relationships and the teaching of academic and life skills (Bridgeland, 1971; Cooper, 1993). Such approaches were seen as being in stark contrast to the rigid authoritarianism which typified standard educational provision (Bridgeland, 1971), where discipline was enforced with legally sanctioned corporal punishment until the 1970s, and where negative, punitive approaches to SEBD were still widely used.

This is not an argument in favour of segregation. The point being made here is that in an unequal society, where the possessors of the greatest share of economic and cultural capital are disproportionately rewarded by the education system at the expense of the most vulnerable, there are ways of exploiting and subverting this grim status quo to the benefit of the marginalized. The wholesale dismissal of nonmainstream educational provision is an act of extreme ignorance, as is the failure to acknowledge some of the achievements of this sector. Worse, this ignorance feeds the very processes of discrimination and marginalization that such views are claimed to challenge. This last point can be illustrated with reference to some of the debate surrounding the phenomenon of Attention Deficit/Hyperactivity Disorder (ADHD), which is one of the most commonly diagnosed of the behavioural disorders.

The Limitations of the Social Model of SEN: The Case of ADHD

ADHD has been dismissed by some commentators as a medical construct that individualizes educational failure and disruptive behaviour (e.g., Lloyd and Norris, 1999; Skidmore, 2004; Slee, 1995; Travell and Visser, 2006). The effect of such individualization, it is argued, is to distract attention from the roles that schools and teachers may play (wittingly or unwittingly) in the construction of learning and behavioural problems, and allow educators to absolve themselves of their responsibility to provide appropriate educational opportunities to certain groups. This is, in essence, the core of the social model of disability, initially proposed by writers such as Barton (2005) which emphasizes the role of social construction in SEN.

This negative reaction is based on a number of erroneous assumptions. The first is that we have to choose between bio-medical and environmental explanations for learning difficulties because they are incompatible. This is expressed in an extreme form by Slee (1995) who complains that 'The monism of locating the nature of [classroom] disruption in the neurological infrastructure of the child is myopic and convenient' (p. 74).

Visser (1997) expressed a similar view 'Rejection of the ADHD label by educationalists is precisely because it offers a view of behaviour which is "nature" without "nurture"' (p. 15).

More recently, Skidmore (2004, pp. 3–4), although attempting to offer a faintly conciliatory nod towards what he terms the 'psycho-medical paradigm', recycles the same false oppositions:

Given its long historical roots, and the undoubted existence of such psychological and medical conditions [as Down's syndrome and autism], it is likely that research into learning difficulties in the psycho-medical paradigm will continue to be conducted, that it will continue to exert an influence on the wider field, and that some of its findings will be found to be of use in the education of pupils who are affected by conditions which are generally recognised to have an organic basis. The difficulty arises when illicit attempts are made to apply this framework to an infinitely-extensible set of putative syndromes or disorders for which reliable evidence of a neurological or organic base is lacking, and where 'diagnosis' rests on value laden, culturally-specific judgements about behavioural or cognitive norms. In the case of ADD [sic] it is arguable that the scientistic discourse of positivism and the rhetorical stance of authoritative objectivity which it engenders have been deployed to disseminate a biological determinist hypothesis for which empirical evidence is wanting, and to legitimise the practice of drugging defiant children into docility, using stimulants whose long-term side effects are unknown, in the service of a tacit project of social control.

These views reflect longstanding suspicion among some British educationists and educational psychologists of explanations of emotional and behavioural difficulties that cite biological factors as possible causes (e.g., Boreham *et al.*, 1995). The distaste for biological determinism is understandable when we consider the horrors of the eugenics movement which marred the early twentieth century in Europe and America (see above). To extend this distaste to ADHD, however, on the grounds that it represents a modern manifestation of an outdated, politically driven and discredited pseudo-science is simply wrong-headed. This view, at best, reflects a profound ignorance of modern understandings of (a) the relationship between biological and environmental factors in human development, and (b) of the scientific and educational literature on ADHD. At its worst, this portrayal of ADHD reflects a wilful misrepresentation of the topic that is likely to hinder the development and dissemination of well informed and effective educational interventions that will benefit many school students directly, and influence the development of educational knowledge practice in ways that will benefit all students.

   It is now necessary to highlight and address the flaws in the arguments presented by Skidmore and others.

Dealing with Challenges to the Validity of ADHD Diagnosis

First, it is claimed that the ADHD diagnosis is somehow bogus or 'illicit' because there is an absence of neuro-scientific evidence. This is patently untrue. As noted above, there is wealth of evidence from many studies over many years which points to:

- consistency in patterns of symptoms associated with specific clinical impairments of inattentiveness, hyperactivity and impulsiveness;
- genetic pathways being implicated in the distribution of the condition; and
- neuro-imaging studies which reveal specific differences between individuals diagnosed with ADHD and those who are not (Sharkey and Fitzgerald, 2007; Tannock, 1998).

The earliest clinical accounts of what we now refer to as ADHD are to be found at the end of the eighteenth century in the writing of a physician named Alexander Crichton (Palmer and Finger, 2001) and a paper by George Still, which appeared in *the Lancet* in the early 1900s is often cited as an early source (e.g., Barkley, 1997). It was during World War I, as a result of opportunities to study extensive numbers of live individuals with serious head injuries, that consistent links were first observed between some of the symptoms of what is now termed ADHD and damage to the frontal cortex of the brain (Barkley, 1997). It was not, however, until the late twentieth century and the advent of advanced brain imaging technology that it became possible to study the functioning of the living human brain in greater detail. This ongoing research continues to produce findings that enrich our understanding of the relationship between cognitive and neurological functioning (e.g., Kelly *et al.*, 2007). In addition to these sources, both twin studies and advanced molecular genetic studies have produced a wealth of data pointing to specific genetic correlates of ADHD (Fitzgerald *et al.*, 2007; Levy and Hay, 2001).

Second, it is claimed that ADHD is an example of biological determinism. The fear of biological determinism is well founded, partly because it denies the importance of human agency (Rose, 2004) and leads, in some cases to an ill-founded sense of fatalism in relation to the developmental opportunities available to some individuals. Having said this, there is, at the time of writing, no definitive account of the biological underpinnings of ADHD. This is hardly surprising; not least because of the complexity of the biological and psychological systems that are implicated. The same would have to be said of other complex conditions, such as Autistic Spectrum Disorders. Another, possibly more significant reason for the lack of a definitive biological cause, is that there may not be one. Not only are there numerous biological pathways implicated in the development of ADHD (Barkley, 1997), but it is also almost certainly the case that ADHD is not biologically determined in the simplistic sense suggested by Skidmore and others. On the contrary, as we have indicated, ADHD is widely argued to be the product of a complex interaction between biological and social-environmental factors.

This argument is consistent with current and recent models of gene-environment interaction, such as that presented by Plomin (1990) and, in relation to developmental disorders, (Frith, 1992). An adaptation of Frith's model of this interaction is represented in Figure 1.1. The model shows that biologically inherited factors (i.e., Genetic endowments) are, from their inception, in constant dynamic interaction with environmental factors. Gene-environment interaction leads to the development of certain patterns in brain architecture (e.g., lobe development) and functioning (e.g., the neurotransmitter systems), which in turn lead to the development of certain cognitive characteristics (e.g., the efficiency of the executive functions, such as those concerned with self talk and working memory). However, the extent to which and the ways in which these cognitive characteristics contribute to presenting behaviours that are functional or dysfunctional is heavily influenced by the environment and experience. For example, an individual who is prone to memory problems can learn mnemonic strategies which help to compensate for the difficulties. Furthermore, positive, affirming relationships with others may encourage the individual to develop a high level of motivation, which they can deploy in attempting to overcome aspects of their functioning which are potentially problematic in social situations. On the other hand, social and cultural differences will influence the judgements that observers make about the behaviours.

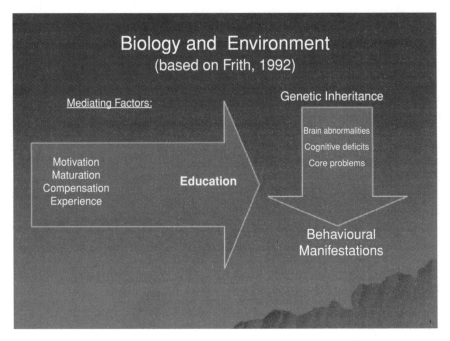

Figure 1.1   The interaction between biological inheritance and environmental factors in the development of behavioural difficulties (based on Frith, 1992).

The essence of this bio-psycho-social approach, therefore, is that while a behavioural disorder such as ADHD is associated with certain neurological and genetic patterns, these patterns do not determine the existence of the disorder. It is likely that there are people who possess the frontal lobe dysfunctions and genes associated with ADHD who do not develop the disorder. The disorder is only triggered when these biological characteristics interact with environmental factors which render the cognitive patterns that flow from the biological make up dysfunctional. Environmental settings which place a high premium on self regulation, sedentary behaviour, passive as opposed to active approaches to learning, and social conformity over individualism, will render the cognitive characteristics associated with ADHD problematic. This helps to explain why ADHD is most strongly associated with the school years, where successful studenthood often equates with obedience and conformity. In the adult world, however, where there is a wider range of opportunities for more individualistic forms of expression, the very characteristics which are rendered dysfunctional in many (if not most) schools and lead to a diagnosis of ADHD, can be reframed in positive terms. The disobedient, erratic and uncontrollable school student becomes (for example) the spontaneous, irreverent, iconoclastic adult, who is praised for his or her individualistic take on life. Prominent contemporary examples might be the actor Jim Carey and the comedian Billy Connolly (Stevenson, 2001). Less exotic examples are to be found in all walks of life: such as those writers, journalists, teachers, barstaff, taxi drivers and party goers who were branded as school failures but who, in adulthood, achieve acceptance and even admiration for the very characteristics that were problematic in their school years.

The key implication of this bio-psycho-social perspective for education is that the more we understand about the biological and psychological correlates of ADHD (and similar conditions), the better placed we will be to provide educational environments that avoid exacerbating difficulties that children may experience and that promote their optimum educational engagement (see below).

It has been argued here that while biological inheritance plays an important role in the development of the characteristics that are associated with ADHD, whether or not these characteristics lead to problems in the school setting that affect the educational and social engagement of the student is largely determined by characteristics of the school environment. Arguments, such as that posed by Skidmore (see above), that portray ADHD as an example of biological determinism simply divert attention from the important process of converting a bio-psycho-social account of ADHD into pedagogical and other interventions. Yet it is pedagogical skills which, according to research by MacBeath *et al.* (2006) and Blatchford *et al.* (2009) referred to above, that are most desperately needed by teachers and teaching assistants.

Third, the ADHD 'diagnosis' rests on value laden, culturally-specific judgements about behavioural or cognitive norms. This criticism combines paradoxical characteristics of self-evident truth and absurdity. It is self evidently true that all judgements about the appropriateness or inappropriateness of behaviour or cognitive expression are socially and culturally based. Culture reflects the values, attitudes and beliefs of a social group, and as such, it helps to hold the group together. On the other hand it is absurd to imply that it is possible for human beings to adopt a culture free stance. Having said this, there are situations where cultural values and assumptions serve to disadvantage members of the social group and require adjustment. The ADHD diagnostic criteria, when considered through a bio-psycho-socially informed educational perspective, offers a case in point.

An important point to observe about the ADHD diagnostic criteria is that it harbours taken for granted assumptions about the kinds of pupil behaviours that are to be expected in properly functioning *classrooms*. These assumptions include the idea that pupils from an early age are expected to internalize and behave in accordance with a set of rules that derive from constraints imposed by a teacher-centred and curriculum focused method of teaching pupils in age related groups. Teacher–pupil ratios create potential problems of social disorder which are met with rules of conduct designed to regulate pupil movement around the classroom and interactions between peers. Externally imposed curricula, as opposed to negotiated curricula, assuming a tight relationship between pupil age and cognitive functioning, tend to be managed by teachers in ways that require pupils to follow a lineal programme of tasks at predetermined times and within strict time limits. It follows from this that teachers often fulfil the role of 'instructors', providing an estimated 80% of the talk that goes on in classrooms (Sage, 2002). Pupils, therefore, are required to be expert in following complex instructions and internalizing behavioural and cognitive routines that, in turn, are intended to establish patterns of self-regulation that become increasingly important as pupils pass through the higher realms of the curriculum and schooling process. It has long been noted that this factory model of education is by no means the only, or even the most desirable model of schooling. At its worst it rewards conformity and passivity at the expense of intellectual curiosity, critical debate and creativity (Silberman, 1971). At its best it favours pupils whose cognitive styles favour systematic reflection and abstract lineal thinking. Schools, of course, have always made these kinds of demands. However, it can be argued that there has developed an increasing discontinuity between the demands of school, in these respects, and the behavioural expectations and activities that pupils commonly experience outside of schools. This makes schooling a problematic experience for many contemporary pupils and provides a major, relatively new source of stress to pupils with attention and activity problems.

In other words, children who are biologically predisposed to develop ADHD are disadvantaged by culturally based assumptions about what appropriate behaviour in schools and classrooms looks like. This is not the fault of the clinicians who drafted the criteria, on the contrary, the ubiquity and persistence of ADHD and its diagnostic forerunners and equivalents reflects, unintentionally, but accurately, one of the most persistent criticisms of Western mass education, namely that it stresses rigid authoritarian values and is relatively unresponsive to individual differences and needs. It follows from this line of argument that schools and teachers (and, indeed, academics and policy makers) who wish to make our schools and other educational facilities more inclusive should be learning from the lesson that ADHD (for example) teaches us about how we might shape the educational environment in order to improve access to learning opportunities. If implemented, pedagogical and organizational interventions based on an understanding of ADHD will not irradicate ADHD, but they are likely to reduce the negative educational implications associated with it.

Importantly, a bio-psycho-social perspective draws a stark picture of the major alternatives facing educators when confronted with students who experience difficulties in engaging effectively in schools: we can either strive to change the educational environment to accommodate the student, or we can attempt to change the student to enable him or her to engage with an unchanging environment. Clearly, in the real world we may often attempt to combine environmental and individual changes. Nevertheless, the use of medication is often best understood as a reflection of the failure of the school to make changes that enable the student with ADHD to engage effectively. This is not the fault of the ADHD diagnosis itself, on the contrary, an understanding of the ADHD diagnosis from a bio-psycho-social perspective can be used to inform the development of effective educational practice that will in some circumstances preclude the need for medication.

Fourth, acceptance of the ADHD diagnosis 'legitimise[s] the practice of drugging defiant children into docility, using stimulants whose long-term side effects are unknown, in the service of a tacit project of social control' (Skidmore, 2004, p. 4). This is perhaps the most insidious and ill founded of all the arguments that are posed against the ADHD construct, not least because its acceptance produces the very result that its proponents claim to abhor, namely the overuse of stimulant medication. This is because the failure to admit the validity of ADHD creates a major obstacle to the development of educational interventions for the condition, leaving diagnosed individuals in a situation in which the only source of informed intervention is the medical practitioner. In circumstances where the school is unwilling to cooperate with medics the likelihood will be that medication will be employed to enable the child to adapt to an unyielding and unresponsive school environment.

In order to avoid this highly negative scenario it is essential to stress the point that informed opinion on the matter argues strongly that medication for ADHD is by no means an essential treatment, and that when prescribed it should always be within the context of a multi-modal treatment programme that includes psycho-social and educational interventions (Barkley, 1997; Maras and Cooper, 2000; National Institute of Health and Clinical Excellence, 2000). Furthermore, it is argued by some authorities that psycho-social and educational interventions should be the first choice of intervention (e.g., BPS, 2000).

A key feature of the latter approach is that it tends to 'reframe' ADHD as a particular cognitive style, rather than a 'deficit' (Cooper and Ideus, 1996; Cooper and O'Regan, 2001). It involves pedagogical strategies designed to exploit, rather than inhibit, some of the characteristics associated with ADHD (DuPaul and Stoner, 1995; Purdie *et al.*, 2002; Zentall, 1995). Zentall (1995), for example, describes strategies designed to increase the active participation of students with ADHD though the provision of visual motor-tasks. A study by Zentall and Meyer (1987) found that such strategies were associated with improved performance and behaviour of pupils with ADHD when compared with their performance on tasks requiring more passive engagement of students. Evidence from studies reviewed by DuPaul and Stoner (1995) supports this view, showing that pupils with ADHD respond well to feedback and reinforcement from teachers when the frequency of these interventions is greater than it is for eliciting desired engagement and responses from 'regular' students. Interventions based on the belief that students with ADHD tend to have an active ('kinaesthetic') learning style have been shown to increase levels of attention to task in pupils with ADHD and reduce disruptive and impulsive behaviours (Hinshaw *et al.*, 1984). Related to this is the insight that pupils with ADHD are particularly prone to the negative consequences of 'recess deprivation' (Zentall, 1995). Zentall and Smith (1992) found that pupils with ADHD self-reported a greater preference for frequent physical activity than pupils without ADHD. Pellegrini and Horvat (1995) found that levels of disruptive behaviour decreased and levels of on-task behaviour increased when periods of 'seatwork' were punctuated by frequent periods in which students were required to engage in structured physical activity. This implies that the redistribution of such time throughout the day at regular intervals will produce positive outcomes.

A major classroom problem associated with ADHD is the tendency of affected pupils to be talkative at inappropriate times. This 'problem' can be exploited for pedagogical purposes by the teacher increasing opportunities for on-task verbal participation by pupils (Zentall, 1995). Studies have found that pupils with ADHD perform better on reading comprehension tasks when they are required to read comprehension passages aloud, rather than silently (Dubey and O'Leary, 1975). Also, the tendency of pupils with ADHD to dominate verbal interactions with peers can be modified by training them to use questioning techniques rather than assertion (Zentall, 1995). Zentall found that this technique works best when combined with social skills training. Zentall (1995), drawing on empirical evidence provided by Rosenfeld and colleagues, suggests that seating pupils in a semi-circle around the teacher, or in small groups produces more on-task verbal participation by pupils with ADHD and more appropriate hand raising behaviours during whole class teaching episodes. Furthermore, there is evidence to support the conclusion that reducing the teacher–pupil ratio, in situations involving teacher–group verbal interaction, improves the quality of engagement of pupils with ADHD. This effect is enhanced when teachers provide behavioural models for active listening strategies (Carter and Schostak, 1980).

The twin pedagogical strategies of behavioural modelling and teacher-direction are strongly associated with a reduction in pupil inattentiveness and impulsiveness in the classroom and positive academic outcomes. These effects are most powerful when teacher direction involves clear and distinct information about performance, behavioural expectations, and expected outcomes. Optimal pupil performance is associated with brevity and clarity of sequences of instruction, the accompaniment of verbal instructions with visual cues and the availability of resources that pupils can refer to for reminders of direction and expectations (DuPaul and Stoner, 1995; Zentall, 1995). The use of pupils as behavioural and academic models through the careful programming of interaction between the pupil with ADHD and preferred role models is also found to be an effective pedagogical tool. It is important though that the opportunities for disruption created by such pupil interaction are controlled by the teacher's use of positive reinforcement for task appropriate and socially desirable behaviour (Zentall, 1995). In accordance with these findings Cooper and O'Regan (2001) provide case study material indicating that pupils with ADHD can benefit from taking on the role of peer tutors with younger, less competent pupils.

In a classroom environment in which extraneous stimuli such as irrelevant noise and other distractors are limited, and where pedagogical strategies of the type described above are in use, opportunities are created to enable the pupil with ADHD to practice self-pacing. Self-pacing, as opposed to external (i.e., teacher directed) pacing is associated with greater accuracy (Zentall, 1995) and pupil self-reported satisfaction (Cooper and Shea, 1999) with learning tasks. This can usefully extend to providing pupils with ADHD with opportunities to remove themselves from classroom situations which they find stressful to a pre-determined quiet area (Zentall, 1995; DuPaul and Stoner, 1995).

In a meta analysis of interventions for ADHD, Purdie *et al.* (2002) found that, in comparison with clinic based interventions, educational interventions, of the type describe above, were most effective in promoting positive cognitive outcomes (defined in terms of non-specified academic performance, language and reading skills, mathematical skills, IQ and memory functions). Although the overall mean effect size was small (.28), it was concluded that educational interventions were the most effective in producing cognitive improvements. School-based cognitive interventions were also more effective than clinic-based cognitive interventions. This highlights the central importance of pedagogical approaches to the amelioration of the negative outcomes of ADHD. Multi-modal approaches (combining medical, psycho-social and educational interventions) were found to be second only to medication in achieving improvements in behaviour, and superior to medication in producing improvements in social functioning.

Fifth, ADHD represents the wrongful medicalization of defiance in school children. As noted above, a medical diagnosis does not necessarily require medical treatment. In fact a bio-psycho-social perspective enables medical diagnoses, such as ADHD, to be used to inform psycho-social and educational interventions that may preclude the need for medical intervention. The development and implementation of such educational interventions, however, depends upon an accurate understanding of the nature of ADHD. The claim, made by Skidmore among others, that ADHD is simply a medical term applied to 'defiant children', if accepted, is guaranteed to produce confusion and inappropriate educational interventions for children with ADHD.

Obviously, children with ADHD are like all children in that sometimes they are deliberately disobedient and defiant. However, ADHD is clearly defined as relating to difficulties in various self regulatory processes, including: sustaining attention, inhibiting responses and controlling motor activity. Crucially, ADHD is non-volitional. Children with ADHD perform differently from other children on tests of vigilance and impulse control (Barkley, 1997). Their failure to comply with the wishes of teachers and parents are theorized to be the result of cognitive deficits, such as problems with executive functions (Barkley, 1997, see above). This helps to explain why ADHD symptoms respond well to pedagogical interventions. Interventions intended to support children whose core problem is that of defiance are quite different.

Defiance, when it reflects a child's dominant style of social engagement, goes beyond appropriate assertiveness and is characterized by an aggressive and uncooperative response to adults and/or other children in the absence of obvious provocation. Defiance, therefore, is often better understood as cognitive distortion, rather than a cognitive deficit. Cognitive distortions require interventions that enable children to examine and reflect on the ways in which they interpret situations and the choices that they make on the basis of these interpretations (Frith, 1992).

This is not to say that children may not combine ADHD with conditions associated with defiance. It is widely reported, for instance, that a high proportion of children with the ADHD diagnosis have comorbid diagnoses of Conduct Disorder or Oppositional Defiance Disorder (Barkley, 1997; McArdle, 2007). Such children will, therefore, benefit from a combination of interventions, some of which address deficits, and others which address distortions. The crucial thing, however, is for teachers to be able to base interventions on a careful assessment of the specific need in the specific situation.

The key point being made here is that an understanding of the differences between cognitive distortions and deficits can be extremely valuable to teachers, while confusion between or the conflation of deficits and distortions are likely to lead to ineffective intervention (Royer, 1999). Unfortunately, progress towards enabling teachers to access the knowledge and skills that flow from the

bio-psycho-social perspective is hampered by the dogmatism of a narrow social perspective which often seems to refuse to engage with the ways in which
individual differences interact with social circumstances.

The problem here is the seductive simplicity of the idea that if we avoid using
language which refers to individual deficits and difficulties, and act in ways which
emphasize the commonalties between diverse individuals then we will succeed
in creating inclusive educational environments. It must be acknowledged that
the value position often associated with this viewpoint is entirely laudable, and
it is shared by the authors of this book. We believe that education should be
characterized by principles of social justice and equality. However, values alone
are insufficient to make inclusion work.

We can illustrate this point very easily through reference to an example which
is included by Booth and Ainscow (1997) in their selection of international case
studies on inclusive education. This case study is set in an American High School.
The author (Ware, 1998) provides an account of the 'inclusion' of Josh, a multiply
handicapped student with severe communication difficulties in a mainstream
'issues theater' class. In spite of the teacher's confidence that Josh is 'included' in
this class, the evidence presented in support of this claim is entirely unconvincing.
Although we are told that Josh's teaching assistant believes Josh to be 'alert,
responsive, charming and smart' (p. 31), at no time is any information given
about what value Josh is getting from being 'included'. In fact, the main purpose
of his inclusion seems to be for the benefit of others, especially his fellow students,
who, apparently, learn to 'empathize' with him, and the teacher who sees him
as a signifier of her value position. The closing words of the chapter are a direct
quotation from this teacher, who states:

> Anytime you try to include a student with disabilities in the classroom – by the
> very act of having them in the classroom – you're making a statement on values.
> It's like when you have something in your home that you set out, you say 'this
> is of value to me, and I want it to be part of my everyday life.' I want to have
> it here because it brings me pleasure or because it's functional, or because it's
> somehow important to me.' . . . Anytime you invite a student with disabilities
> into your classroom, you're saying, 'I value humanity, I value an open attitude,
> I believe all persons are created equal, and I'm going to live up to that . . . to
> walk the walk, you know?' (Ware, 1998, p. 42).

Empathy and socially progressive values are important, however, they are, alone,
an inadequate basis for an educational experience. This teachers' understanding
of the term 'empathy' is also very suspect. In this case she concludes that students
are empathizing with Josh because they speak for him, not on the basis of what
is known about his view of the world (they mostly believe that he is unable to
communicate), but on the basis of their own projections about what they think
he might be thinking. In short, in spite of the rhetoric of the author and the
featured teacher, Josh is no more 'included' in the events described than if he were
physically absent from the setting. Not only is there no evidence of his *engagement*

in the classroom activities, the teacher shows a shocking lack of interest in what, if anything, Josh is getting out of the experience. It is as if the teachers' values are *all* that matter.

This example provides unintentional support for MacBeath *et al.*'s (2006) complaint that inclusive education fails when there is an over emphasis on values, and an insufficient emphasis on teachers' knowledge and teaching skills. In this case, the nature of Josh's disability – limited physical and communicative competencies – serve to insulate Josh's peers and the teacher from negative consequences that might otherwise arise from inappropriate educational intervention. In other circumstances, however, as MacBeath *et al.* show (2006), SEBD can be exacerbated and even created through such mistakes. In Josh's case it would appear that whatever his emotional reactions are to the situation in which he finds himself, they are less important than what his physical presence signifies about the values of his teacher.

This discussion leads us to the obvious conclusion that the achievement of social justice in education depends on creating the circumstances through which individuals are enabled to access and master knowledge and skills which enable them to engage socially, emotionally and cognitively with the world, in ways which lead to the most effective expression of their abilities, talents and wishes. This brings us to the concept of 'educational engagement'.

Educational Engagement

Educational engagement is concerned with the ways in which a learner is involved with the social and academic aspects of learning. In this sense, 'engagement' can be thought of as incorporating cognitive, social and emotional dimensions. The 'cognitive' dimension relates to the thoughts and thought processes that the learner employs in learning situations. These include perceptions of self and others, memory, reflection and problem solving approaches. The 'social' dimension refers to the ways in which the learner interacts with other people in the learning situation. Significant aspects of social engagement include those behaviours and orientations that can be described as either pro- or anti-social. The 'emotional' dimension relates to the feelings and unconscious motivations that all individuals possess. These include the individual's sense of emotional security (i.e., safety), fears, anxieties, happiness, jealousy and so on. These dimensions of human development interact with one another in important ways and the outcomes of these interactions have significant consequences for the ways in which students engage with learning activities in schools and classrooms.

The concept of educational 'engagement' refers to something much broader than a simply cognitive model of learning. Thought processes are clearly at the heart of learning in schools. Recently there has been a great of interest in moving beyond the idea that cognitive processes are concerned with academic skills, such as problem solving and memorization, and recognizing the role that cognition plays in the management of emotions (Cefai, 2008). However, the management of emotion through the application of Emotional Intelligence or Emotional Literacy skills, is different from the facilitation of particular emotional states. Educational engagement is concerned with the full range of social (including behavioural), emotional and social functions involved in learning and development, from the creation of a school and classroom climate that is conducive to feelings of emotional well-being, to the development of mental skills for understanding and the management of information, to the promotion of positive social relationships and the development of positive self esteem. This is what is meant by positive educational engagement.

Educational engagement and attachment to school

When students are educationally engaged they are 'attached' to schooling, in an emotional sense. Attachment to school (Smith, 2006) can be defined in terms of the degree of commitment towards and engagement with schooling that a student feels. Students who have a strong attachment to school believe that schooling is a worthwhile experience in itself and that success in school will lead to significant rewards both in the short term and in later life. Weak attachment to school is characterized by indifference or hostility towards teachers and scepticism or disbelief in relation to the value of schooling.

The concept of educational engagement is not incompatible with the broadest definitions of 'inclusive education', though it places a stronger emphasis on the interaction between social and psychological factors. A key underpinning of the construct of educational engagement, as we see it, is a bio-psycho-social perspective which recognizes that there is a wide range of human diversity, which when properly understood enables schools and teachers to make accommodations. Furthermore, we argue that when we develop such understandings we learn things about human functioning in general that enable us to improve learning environments in ways which benefit all students. For example, an informed understanding of ADHD raises awareness of the mechanisms of human self regulation and the environmental factors which can help or hinder the efficient functioning of these mechanisms. Our definition of educational engagement, therefore, rejects the view that diagnostic categories are necessarily discriminatory and stigmatizing. This is not to say that they cannot be used in negative ways. We argue for a responsible and informed approach to their use. We also point to the damage that can be done when diagnoses are ignored and/or belittled sometimes from perspectives that are claimed to be informed by (sometimes questionable) readings of postmodern philosophy (e.g., Runswick-Cole and Hodge, 2008). In particular, we are conscious of the barriers to multi-agency cooperation that can be created by arid arguments about language and terminology, which in turn distract attention from what should be the primary focus of educational services: to promote the fullest possible educational engagement of all students. In this sense we concur with James Kauffman *et al.*, 2002, p. 154) when they state:

> Deconstructivism and related 'postmodern' philosophies may appear to promote equality among ideas, but ultimately they create intolerance and tribalism by pitting individuals and groups against each other because there are no universal truths that grant power – except, ironically, the absence of universal truth.

We would add that such approaches can also contribute to the disastrous consequences witnessed by MacBeath *et al.* (2006) that were reported earlier in this chapter. By denying the legitimacy of certain approaches to understanding the serious difficulties that some students face in attempting to engage with certain social and learning situations, the proponents of such antagonistic positions are placing obstacles between teachers (and other front line professionals) and a whole field of knowledge and skills that has the potential to inform effective pedagogy for both students with SEN and students in general (see Lewis and Norwich, 2005). There is a deep irony here which reminds us of Tomlinson's words, already quoted in support of a different point:

> education systems and their parts do not develop spontaneously . . . and they do not develop out of purely humanitarian motives. They develop because it is in the interests of particular groups in society that they should develop, and that they should develop in certain ways (1982, p. 27).

So whose interests are served when educationists abandon the quest to understand the mechanisms of 'effective teaching and learning' in favour of debates about the kinds of language that we should be allowed to use before we can make a legitimate contribution to a discussion of these issues? Apart from the journal editors and book publishers who welcome and celebrate this discourse, and those who build academic careers and comfortable lifestyles on the basis of it, there are serious and thoughtful people who are dedicated to it. They rightly believe that simplistic biological determinism is an appalling and dangerous influence that must be challenged and defeated. However, they wrongly believe that perspectives informed by biological insights are, by definition, representative of a biological determinist viewpoint. In our reading of the literature, they are universally ignorant of the bio-psycho-social perspective. As a result, teachers, parents and students who are influenced by the anti-perspective are disarmed and left helpless. This is a superb recipe for creating and exacerbating Social, Emotional and Behavioural Difficulties (SEBD) in schools, and beyond.

Moving the Debate Forward

SEBD is a major problem in our schools that creates barriers that affect everyone. As we have shown, it is a significant area of SEN in itself. Furthermore, it might be seen as the 'elephant in the living room' of the inclusive education agenda. There is a need to take a serious look at this issue within the context of the educational needs of the student population as a whole. As we have already stated, there are unhelpful ways of thinking about 'inclusive education' which divert attention from the all important issue of 'educational engagement'. The central intention of this book is to focus on what the existing evidence base tells us about what is known about effective interventions for promoting educational engagement, with particular reference to the challenges posed by SEBD. The key question is: what does the current research evidence base tell us about the kinds of knowledge and skills that teachers and other school personnel need in order to promote the educational engagement of students?

The main body of the book focuses on published accounts drawn from a comprehensive range of international sources, including research papers in scholarly journals, books, published conference proceedings and research/evaluation reports produced by research, governmental, charitable and other organizations. A key purpose of the book is to identify best practice models for supporting children and young people with SEBD.

This Book

The main purpose of the book is to draw attention to the best available evidence for determining which approaches to promoting the educational engagement of students with SEBD are most promising. This means that our approach is both descriptive of the range and nature of sources, and evaluative, in terms of the quality and empirical rigour of evidence presented. In this sense, the effectiveness of an intervention is determined by its impact on students' functioning and development as shown empirically through the application of qualitative and/or quantitative research techniques. The following hierarchy of study types (based on Nathan and Gorham, 2002) will be employed to differentiate between studies in terms of their quality, with rigorous, large-scale random controlled trials providing the strongest form of evidence of success that is *generalizable* across different settings and *maintained* over time.

Type 1: randomized prospective trials with control/comparison groups;
Type 2: clinical trials with some type 1 characteristics missing;
Type 3: prospective 'naturalistic studies' with control/comparison groups;
Type 4: prospective 'naturalistic studies' without control/comparison groups;
Type 5: retrospective studies; pilot studies.
Type 6: reviews with secondary data analysis/ meta analyses.
Type 7: reviews without secondary data analyses.
Type 8: case studies; and
Type 9: audits; essays; opinion papers

Inclusion and Exclusion Criteria for Studies

Since the literature is extensive, inclusion and exclusion criteria were established. The main review included published sources:

- relating to children and young people up to age 18;
- published since 1980; and
- those which generated data and were experimental in form (generally Types 1–4 and Type 8) while Types 6 and 7 were used only to give overviews. Type 5 studies were used infrequently, and merely to support other data. Type 9 studies were not regarded as useful or pertinent to the main body of this review.

The review included only studies that could contribute empirical evidence thus contributing to evidence-based practices. The main review did not include:

- studies not published in peer reviewed journals or not published by respected academic publishers;
- studies not assessing the effectiveness of interventions for SEBD;
- studies not having a *direct* relationship to education, that is, those studies which were conducted in mostly clinical settings, in youth work settings, or involving dietary or pharmacological interventions;
- studies not specifying methodology;
- studies on children of below pre-school age, with the exception of those which were on-going for several years, beyond entry into school;
- studies on learning difficulties and physical disabilities;
- opinion-based secondary sources which cited no original data; or
- reviews of international policy issues, except where strictly relevant.

Given that a major purpose of this book is to highlight the most persuasive research evidence, we have tended to focus on rigorous, large-scale random controlled trials, where these are available, because they provide the strongest form of evidence of success that is generalizable across different settings and maintained over time (Nathan and Gorham, 2002). We have made use of this typology throughout the book, sometimes by referring to it directly by designating a study by its type number, in other places we describe the methods used in detail. The reason for this is that while some study types, such as types 1 and 2, tend to adhere to a common design pattern, others (such as types 3, 4, 5 and 8) are far more diverse in their designs. Therefore, while it is often reasonable to refer to a type 1 or type 2 study on the basis that the reader will be able to understand the main features of the design, with types 3, 4, 5 and 8 it is necessary to offer more by way of description of the actual methods employed. Types 6, 7 and 9 are, again, more helpfully understood in relation to the specific characteristics of the individual output, rather than in relation to its numerical designation.

Clearly, the quality of a research study cannot be judged on the basis of study type alone. The quality of a study depends on its clarity of purpose, the precision of its research questions, the appropriateness of the research strategy and methods and the suitability of the methods of data analysis and interpretation. Furthermore, implementation issues and matters such as sample selection and size, as well as the gap between intended and achieved sample, or, in longitudinal studies, attrition, are also of vital importance. There is insufficient space in a book such as this to provide detailed commentary on all such aspects of every study that we have reviewed. We have, however, endeavoured to favour studies which conform to the highest standards of rigour in relation these quality markers. Where there are issues of concern in relation to quality we have commented on this and its implications for the power of the study. In Chapter 9 we summarize and evaluate the relative merits of the different studies reviewed.

Therefore, the studies to which we attribute the highest power are usually those which are type 1 or type 2 in design and conform to the highest standards of rigour in relation to the quality markers outlined above. Moderately powerful studies are usually those which are type 1 or 2 design but fail to reach the highest quality standards in certain respects. Other studies which we rate as moderately powerful include those which are types 3–6 and reach the highest quality standards for studies of these types. Those studies which we designate as low power are good examples of types 7–9, or types 1–6 with significant though not, in our view, fatal flaws.

Outline of the Rest of the Book

The book is divided into the following chapters.

Chapter 2 deals with some basic theoretical considerations which underpin much of what is to follow. This is coupled with brief reference to the development of educational interventions for SEBD prior to 1980.

Chapter 3 reviews key evidence on effective resources for SEBD in the classroom and school that can be used by individual staff members, and environmental issues which should be addressed. It also deals with those personal qualities which research has shown to contribute to effective teaching.

Chapter 4 addresses the question: which practical classroom strategies and interventions for dealing with SEBD in the classroom are likely to be of greatest value to teachers and other 'front-line' personnel, such as classroom assistants, and their students?

Chapter 5 considers whole-school approaches to dealing with SEBD, including behaviour support initiatives, and approaches embedded in the curriculum, as well as 'universal' approaches which operate within school and community. This chapter also deals with off-site provision.

Chapter 6 deals with strategies used to provide alternative provision for smaller numbers of students. This may be on the school premises or sited elsewhere.

Chapter 7 is devoted to the research evidence on the effectiveness of different approaches to encouraging positive engagement between families and schools.

Chapter 8 explores the research literature on multi-agency cooperation in relation to SEBD in schools. Of particular interest here are projects which illustrate effective ways of working in multi-disciplinary teams.

Chapter 9 provides a brief summary of the findings from our review of the relevant research literature.

Chapter 10 presents the main conclusions to be drawn from the preceding chapters in terms of the knowledge and skills required by staff in schools. It also gives consideration to broader training needs and related issues.

2

SEBD

The Evolution of Intervention and Current Theory

Overview

Having established, in the previous chapter, that Social, Emotional and Behavioural Difficulties (SEBD) are the elephant in the living room of inclusive education, this chapter provides a brief outline of some of the key challenges posed by SEBD and some of the issues underlying these problems. Emphasis is given to the ways in which intervention has developed over the past century and the main theoretical dimensions relating to this evolving picture.

The Problem of SEBD

Social, Emotional and Behavioural Difficulties (SEBD) is a problematic term. On one level, SEBD is used as a label for individuals who are found to be problematic. Their problematic status may be awarded because they are disruptive or threatening, or because they are emotionally vulnerable or socially inept. There is, of course, a serious problem here, simply because behaving in problematic ways is sometimes a legitimate response to intolerable circumstances (Cooper *et al.*, 1994). There is a fairly long history of research and writing which declares that what might now fall under the category of what we are calling SEBD might be the product of legitimate resistance to oppressive circumstances (Cooper, 1993; Schostak, 1982). SEBD may also be socially constructed, which means that societies, families and school systems and individual staff may be 'deviance provocative' and create circumstances in which deviant identities are at first predicted and then confirmed through a process of 'typing' (Hargreaves *et al.*, 1975). SEBD are always context specific, though in sometimes complicated ways.

From Inclusion to Engagement: Helping Students Engage with Schooling through Policy and Practice
By Paul Cooper and Barbara Jacobs © 2011 John Wiley & Sons, Ltd

Young people may be socialized into ways of behaving that the wider culture construes as deviant, as in the case of the child who has been brought up to use a coercive social style in order to meet personal needs (see references to Patterson *et al.*, 1992, below). This means that they are, effectively, trained in deviant ways if behaving. On the other hand young people may apply a non-deviant, socialized cognitive and or behavioural approach to what might be termed a deviant situation (for example, to use physical force in resistance to some form of physical abuse), which may be misconstrued as a deviant response. In other circumstances individuals who have been exposed to deviant environments might, unwittingly, respond in non-deviant environments in deviant ways, because they misread the situation on the basis of prior experience.

These insights mean that it is necessary to be alert to the dangers of using a term such as social, emotional and behavioural difficulties lightly. At the forefront in our thinking should always be that the term SEBD (and its many variations – see below) should always be seen as a loose descriptive term that may be subject to change as we learn more about the situation in hand. It is particularly important to understand that what might be at first construed as a problem emanating from within an individual, may turn out to be the symptom of a problem in the individual's environment. For example, a student may become morose, oppositional and disruptive in class in response to an emotional trauma in the family situation, or as a consequence of bullying in the school setting. On the other hand, repeated patterns of behaviour which are deemed problematic across a wide range of different settings and over an extended time frame, may suggest something more deep seated in the form of a persistent social and/or cognitive style which may, in turn, be rooted in the individual's social experience, or even in a combination of their social experience and a biological disposition. In any event, where problems are deep seated and pervasive there is likely to be a need for the individual to be helped to learn new ways of thinking and behaving. This will often involve making adjustments to the environment as well as helping the individual directly.

This brings us to the heart of what we mean by the term SEBD. SEBD can be said to exist when aspects of observed behaviour are interpreted as being disturbing and/or disruptive to a social situation to a serious degree. Disturbing behaviours are often interpreted as being indicative of underlying emotional problems. It must be emphasized, however, that the surface appearance of SEBD may, on closer investigation, be less a matter of individual dysfunction and more a matter of dysfunction in the social environment of the individual.

Understanding SEBD

Core features shared by children who present with SEBD include the manifestation of disturbing and/or disruptive behaviour that interferes with social functioning and academic performance. Children with these difficulties may be termed as 'acting-out' (i.e., disruptive) or 'acting-in' (i.e., showing withdrawn and/or avoidant behaviour). Many of these children come from socially deprived or disrupted family backgrounds, although this is by no means always the case.

Emotional disturbance of one kind or another is often an associated feature of both 'acting-in' and 'acting-out' types as either an underlying or outcome factor.

There is a wide range of terminology used to describe children presenting the kinds of difficulties referred to here that are employed in the published literature. These include: *Social, Emotional and Behavioural Difficulties*[1] (Scotland), *Behavioural, Emotional and Social Difficulties* (England), or *Emotional and Behavioural Difficulties* (Northern Ireland) – these are variations of an educational concept that are in current use in parts of the United Kingdom and Northern Ireland. They refer to disturbances to social, emotional and/or behavioural functioning that have a direct and significant impact on the educational engagement and progress of students in schools. This is a deliberately loose definition which owes much to the UK 1981 Education Act's (HMSO, 1981) generalized definition of 'Learning Difficulty' which deliberately eschews a focus on medical or psychological disorders in favour of an emphasis on educational functioning. Therefore, children may be classified as having a special educational need as a result of SEBD on educational grounds in the absence of a medical diagnosis. Conversely, children with a formally diagnosed behavioural disorder will not necessarily be deemed to have a special educational need if their condition is being managed in a manner which requires no educational resources beyond those routinely available to all children. This said, it is acknowledged that there is likely to be a strong overlap between the population of children and young people with SEBD and that of those with diagnosed disorders (DCSF, 2008) (see below). An important point about the term SEBD is that it is usually taken to refer to the student within his or her social context. In this sense the term relates to a now outmoded term: 'maladjustment' (e.g., Ministry of Education, 1955), which referred to individuals who were poorly adjusted to their environments. The difference between these terms is that SEBD acknowledges that the problem may reside primarily in the environment rather than the individual.

Challenging behaviour

This is a term that is sometimes used in the United Kingdom in health, social care and educational circles to refer to students whose behaviour is experienced by those around them as disturbing and or threatening, and is most often associated with students who have serious cognitive impairments (e.g. Harris *et al.*, 1996).

Emotional and behavioural disorders

This term has international currency in medical/psychiatric circles, and is used in the United States in educational legislation, as well as psychological and educational research and professional literature. The term refers to specific psychiatric

---

[1] The authors of this book employ the term 'Social, Emotional and Behavioural Difficulties' as this is the longest established and most comprehensive term currently in use in the field.

conditions the diagnostic criteria for which are published by bodies such as the American Psychiatric Association (2007, DSM IV- TR) and the World Health Organization (1991). These conditions include:

conduct disorder – a disruptive behavioural disorder in which the individual shows marked aggression towards other people, as well as violent and destructive behaviour;

oppositional defiant disorder – a disruptive behavioural disorder characterized by interpersonal oppositionality, uncooperativeness and verbal aggression;

attention deficit/hyperactivity disorder/ hyperkinetic disorders – a behavioural and cognitive disorder characterized by difficulties in sustaining attention to tasks, impulsiveness and, in some cases, difficulties in regulating physical movement (i.e., hyperactivity);

anxiety disorders – emotional disorders in which the individual becomes distressed, fearful and hyper-aroused; and

depressive disorders – emotional disorders in which the individual becomes withdrawn, unmotivated and prone to feelings of low self worth.

An important issue here is that presenting, surface behaviours may be described in different ways by different professionals. Furthermore, theories of underlying causation may vary widely, from those which emphasize a *within-person* (bio-psychological) set of causes, to those which emphasize primarily *environmental* (social) causes.

As we argue later in this chapter, there is a great deal to be gained from drawing these perspectives together in a bio-psycho-social model. However, one of the consequences of widespread poor quality interdisciplinary communication is a tendency for views to be polarized. This is particularly so in the case of certain sociologically-informed educational critiques which tend to misconstrue and denigrate bio-medical and bio-psychological models (e.g., Skidmore, 2004; Slee, 1995; see Chapter 1).

On the other hand, there is sometimes a tendency for the more sophisticated educational perspectives to be ignored by those who operate within a predominantly bio-medical paradigm. This was illustrated in the United Kingdom by the National Institute for Clinical Excellence (NICE, 2008) in its advice on the treatment of children with ADHD. Although claiming to be informed by an educational perspective, the educational content related only to behaviour management strategies, making no reference at all to psycho-educational interventions which have been shown to be effective with students with ADHD (e.g., Purdie et al, 2002).

The Challenge of SEBD

SEBD among school pupils represent a unique problem within the educational sphere. No other educational problem is associated with such a level of frustration, fear, anger, guilt and blame.

As we have already noted, SEBD are not only manifested in outwardly disruptive terms, they can be 'internalizing', so that the threat, rather than being disruptive to others, is to the individual's own safety and well-being. In spite of this, it has long been the case that practitioners, policy-makers and researchers, particularly in the education field, have tended to focus their attention on the externalizing, disruptive students, to the relative neglect of the internalizing students. As a result, and as the following sections of this chapter will show, we know a great deal about the nature of disruptive behaviour and its effects on classrooms, teachers and students. We have a much shallower database to draw on in relation to internalizing students. This is demonstrated in a review of research by Shoenfeld and Janney (2008) which identified only eight research-based articles published in the previous 20 years which dealt with the academic effects of anxiety disorders. The serious academic effects associated with anxiety disorders cited include:

- academic impairment and relatively low levels of achievement among anxious children compared to children in the general population;
- teacher perceptions of academic difficulties among anxious students on a par with those of children with externalizing difficulties;
- difficulties reported by anxious students in performing school-based tasks including giving oral reports, concentration and completing homework tasks; and
- anxious students being more likely to opt out of schooling owing to feelings of anxiety.

As will be shown later, there is a concomitant imbalance in the educational intervention literature between studies focusing on externalizing as opposed to internalizing students.

In relation to both 'acting-out' and 'acting-in' problems, however, it is a source of concern that prevalence rates for mental health problems among school students appear to be increasing and have been for some time (Rutter and Smith, 1995). While this phenomenon may be in part due to changes in diagnostic criteria and developments in assessment techniques and service delivery – factors which help determine what constitutes a 'disorder' and whether or not it is identified – this is unlikely to be the sole explanation (Fonagy *et al.*, 2002). There is also evidence to suggest that widespread, culturally-based changes in the life experiences shared by young people, which have in turn led to changes in the very nature of social constructs such as 'childhood' and 'adolescence' and the ways in which adults relate to young people, have created a more SEBD-provocative world (e.g., Cunningham, 2006; Layard and Dunn, 2009; Gibson-Klein, 1996).

Recently, the United Kingdom's British Medical Association (2006) estimated that 20% of young people experience a mental health problem at some point in their development, and 10% experience these problems to a level that represents a 'clinically recognizable mental health disorder'. The range of problems includes: emotional disorders (such as anxieties, phobias and depression), self-harm and suicide, conduct disorders, hyperkinetic disorders/ADHD, autistic spectrum disorders, psychotic disorders, eating disorders, and substance and drug abuse. In the United Kingdom 20% of this group of young people are diagnosed with two or more disorders.

There are no simple demarcation lines in SEBD. Delinquency among young people often overlaps with mental health problems, and both of these major areas seem to relate to adverse social circumstances in the communities where young people live and the schools they attend. The young person who exhibits mental health problems and/or social deviance (including delinquency) is likely to have difficulty in engaging with the school experience and, in the absence of effective intervention, is at great risk of experiencing deterioration in their presenting difficulties as they move towards and through the adolescent years (Rutter and Smith, 1995).

Influences in the Development of SEBD – A Brief Theoretical Review

There are many theoretical models which attempt to explain the aetiology of SEBD. It would be impossible to review all of these in the context of the current book. In this section we attempt to offer a brief account of some of the major theories. As the reader will see, these tend to relate quite closely to the various approaches to intervention that we identify later in the chapter.

Gullotta (1996) is helpful here. He provides a typology of four approaches.

* *Psychological theories* emphasize the role of intrapsychic processes in the development of SEBD. These include psychodynamic theories, which emphasize the importance of early life experience on later psychological functioning, and social psychological theories which deal with the ongoing influence of social experience on the development of personality traits. Behavioural theories emphasize the importance of reinforcement in the development of behaviour.
* *Social psychological theories* deal with the ways in which people influence one another in their day to day interactions in dyads and small groups often focussing on the ways in which social mechanisms influence thought processes. This approach differs from a purely psychological approach because it places far less emphasis on the ingrained intrapsychic patterns (i.e., personality) and much more emphasis on the common ways in which human beings can spontaneously respond to immediate social stimuli.
* *Socio-cultural theories* emphasize the influence of the wider culture or social system on the individual. Structural functionalist theories emphasize the role of social and political power in influencing an individual's perception of reality. Systems theory, on the other hand, offers a less 'top down' view, emphasizing the interactive features of social systems. Systems theory shows how patterns of behaviour that may be construed as personality traits can be understood as the product of social feedback.

- *Biological theories* take many forms, including chemical and family genetic approaches which explore the relationship between genetic inheritance and behavioural patterns. This approach also considers the role of neurological insult on behaviour. Cognitive neuroscience focuses on the correlations between behaviour, cognition and the physical and chemical make up of the brain.

We would like to add to this typology the *bio-psycho-social* approach which is concerned with the ways in which inherited biological factors interact with environmental influences of various kinds to produce particular patterns of behaviour. (See below for more detail on this approach).

Each of these approaches has important insights to offer. This will become evident when we move on to discuss intervention. However, for present purposes we choose to emphasize a social learning model owing to its particular applicability to the school setting. At the heart of social learning theories is the recognition of the importance of repeated patterns of social reinforcement in the formation of deeply ingrained patterns of behaviour. Schools tend to be places where social routines are established in order to establish order, and where social categorization (labelling) performs an important organizational role. These features make social learning theory ideal for exploring the interactions between environment and social behaviour.

The Development of SEBD – A Social Learning Model

Patterson *et al.* (1992) propose a social learning model to describe the life course of individuals who become what they term 'career anti-social adults'. This model is based on intensive studies of incarcerated adult males who are defined as being anti-social. Common features in the life histories of individuals studied by Patterson *et al.* were experience of:

- social disadvantage;
- ineffective parental discipline;
- lack of parental supervision;
- parental use of physical punishment;
- parental rejection;
- peer rejection;
- membership of deviant peer group;
- academic failure; and
- low self esteem

What is interesting about the model is the account of how these factors appear to have interacted in the lives of the incarcerated adults. They describe a 4-stage process.

Stage 1: Basic training

This is the pre-school phase in which the child is 'trained' in coercive behaviour in the home setting. Parents and family members are often unwitting trainers who provide models and reinforcement for coercive behaviour through their daily interactions with the child. Their lives (and those of others) are made difficult by the coercive behaviour of the child, but the parents lack resources, knowledge and/or skills necessary to change the child's behaviour.

Stage 2: The social environment reacts

Behaviours that were functional for the child in the home setting are challenged when entering school. The school's attempts to challenge the child's behaviour through punishment or coercion, or unsuccessful attempts at remediation, cause the child's coercive behaviour to escalate. This leads to the pupil being engaged in further conflict with, and being rejected by, parents, peers and the school.

Stage 3: Deviant peers and polishing anti-social skills

The experience of rejection combined with affiliation needs lead the child to seek out like-minded children, and they form a deviant peer group. Here the skills of coercion are further reinforced and developed.

Stage 4: The career anti-social adult

The adult is socially marginalized. The main way of relating to others is through coercion. They experience disruption in personal relationships and have difficulty securing and sustaining gainful employment. Risk of mental health problems, substance abuse, criminality and imprisonment also increases.

This model deals specifically with an extreme form of deviance that is based on a study of males only in the original study. However, it illustrates very clearly the way in which elements in a constellation of influences interact with one another to produce an effect whereby an individual is channelled towards a deviant career. No single factor can be identified as the cause of the deviance. From the individual's point of view the opportunities to escape from the deviant identity that gradually takes over are severely limited.

The central importance of the educational context in the model (particularly at stages 2 and 3) is clear, and has important resonance with the findings from research by MacBeath *et al.* (2006) and Blatchford *et al.* (2009) on the consequences of ineffective intervention in the name of 'inclusive education'. Highlighted here are failures to take advantage of opportunities that might exist for channelling the student towards more prosocial ways of behaving, and the way in which the school plays an unwitting role in maintaining and promoting the deviance.

The Importance of Education, Schooling and the Social Context in Relation to the Experience of SEBD

In the 1960s and 1970s emphasis was placed on exploring the power of the educational context to socially construct deviant identities among students from low SES backgrounds and vulnerable minority groups. This theme is well illustrated in the sociological and educational research literature dealing with labelling theory and the self-fulfilling prophecy (Hargreaves, 1967; Hargreaves *et al.*, 1975; Rosenthal and Jacobson, 1968). Researchers in the United States (Bowles and Gintis, 1971; Silberman, 1971) and the United Kingdom (Sharp and Green, 1975; Willis, 1977) revealed how the cultural lives of schools often reflect and reproduce tensions and inequalities in the wider society, leading to disenchantment and disengagement from education among students from certain sections of society, such as lower SES groups and ethnic minorities (Coard, 1971; Willis, 1977)

This led to a shift in emphasis in policy approaches in the United States and the United Kingdom away from individualized, medicalized, within-child approaches, to understanding and dealing with SEBD in favour of more socially-oriented approaches which highlighted the impact of negative social experience on the development of SEBD and delinquency among young people. In educational terms this policy shift was reflected in efforts to improve equality of opportunity in education, through, for example in the United Kingdom, the widespread abandonment of selection by ability at age 11 and the introduction of comprehensive secondary schools. In the United States large-scale state-wide and community-based early interventions were pioneered, combining an aggressive approach to tackling the poverty and unemployment with compensatory education programmes (e.g., 'Operation Headstart'). The recently developed 'Sure Start' in the United Kingdom offers a similar approach. Urban regeneration initiatives, such the UK government's 'New Deal' programme, which targeted areas of severe social deprivation with the injection of funds to improve the physical infrastructure, including the public-owned housing stock, community facilities and educational provision, are reflective of this recognition of the relationship between poor living conditions, economic hardship and social and educational engagement. It has been argued that this concoction, at its most negative, results in the development of an 'underclass', members of which effectively operate outside the boundaries of mainstream civil society to the detriment of both the wider society and themselves (MacDonald, 1997). It should be acknowledged that the underclass construct has been challenged by some commentators (Nolan and Whelan, 2000). We argue, however, that at the very least the construct provides a useful metaphor for understanding the experience of marginalization, helplessness and despair that is experienced by people who find themselves cut off from the comforts and rewards that tend to come with relative educational success, stable employment and membership of an aspirational community. This is particularly resonant in educational research studies which have repeatedly revealed that highly stratified educational systems often provoke the development of anti-social and anti-school sub-cultures among those who find themselves at the lowest strata (Cefai *et al.*, 2008; Hargreaves, 1967).

A further dimension of the shift towards institutional interventions aimed at preventing educational failure and disaffection can be found in the school effectiveness (Mortimore *et al.*, 1988; Purkey and Smith, 1984; Reynolds and Sullivan, 1979; Rutter *et al.*, 1979; Smith and Tomlinson, 1989), and school improvement literature (e.g., Fullan, 1992). This research endeavour is rooted in the unremarkable, but potent, recognition of the fact that the quality of a school makes a difference to pupil academic attainment. This was well known before the major school effectiveness studies of the 1970s and 1980s on the basis of Douglas' large-scale research in primary (Douglas, 1964) and secondary schools (Douglas et al., 1971).

The accumulated research on school effectiveness produced a range of characteristics which appeared to differentiate between high and low performing schools (in terms of students' behaviour, attendance and attainment) with demographically-similar profiles. Core characteristics included: consultative approaches by school leaders; a curriculum tailored to pupils' needs coupled with high expectations; positive teacher–pupil relationships and preventive rather than remedial approaches to behavioural problems and pastoral needs (Mortimore, 1997).

Coupled with this socially-oriented approach is a scepticism towards 'non-mainstream' approaches to dealing with SEN and an emphasis on 'inclusive' education (e.g., Sebba and Sachdev, 1997; Skidmore, 2004). Unfortunately, as we noted in Chapter 1, there is often a wide gap between the aspirations towards inclusive education and practice.

The Importance of Attachment to School

As we noted in the opening chapter, a crucial factor that can be both a cause and effect of SEBD is what David Smith, in the Edinburgh Study of Youth Transitions and Crime, describes as 'attachment to school' (Smith, 2006). Attachment to school can be defined in terms of the degree of commitment towards and engagement with schooling that students feel. Students who have a strong attachment to school believe that success in school will lead to significant rewards in later life. Weak attachment to school is characterized by indifference or hostility towards teachers and scepticism about the value of schooling.

Weak attachment to school is not necessarily related to mental health difficulties, delinquency or social deviance, but is often a problem in itself that can lead to disaffection and alienation. These are problems of a psychological nature that impair the individual's capacity for social and academic engagement that can, in turn, lead to reduced life chances.

Possibly because of the disturbing, dramatic and traumatic impact of SEBD they are subject to sometimes extreme, bewildering and contradictory ideas about how they should be addressed. With no other educational problem is it considered legitimate to apply legally sanctioned punishment and exclusionary practices.

This is not to say that the exclusion option is always inappropriate. There are times when a relationship breaks down to such a degree that the temporary or permanent cessation of the relationship provides the best available opportunity for a new beginning. However, there is evidence to suggest that our most socially and emotionally vulnerable school students are likely to have the least satisfactory experience of schooling. A recent study by Barnardo's (2006) found strong associations between social disadvantage, educational failure and SEBD, with, in 2005, only 6% of care leavers achieving 5 GCSE's at A*–C (against a national average of almost 50%), and 36% of care leavers not sitting any GCSE or equivalent examinations (compared to a national average of less than 10%). Furthermore, Looked After Children (LAC) are more likely than other children to experience:

- repeated school moves;
- exclusion from school;
- a lack of carer representation at parent evenings;
- being bullied;
- lack of access to praise and rewards;
- a lack of involvement in decision making about their futures; and
- Stigmatization at school.

These findings echo an earlier study by Hayden (1997) which found primary school pupils with SEBD seriously over-represented in exclusion figures, suggesting a tendency towards the application of punitive responses to SEBD.

Other studies have also focused on the ways in which schools help to create the problem of disaffection and exacerbate SEBD. Klein, an educational journalist, noted that 'disaffection in schools is endemic in American and British societies' (Klein, 1999, p. xii). Drawing on contemporaneous research evidence, she then proceeded to list some of the key factors that 'tip the un-resilient, at risk child over the edge and into the quagmire of disaffection' (p. xv). These include:

- an over-emphasis in schools on a one-dimensional form of academic achievement that fails to take account of the different ways in which children learn and express their knowledge and understanding;
- the use of ability-setting in schools;
- a punitive emphasis in approaches to school discipline;
- the school curriculum's lack of relevance to pupils' everyday lives;
- a school ethos that reflects a 'them and us' polarity between staff and students, and their parents; and
- teaching methods that fail to meet diverse needs.

A study by Cooper *et al.* (2000), which drew heavily on the first-hand accounts of school students, many of whom were perceived to exhibit social, emotional and behavioural problems, paints a similar picture. For the pupils in this study, who were drawn from the full 5–18 age range, a key concern was the extent to which they felt themselves to be acknowledged and respected as human beings. School regimes that were characterized by a mechanistic and impersonal approach to pupil management were associated with pupil disaffection, whereas regimes that pupils and staff experienced as being underpinned by values of respect and care for all persons were associated with positive challenges to disaffection and lower levels of exclusion.

Many of these findings were echoed in a study of 33 pupils excluded from UK schools (Pomeroy, 2000). For these students problematic relationships with teachers were referred to as the most common sources of difficulty. Among the concerns these students cited were:

- teachers refusing to listen to young people's views or to 'hear their side of the story';
- teachers not intervening to provide pastoral care, particularly in relation to conflict with peers;
- teachers humiliating and/or antagonizing pupils by shouting at, insulting, speaking sarcastically to, and being rude to pupils;
- teachers treating pupils unequally; and
- teachers not providing sufficient help to pupils struggling to do schoolwork.

Pomeroy's study clearly shows that for this group of pupils the impersonal, disrespectful and unsympathetic experience of school described by pupil research participants in the 1960s, 1970s, 1980s and 1990s, were still relevant in the year 2000.

More recently still, a study of over 2000 pupils in secondary schools in Ireland found that pupils were preoccupied with concerns about the ways in which adults in their schools exercised power over students. In particular they were concerned that pupils had few rights in relation to the ways in which staff controlled and punished pupils (Lodge and Lynch, 2003). This study also found attitudes among students that reflected the marginalization of minorities, such as students from minority ethnic groups, those with disabilities, those who were gay, lesbian or bisexual, and those 'professing minority religious beliefs' (Lodge and Lynch, 2003, p. 16).

It is salutary to note not only the similarities between these studies in terms of the consistent story they tell about how young, vulnerable people experience rejection and exclusion in school, but also the fact that these same concerns are reflected in the research literature spanning almost the last 50 years. Empirical studies, drawing on the first-hand accounts of disaffected pupils, by Cooper (1993), Cooper *et al.* (2000), Cronk (1987), Garner (1995), Hargreaves (1967), Hargreaves *et al.* (1975), Hughes and Cooper (2007), Lawrence *et al.* (1984), Marsh *et al.* (1978), Schostak (1982), Silberman (1970) and Tattum (1982) tell a similar story.

Early Twentieth Century Precursors – The Work of 'The Pioneers'

In the opening chapter we referred to an earlier body of literature, more reflective than empirical in nature, which foreshadows a similar set of concerns in relation to the failure of adult society, particularly as reflected in the mainstream schools of the day, to recognize and meet the emotional needs of young people. These individuals particularly concerned with 'maladjusted' youngsters who were vulnerable and often emotionally scarred as a result of social and emotional deprivation and sometimes abuse (see, for example, Bridgeland, 1971; Neill, 1968; Wills, 1963).

A simple, and yet profound feature of the residential communities for the 'maladjusted' established by these pioneers was what we might now call 'person-centeredness'. A.S. Neill, David Wills and other enlightened workers in the maladjustment field in the first half of the twentieth century believed that only if we treat our students as if they are people who need to be known and respected, can we expect reciprocal treatment from them (Bridgeland, 1971). The process of creating a reciprocal, respectful relationship involves the recognition of responsibilities and obligations on both sides. These simple ideas have critical resonance today, and are being implemented in some forward-looking schools as well as being recognized by policy-makers. The recent trumpeting of ideas of emotional literacy and emotional intelligence reflect these values. The UK government's 'Every Child Matters' (DfES, 2003) agenda, with its emphasis on the importance of emotional safety as a foundation-stone of educational engagement is also reflective of this view.

Resilience in Education

Although negative personal outcomes, such as SEBD and delinquency, are associated with particular risk factors, such as social deprivation, low income, family dysfunction, and early life trauma (e.g., family bereavement, physical, sexual and/or emotional abuse), it is a fact that the majority of people who experience such circumstances do not develop SEBD or become delinquent. This has led to an interest among researchers in the concept of 'resilience', that is, the study of factors, such as personal qualities and protective mechanisms, associated with successful adaptation, including the achievement of academic and social competence (Luthar *et al.*, 2000), in people who have had prolonged exposure to high risk environments (Benard, 2004).

The earlier studies focused on individual characteristics, which protect children and young persons growing up in a difficult environment and enable them to achieve success. As later studies were to show, however, positive outcomes in the face of adverse circumstances are influenced by various processes besides individual characteristics, including the family, the school and the community. Development is the result of the dynamic interaction between the various systems impinging in the child's life (Bronfenbrenner, 1979) and it is the interaction between the child and his or her environment that finally determines the adaptive process.

Seminal studies, including those by Werner and Smith (1988, 1992) and Garmezy and Rutter (1983) found that despite the high-risk environments in which their participants grew up, the majority developed into healthy, successful young adults. They concluded that protective factors have a stronger impact on children's development than risk factors. In 1963 Werner and Smith began an on-going investigation of the impact of social disadvantage on development over the lifespan of a group of 600 individuals living in Hawaii, from birth to adulthood. All the participants were from socio-economically impoverished backgrounds, and one third of them experienced multiple risk factors. At the age of 32, the majority (70%) had developed into healthy and successful young adults in spite of the high-risk environments in which they grew up. The study suggests that individual and external protective factors had a stronger impact on children's developmental trajectory than environmental risk factors. Three sets of protective factors were identified:

- dispositional attributes of the individual such as sociability and competence in communication skills;
- affectional ties within the family, providing emotional support in times of stress, and supportive relationships; and
- rewarding external support systems, such as school and work (Werner and Smith, 1988, 1992).

These findings are supported and augmented by other studies which show that the interactions between these three protective systems in the child's life eventually lead to success in the face of adversity (Pianta and Walsh, 1998; Wang and Haertel, 1995; Werner and Smith, 1992). Individuals with high levels of these personal and social protective factors are thus more effective in coping with adversity than individuals with lower levels of protection.

Resilience (Cefai, 2008) is a dynamic process that occurs as the result of the person in interaction with his or her environment. Contexts such as home, community, schools and classrooms have been shown to provide protection to children and young persons at risk by helping to influence their development in the direction of positive and healthy psychological and social pathways (Cefai, 2008; Crosnoe and Elder, 2004; Pianta and Walsh, 1998; Rees and Bailey, 2003). Schools have a particularly important role to play in promoting resilience.

As we have noted already (see above), 'attachment to school' (Smith, 2006) is an important protective factor against delinquency, this is because schools provide a major and continuing context for cognitive and socio-emotional development. Numerous studies have shown that the positive effects of school experience seem most evident among pupils who are vulnerable and have few other supports (Rutter, 1991). In the Isle of Wight epidemiological study (Rutter *et al.*, 1971), one of the most comprehensive epidemiological studies undertaken to date, the development of children from socially disadvantaged backgrounds and families with parental psychopathology was studied. It was found that most of these children did not develop social, emotional and behavioural difficulties despite these negative experiences, and attributed their successful adaptation to both individual and social factors, among which were school factors such as the promotion of sense of connectedness and achievement.

Various studies have found that high achieving pupils tend to contrast with their low achieving peers, by reporting more positive views of their educational experiences, being more engaged in classroom activities, and in viewing their teachers as supportive and encouraging (Waxman *et al.*, 2004). A study by Wehlage *et al.* (1989) of 14 high schools identified as being successful with at risk children in terms of increased literacy performance and school attendance, found that students who identified themselves with the mainstream school culture and had established a social bond with peers and adults in the school, were more likely to participate in the life of the school and to achieve. These successful schools were characterized by a teacher culture predicated upon a moral obligation to serve young persons.

These findings are echoed in a range of other studies which have focused on the capacity of schools to promote resilience among vulnerable groups. In a longitudinal study of primary pupils' academic and social competence and connectedness to school in high-crime areas, Hawkins *et al.* (1999) reported greater pupil commitment and attachment to school, less misbehaviour, and better academic achievement, particularly among pupils coming from poorer families, following the introduction of a school-based programme designed to promote pupils' academic and social competence and connectedness. An analysis of the *Minnesota Adolescent Health Survey*, which compiled a large database from a state-wide survey of over 36 000 7th to 12th grade students, revealed that the experience of being catered for and the feeling of connectedness resulted in demonstrably greater well-being and correspondingly less risky, health-compromising behaviours among students in general, particularly those considered 'at risk'. School connectedness was the most important protective factor for students against anti-social behaviour (Resnick *et al.*, 1997).

Being cared for and respected in school, both by staff and peers, has been found to make a significant contribution to the development of resilience. The Child Development Project, which was begun on several different sites in the United States in the 1980s, and is currently ongoing (Solomon *et al.*, 1997a, 1997b, 2000) sought to build a sense of caring community in schools. Pupils attending the CDP schools scored significantly higher than controls on outcomes such as general social competence, conflict resolution, empathy and self-esteem, and school-related variables such as liking for school, achievement, motivation, and reading comprehension. Teacher practices that encouraged pupils' active participation, collaboration, and interpersonal support through an emphasis on prosocial values, elicitation of pupil thinking and ideas, and encouragement of cooperation and supportiveness, were related to pupil engagement, influence and positive behaviour. These findings held for a broad variety of pupils including pupils from low socio-economic status, urban areas and ethnic minorities. They are also echoed in studies which highlight the importance of social acceptance by peers and friendship in school in the promotion of resilience. Criss *et al.* (2002) carried out a longitudinal study of 600 young children experiencing adverse family situations in three different sites in the United States. They found that peer acceptance and friendships at school moderated the effects of family adversity, protecting children from developing anti-social and aggressive behaviours.

A programme of studies of school and classroom practices associated with the promotion of resilience in inner-city schools by Wang and Haertel (1995) high-lighted the importance of a consistent pattern of organizational and staff char-acteristics. Teacher actions and expectations and effective instructional methods and curriculum, played key roles in pupil motivation, positive attitudes towards school, achievement, and prosocial behaviour. Important teacher characteristics included:

- concern for and sustained close relationships with pupils;
- high expectations for all pupils;
- the tailoring of pedagogy to meet the needs of individual pupils;
- engaging pupils in setting goals and making learning decisions; and
- shared interests and values.

These characteristics were associated with a high degree of student engagement and pupil satisfaction with learning experiences. These factors were, in turn, consistently associated with enhanced pupil cognitive and affective outcomes. These studies underline the point that the school practices most associated with resilience-enhancement were classroom practices, such as classroom relation-ships, classroom management approaches and pedagogical practices.

The resilience literature seems to agree on a number of key school qualities which have been found to promote positive academic and social outcomes, and compensate for risk factors such as socio-economic disadvantage (Benard, 1995, 2004; Pianta and Walsh, 1998; Rees and Bailey, 2003). Benard (2004) grouped these factors into three key processes.

- Caring relationships between pupils and teachers based on teacher concern, care, respect and support towards the pupils. Being there, unconditional love, compassion, listening, patience, and basic trust/safety are some of the processes underlying such relationships.
- High expectations for pupils to do well through teacher practices which are child-centred, use pupils' own strengths and interests, and tap their intrinsic motivation for learning.
- Pupils' meaningful involvement and responsibility, with opportunities to ex-press opinions, make choices, solve problems, and work with and help others in a caring and healthy environment.

The way in which these processes are actually implemented in schools and class-rooms, however, should be tempered according to the needs of the particular contexts where they are implemented. It would be counter-productive to seek to provide quick-fix solutions to be implemented across cultures and contexts (Ce-fai, 2007; Howard *et al.*, 1999; Rutter, 1991). Some studies have also indicated that approaches to the promotion of resilience are more likely to be effective when they are integrated as part of the daily curriculum rather than presented as one off, off-the-shelf packages (Carter and Doyle, 2006; Crosnoe and Elder, 2004; Pianta and Walsh, 1998). Finally, as we have already noted, the school is one of a number of systems in the child's world which may serve as a protective context for the healthy development of children and young people. It follows that it needs to work in close collaboration with families, communities and other social organizations and entities in enabling effectiveness in the healthy social and academic development of children and young people (Benard, 2004; Wang and Haertel, 1995).

The distinctive contribution of a 'resilience' approach resides in its emphasis on interactivity. In this sense the resilience construct reflects the ways in which positive factors in an individual's life may interact to provide protection from potential dangers, just as the Patterson *et al.* (1992) model (see above) illustrates how negative outcomes follow from the interaction of negative factors. Many of the issues which have been aired in this section will be dealt with in more detail in research studies reviewed below. A crucial intention here is to show how social and emotional resilience can be initiated, promoted and supported through an understanding of the nature of SEBD and through intervention of various kinds which flow from this understanding.

The Evolution of Theory in Relation to SEBD

In this section we review the historical development of the theoretical under-pinnings of educational interventions for SEBD. We begin with a brief overview of key developments before developing a more detailed account of the different intervention approaches. For a graphical illustration of what follows, please see Appendix I.

We argue that the history of educational-psychological interventions for SEBD can be usefully understood as following a course which reflects the developing field of therapeutic psychology and psychiatry. Early approaches, which can be traced back to the first half of the twentieth century and dominated SEBD-focused provision in both the United States and the United Kingdom, were heavily influenced by Freudian psycho-analytic theory. In the 1960s concerns about the psychodynamic emphasis on individual pathology led to a widespread adoption of behavioural approaches in schools, based on the seminal theories of Pavlov, Watson and Skinner, which have their origins in the 1920s. To this day behaviourism continues to have strong influence on educational approaches to SEBD. The 1980s saw the application of humanistic approaches into schools, largely on the basis of the writing of Carl Rogers (1980). Again, the theoretical basis of this approach lies much earlier in the 1940s and 1950s. The shift towards humanistic approaches was influenced by concerns about the association between behavioural approaches and a coercive approach to social control. Humanistic approaches, on the other hand, emphasize the primacy of the individual's sense of self and the development of self concept and self esteem.

Cognitive behavioural approaches, though originating much earlier, began to make a significant impact in educational settings in the 1990s. These approaches combine the precision of behaviourism with the emphasis on personal agency that is a key feature of the humanistic approach. The systemic (or ecosystemic) approach to SEBD was first applied in educational settings in the United States in the 1980s, and was further developed in the United Kingdom in the 1990s.

The systemic approach focuses on the ways in which SEBD can be understood as the product of interactions between individuals and groups. This approach is often employed in conjunction with other approaches. It is important to note that all of these approaches are in current use in educational settings throughout the world, though psychodynamic approaches are less frequently used, while behavioural and cognitive behavioural approaches are most commonly used.

We will now deal with each of these approaches in more detail. (See Appendix I for the evolution of interventions for SEBD in relation to major educational Interventions.)

1 Therapeutic interventions/psychodynamic approaches

Psychodynamic therapies (origins c. 1900) involve the establishment of therapeutic relationships which enable the individual to reveal and explore analytically the life experiences that have influenced the development of dysfunctional ways of thinking and behaving.

Bridgeland (1971) reminds us that as early as the mid nineteenth century there were prominent critics of the practice of treating juvenile and deviant children as criminals in need of harsh, often corporal, punishment. Mary Carpenter and Dr Barnardo are cited as leading philanthropists of this period who established settings for vulnerable children that emphasized the therapeutic power of nurturing environments that were modelled on the template of caring families.

Some time later the American therapeutic pioneer, Homer Lane, set up residential communities for 'delinquent, deprived and disturbed children' (Bridgeland, 1971). The most famous of these was 'The Little Commonwealth', which was run on democratic lines, with the children being organized into family units. Although there is a clear continuity between Lane's Little Commonwealth and the practices developed by Carpenter and Barnardo before him, Lane's work was explicitly influenced by the then new science of psychology and, in particular the psychoanalytic theories of Freud which gave rise to a range of psychodynamic approaches to understanding and dealing with SEBD.

This approach is concerned with the ways in which an individual's current behaviour is associated with feeling-states that relate directly to their early life experience. Unresolved problems relating to childhood relationships with significant others, such as parents, create a barrier to the formation of trusting social and personal relationships in later life, because the individual is unconsciously preoccupied with the consequences of the unsatisfactory early relationship. This relationship is sometimes relived through the process of 'transference', whereby the individual identifies a different individual, for example a teacher, with the object of the unresolved relationship, for example, his or her father. Interventions based on this approach focus on the establishment of ego-strengthening relationships which enable the individual to form reciprocal attachments with others, and through these gain a sense of self-worth and psychological independence.

Interventions that emerge from this orientation are often described as 'therapeutic', and can take a wide range of forms, from one-to-one forms of intervention, such as psychotherapy and counselling, to whole-institution approaches (e.g., schools run as 'therapeutic communities'). The common factor uniting all of these approaches is the importance placed on interpersonal relationships. The purpose of the therapeutic relationship is to enable the pupil to develop a positive self-image whereby they come to see themselves as autonomous individuals worthy of the respect of others and accepting of themselves. Self-acceptance involves knowing one's strengths as well as one's limitations. A psychologically-healthy individual does not dwell on their faults and inadequacies, but, rather, attempts to work constructively to overcome problems associated with these limitations.

As noted earlier, the psychodynamic approach is most strongly associated with a number of residential schools and communities that flourished in the United States and the United Kingdom mostly between the 1920s and the 1970s (Laslett *et al.*, 1997). It should be pointed out that accounts of the working practices of staff in these settings by external commentators (Bridgeland, 1971; Burn, 1956) as well as by some of the practitioners themselves (Neill, 1968; Shaw, 1965; Wills, 1960) suggest that there were wide variations between the schools in terms of the ways in which they employed the psychodynamic approach. While some used psychotherapy; some did not. What the schools tended to share, however, was a broadly similar philosophical approach that was informed by psychodynamic thinking. The schools tended to be characterized by a caring ethos in which students were seen as partners with their staff in their own therapy. This meant that the schools were often run on democratic lines with students taking responsibility for certain aspects of the running of their communities. In extreme cases the heads of these schools advocated total freedom as a major requirement for effective intervention, with students having absolute parity with adult staff (Neill, 1968), while others defined their approach to student engagement in more structured terms referring to 'shared responsibility' (Wills, 1963) and committee structures (Shaw, 1965). A key aspect of the notion of freedom was the psychodynamic concern for the importance of students having the freedom to 'act out' their repressed emotions in a safe and non-judgemental context (Dawson, 1981).

The importance of relationships, which lies at the heart of the psychodynamic approach, has long been recognized by educators. Positive adult–pupil relationships often act as protective and remedial factors in the lives of young people with SEBD. Students with SEBD interviewed by Cooper (1993) referred to three positive effects of the residential special school experience.

Respite – they saw their residential schools as havens where they were protected from negative influences in their home settings, such as aversive family relationships, delinquent peers and deviance provocative mainstream schools.

Relationships – they developed trusting, mutually-respectful and supportive relationships with adults in the SEBD special schools they attended, and saw these as central in helping them develop more positive self images. They also cited these relationships as a source of therapeutic support.

Re-signification – they referred to ways in which they learned to define themselves in new and positive ways by being given support in tackling personal, social and academic challenges that previously they had felt to be beyond their realm of competence. In this way many of those interviewed described a personal transition from accepting a negative self-label to embracing a positive self-label.

Crucially, both students and staff interviewed referred to the importance of all three of these elements being interactive and essential to positive outcomes. It is interesting to note the way in which the identification of these factors prefigures the three processes associated with resilience described by Benard (2004) above.

2 Behavioural approaches

Behavioural therapies (origins c 1920) are based on the ways in which behaviour can be understood in terms of involuntary responses to external stimuli. Behavioural interventions exploit this theory by encouraging desired behaviours and extinguishing undesired behaviours through the manipulation of the stimuli which precede target behaviours and the consequences which follow from target behaviours.

Unlike psychodynamic and humanistic approaches, behavioural approaches concern themselves not with internal processes, but with the ways in which external factors influence and shape behaviour (Pavlov, 1927; Skinner, 1971; Watson, 1924). Kounin (1970), in the United States and Wheldall and Merrett (1984) in the United Kingdom were among the most prominent early advocates of the application of a behavioural analytic approach to classroom discipline. This approach assumes that the individual has not learned appropriate forms of behaviour, and may have learned unacceptable, alternative forms of behaviour. Interventions based on this approach involve training the individual to behave in desirable ways through the manipulation of rewards, sanctions and other contingency management strategies.

Examples of behavioural approaches designed to reinforce positive behaviour and discourage negative behaviour include:

- *Token economies* – Providing pupils with tokens (e.g., stars on a star chart) for performing target behaviours in return for specific rewards.
- *Rules-praise-ignore* – Publicly ignoring (i.e., failing to provide reinforcement for) a rule infringement by one pupil, while publicly praising (reinforcing) compliance with the rule by another pupil and making explicit reference to the rule concerned.
- *Time out* – removing a pupil from sources of reinforcement in the classroom.

The contrast between the psychodynamic and behavioural approaches is striking, and indicates the importance of matching the intervention to the needs of the individual. One is concerned with underlying emotional difficulties which give rise to problem behaviour, the other is concerned with dysfunctions of observed behaviour. This highlights the problem that is commonly cited, of some current approaches to SEBD being overly preoccupied with surface behaviour to the neglect of underlying emotional processes (Bowers, 2004). However, the ascendancy of behavioural approaches in schools since the 1960s is strongly related to the widely acknowledged need for teaching staff in schools to develop group-management skills, owing to the ways in which schools tend to be organized, with large numbers of students to relatively few supervising adults (DCSF, 2005; DES, 1989).

Behaviourism continues to be dominant among approaches to understanding and intervening with SEBD throughout the world. Wheldall (1987) claims that early ethical concerns about an over-reliance in some behavioural approaches on punishment were resolved as a result of more modern behavioural approaches being focused on the reinforcement of positive behaviour (Meichenbaum, 1977), though the legacy of this negative approach is still to be found in the practice of some teachers. In fact, a still widely-used version of this approach known as Assertive Discipline (Canter and Canter, 1976) places a strong emphasis on punishment, and might be seen as reflecting a somewhat intolerant approach to young people. However, it is important to stress that the considerable research base, on which behavioural approaches to SEBD rests, indicates that behavioural and cognitive behavioural approaches often need to combine both positive reinforcement (i.e., praise and reward) and response-cost strategies (i.e., punishment) in order to be optimally effective.

A typical behaviourist study was carried out by Walker *et al.* (1995). It describes and evaluates a series of behavioural interventions aimed at reducing negative-aggressive behaviour among elementary school-age boys. The interventions employed were adult praise, token reinforcement and cost contingency (i.e., the loss of previously awarded points as a form of punishment). Two groups of six students were studied. They were assigned to two different experimental conditions one after the other, each for three months. The difference between the two experimental conditions related to the combinations in which the interventions were applied. Outcomes of the study indicated that the use of social praise alone was extremely ineffective in promoting prosocial behaviour and reducing negative behaviour. By contrast the combination of social praise, tokens, and cost contingency was found to be highly effective in achieving positive change in the experimental setting.

The advantages of behavioural approaches, when they are effectively implemented, lie in their precision, in terms of the focus for intervention and relative ease with which the effectiveness of the interventions can be measured. Although Applied Behavioural Analysis can be complex, it enables changes in behaviour to be measured accurately. A major disadvantage, however, is that the focus on surface behaviour may lead to the neglect, masking, or even exacerbation of underlying intrapsychic problems.

3 Humanistic approaches

Humanistic therapies (origins c 1950) focus on ways in which self-concept is created and developed through social and interpersonal relationships. Interventions based on this approach, such as Rogers's Person-Centred approach, emphasize the therapeutic value of unconditional positive regard, empathy and honesty in relationships.

While the psychodynamic approach focuses on the ways in which individuals can explore the processes by which their attitudes towards themselves and others have been formed and in re-visiting early experiences remediate deep seated problems, the humanistic approach focuses on relationships in the here and now. At the heart of this approach to SEBD is the idea that humans function most effectively when they reach a point of self-acceptance based on an honest appraisal of themselves as human beings. Key features of the humanistic approach are the three 'core conditions' identified by Rogers (1980) in his client-centred therapy, or the person-centred approach, which provide the basis for functional human relationships that lead to positive mental health and a sense of well-being. These conditions, in a pedagogic environment, are:

Empathy is the ability of the teacher/facilitator to see the world through the eyes of the pupil and explicitly acknowledge the right of the pupil his or her own view of situation, no matter how contrary this might be to the teacher/facilitator's habitual view. This validation of the pupil's view of the world by another, significant person can help to break down the feelings of isolation felt by many individuals with SEBD. It can, in turn, create a capacity for empathy within the pupil, thus opening the way to the development of alternative (and possibly more functional) ways of thinking about and seeing the world and themselves.

Unconditional positive regard refers to the ability to split disapproval of the pupil behaviour from disapproval of the pupil as a person. The teacher/facilitator must always be accepting of the pupil/client as a person and show respect and personal warmth towards them. This process is essential in helping the pupil develop a sense self respect and, through this, respect for others.

Honesty (or 'congruence'), within the context of the first two conditions, involves the teacher/facilitator in being direct with the pupil about aspects of his or her behaviour that they perceive to be dysfunctional.

A crucial feature of Rogers' person-centred approach is that it is non-directive. This means that the teacher/facilitator avoids offering explicit advice about how the pupil should behave, but rather acts as a sounding-board for the pupil, enabling him/her to reveal their own ways of thinking and feeling, take ownership of these, and, thereby, become well-placed to make decisions and changes.

In the classroom this approach seeks to promote pupil engagement through a consultative approach to teaching. This would include such strategies as:

- finding out what interests the pupil;
- finding out what the pupil knows already;
- allowing the pupil to teach others (including the teacher/facilitator) what s/he knows about the topic; and
- teaching through questions rather than lecturing so that pupils extend their understanding by drawing on knowledge they already possess.

Another important application of this approach is in the promotion of Emotional Literacy. This involves:

- encouraging pupils to talk about their feelings in order to help them to develop a wide vocabulary of emotion words and concepts;
- using songs, stories, poetry and other literature to explore feelings; and
- using pictures, drawing and painting to explore feelings.

A key aspect of the humanistic approach is that it can be applied in virtually any setting and lends itself well to conventional day school settings. The psychodynamic approach, on the other hand, has often been considered most effective when applied within a highly controlled environment, such as the residential setting (Bridgeland, 1971). Humanistic approaches are also less intensive than traditional psychotherapy, relatively easy to learn and claimed to be more immediate in their effects (Rogers, 1951). These features all led to the humanistic approach being adopted with enthusiasm in the context of a greater focus on the mainstream school as a major site where SEBD and related difficulties could be addressed. Having said this, elements of the psychodynamic approach combined with a humanistic approach can be found in certain contemporary, mainstream-based approaches to supporting children with SEBD, such as Nurture Groups (Cooper and Tiknaz, 2007).

4 Cognitive behavioural approaches

Cognitive behavioural therapies (origins c. 1970) are concerned with the ways in which the relationship between external stimuli and target behaviours can sometimes be influenced by thought processes. The aim of Cognitive Behavioural therapy is to encourage the development of functional ways of thinking by challenging and changing dysfunctional ways of thinking.

The cognitive behavioural (CB) approach has its origins in the insights of Lev Vygotsky (1987–1999), who, arguably, from his vantage point of the 1930s continues to be the single most influential cognitive psychologist in the twentieth century and beyond. Among Vygotsky's most enduring insights is, first, that the higher human cognitive functions, such as spoken language and reflexive thinking, have their origins in human social interaction, and, second (following from this), that human beings use covert language (i.e., internal dialogue) as an important strategic tool in problem-solving and in mediating between external influences and their behaviour.

On the basis of this theoretical foundation CB interventions are directed at influencing the thought processes of target persons by enabling the individual to exert control over their behaviour often through applications of and adjustments to the 'self talk' process (Altepeter and Korger, 1999). By and large, CB interventions are intended to help individuals make conscious positive choices about how they behave, both in relation to themselves and others. This often involves identifying patterns of thinking, feeling and behaving that commonly accompany the expression of particular SEBD, and replacing these with more functional routines (Royer, 1999). CB interventions usually involve helping the individual to develop self-awareness and self-control through the application of self-monitoring strategies. This enables the individual to identify the onset of problematic situations and the triggers to dysfunctional behaviour. The next strategy is to learn problem-solving skills, which usually take the form of a series of steps which they learn first to verbalize overtly and later to verbalize covertly (Altepeter and Korger, 1999; Royer, 1999).

5 Systemic approaches

Systemic therapies (sometimes referred to as *eco-systemic approaches*) (origins c. 1970) are concerned with the patterns of interactions within and between groups of people. The central insight of the systemic approach is the idea that human beings exist within and depend upon social systems, and that the individual's personal needs are ultimately subordinate to those of the overarching system. Individuals' personal identities and social-emotional functioning are shaped by the roles they are required to perform in order to sustain the social systems they inhabit. Therapeutic intervention is required when an individual shows signs of social-emotional dysfunction as a result of their manner of engagement with a particular system or sub system. Systemic therapies are designed to enable individuals to continue to participate in key social systems (such as families, partnerships and work places) in ways which are functional in relation to their mental health. Systemic interventions involve behavioural and cognitive behavioural strategies, and therapists often employ humanistic insights.

Systemic approaches represent the newest family of strategies for intervening with SEBD, with their origins lying in the late 1960s. Drawing on von Bertalannfy's (1968) theory of interactional systems in biology and physics, Bronfenbrenner (1979) was among the first to apply a systemic analysis to human social interaction and educational systems and sub systems. It was, however, Minuchin (1973), de Shazer (1985) and Selvini-Palazzoli *et al.* (1973) who were among the first to exploit the therapeutic potential of these ideas in a revolutionary approach known as systemic family therapy. It was later that Molnar and Lindquist (1989) in the United States, and Cooper and Upton (1990) in the United Kingdom, drawing in particular on systemic family therapy, applied this approach to SEBD in schools under the title of 'ecosystemic' approaches. The term 'ecosystemic', therefore, applies specifically to those approaches that adapt systemic family therapy interventions for use in relation to SEBD in schools.

Central to the ecosystemic approach to SEBD is the idea that simple cause and effect theories of human behaviour, such as the Pavlovian stimulus-response model, while being demonstrably effective in shaping behaviour in a given context depend for their effectiveness on the ability of the interventionist to exert control over the perceived causes and/or consequences of problematic behaviour. Similarly, psychodynamic, humanistic and cognitive behavioural approaches also rely on cause and effect principles in relation to emotional, cognitive and interpersonal/social functioning. Such approaches are effective, but not always so. The ecosystemic approach comes into its own when these 'lineal' approaches fail, looking beyond the obvious cause and effect explanations and applying a 'systemic' analysis to the apparent problem.

A systemic analysis considers apparent problems as being subject to a wide range of possible influences. In the case of classroom behaviour problems, for example, the student who may be seen as the 'culprit' is located in relation to other sub-systems in the classroom, such as individual students, sub-groups of students, and the teacher. Furthermore, the classroom is a sub-system within the school and its rule structures. The school sub-system is, in turn, related to the family sub-system of the student and so on. It is the nature of sub-systems to be in permanent dynamic interaction with one another, the purpose of which is to maintain a stable (homeostatic) state. Where a behaviour problem is intractable, therefore, the problem will be serving some purpose that is not immediately apparent to those present in the sub-system where the problem is visible (as in the classroom). The problem may be being maintained in order to serve a need in a related sub-system (such as in the family). A further principle that follows is that change in any part of an ecosystem (i.e., a collection of interacting sub systems) will affect other parts of the ecosystem, though not always in a predictable (lineal) way.

Various kinds of psycho-educational interventions follow from this approach that are modelled on therapeutic approaches employed in systemic family therapy. A classic example of an ecosystemic intervention is 'reframing' (Molnar and Lindquist, 1989) which involves redefining the apparent problem in new terms and then acting in accordance with the new definition, no matter how counter-intuitive this may appear. This often involves constructing a version of the supposed problem which shifts the focus from the individual who is the supposed heart of the problem to people and circumstances outside the individual and the related patterns of interaction. The proclaimed value of a systemic approach is that it encourages lateral thinking and innovative action in situations which appear to be deadlocked.

Systemic approaches are most effectively used in community settings. The most noted exponent of this approach is Henggeler *et al.* (1999) whose Multi-Systemic Approach is a multi-agency intervention strategy that employs systemic thinking. It is cited by Kazdin (2002) as one the most empirically-effective interventions for dealing with teenage conduct disorders.

The Application of Psychological Principles to SEBD – Changing Values and Practices Over Time

As we have shown, key educational intervention for SEBD are based on therapeutic approaches. This is unsurprising, given that therapeutic approaches are based on theories of social and emotional *learning*. Therapeutic interventions exploit such theories to influence social and emotional learning. In this way, therapeutic approaches can be seen as methods of *teaching*. Choice of teaching methods is influenced by many factors which include efficacy of approach, practicality of approach as well as ethical and ideological considerations. These factors have played an important role in the changes in educational approaches to SEBD that have occurred over the years.

There are three major factors which have influenced changes in approaches to dealing with SEBD among school-aged students. They are:

1. ethical concerns about the relationship between SEBD and individual psycho-pathology;
2. the recognition that differences in educational outcomes reflect social in-equalities to a greater degree than they reflect differences in measurable 'ability'.
3. changing perceptions of the nature and role of childhood and the growth of interest in 'the rights of the child'.

We will now demonstrate briefly, the ways in which these factors have influenced changes in educational approaches to SEBD.

The rise, fall and partial-rehabilitation of psychodynamic approaches

As we noted above, the 'therapeutic education' movement, which had its heyday in the first half of the twentieth century in what have been termed 'pioneering' residential schools (Bridgeland, 1971), drew heavily on psychodynamic theories. This manifested itself in an explicit commitment to a psychoanalytic orientation; the extension of 'unconditional affection' to all staff and students; the advocacy of school climates which emphasized the value of freedom of expression and the acting out of emotional symptoms as step towards resolution of difficulties; and a commitment to the development of internalized controls through 'self government' or 'shared responsibility' rather than the imposition of external discipline (Dawson, 1981). This essentially British tradition lives on in a small number of institutions most notably The Mulberry Bush School in Oxfordshire, and in a very different form at Summerhill School in Suffolk. Elements of this tradition live on also in 'Nurture Group' intervention, which is currently widely used in schools throughout the United Kingdom.

In common with developments in the psychotherapeutic world, such explicitly psychodynamic approaches to the education of students with SEBD have largely given way to a wider range of therapeutically-informed interventions. In both the clinical and educational contexts this shift in emphasis was influenced by two factors. In order of importance, the first is a matter of principle, and the second a matter of pragmatism. The second factor is the easier to explain: psychodynamic interventions were complex and lengthy and required the therapist to have en-gaged in an extensive period of training and analysis. There was a growing sense that many of the problems that were presented to psychodynamic psychother-apists would probably be amenable to less intensive forms of intervention. The first objection, however, was more profound. The 1960s witnessed a significant and highly public debate about the nature of mental disorder. At the centre of this debate was a radical challenge to the individual pathology model at the heart of the psychodynamic approach. The main challengers argued that mental illness is a self-justifying and self-perpetuating social construction, which serves the interests of social control by individualizing what are essentially social problems (Bateson, 1970; Laing, 1960; Szatz, 1960). In the educational sphere this argument had its equivalent in the concerns about selective education and the construct of 'ability'. Radical critiques challenged the construct of general intelligence as an innate quality, and were able to demonstrate empirically the primacy of social and economic factors in determining outcomes that were commonly attributed to ability (Douglas, 1964). This argument was built upon by proponents of the 'New Sociology of Education', who specialized in demonstrating the ways in which the processes of social construction operated at the micro level of schools and classrooms (Hargreaves *et al.*, 1975; Young, 1971).

This social constructionist tradition in extreme form led to the view that SEBD is entirely the product of social factors. This view is often coupled with a rejection of a 'medical model' in general (e.g., Skidmore, 2004), which is portrayed as distracting attention from the social influences on SEBD in the interests of social control. The association between the psychodynamic approaches and residential schooling – on the face of it, the least 'inclusive' form of educational provision – have made the approach appear completely at odds with a modern social inclusion agenda. It is interesting to see, however, a return to prominence of certain theoretical approaches that are associated with that of the psychodynamic tradition, such as Bowlby's attachment theory which is evident, for example, in the widespread adoption of Nurture Groups throughout the United Kingdom (Cooper and Tiknaz, 2007).

The problem of behaviourism

What appears to have followed from the debates in the 1960s and 1970s was a widespread rise in the application of behavioural psychology in education both in relation to curriculum delivery and the growing field of 'classroom management' (Kounin, 1970). A particular feature of these approaches has been the use of contingency management strategies employing rewards and punishments, with an increasing emphasis on positive reinforcement as the intervention principle of choice (Wheldall and Merrit, 1984). The main message of these approaches is that schools and teachers experience the pupil behaviour that they deserve as a result of the patterns of reinforcement that are set up, either wittingly or unwittingly.

The widespread application of behaviourism in education has not been without its critics. Concerns have been aired about the ways in which behavioural interventions may lend themselves to manipulation – a view which is reflected in an aversion to the term 'management', which is often used in educational applications of behaviourism. The concept of 'conditioning', which is central to

therapeutic and educational applications of behaviourism, has come to be associated with the suppression of free will, and, therefore, as a potential threat to
human rights.

Behaviourism poses difficulties on the one hand because of its ethical neutrality
and, on the other, because of the fact that it is highly effective. Like any powerful
technology it can be used for moral or immoral purposes.

The humanistic solution

One response to concerns over the pathologizing influence of a psychodynamic
approach and the potential for dehumanization inherent in the behavioural approach has, since the 1970s and 1980s, a preference for humanistic approaches,
which have played an important role in the development of the concept of 'pastoral care' in schools, and have led on occasions to the employment of counsellors
in schools in many parts of the world (Hamblin, 1979). The approach is perhaps
most reflected in the emphasis on 'person-centred' approaches to promoting
student engagement in schools. Specifically, this approach can be seen in the
popularity of approaches such as 'Circle Time', which is widely used in schools in
many parts of the world.

At the heart of a humanistic approach is the principle that all human beings
are deserving of respect by virtue of the fact that they are human beings, and
a carefully constructed theory which states that solutions for many social and
psychological ills reside in the rigorous application of this principle. This is very
much in tune with contemporary perspectives on human rights, and in particular
the rights of the child. This helps to account for the popularity of this approach.

The cognitive behavioural solution

The rise of cognitive behavioural approaches follows from a dissatisfaction with
radical behaviourism. Cognitive behavioural programmes for social skills training
and anger management are, as we will show, widespread in the SEBD field. Cognitive behavioural approaches are, at least in their intention, far more emancipatory
than purely behavioural approaches. While behavioural approaches emphasize
the influence of external factors on behaviour, CB approaches are concerned with
shaping internal (intrapsychic) influences. The purpose of a CB intervention is to
identify distorted ways of seeing the world that are associated with social and/or
emotional dysfunction, and then to produce interventions that empower the individual to correct the distortion. Once again, the ethical standpoint of those
applying the intervention remains paramount.

The systemic synthesis

Systemic approaches are distinctive in that they offer a way of understanding
SEBD that transcends the linearity of many of the other approaches. The systemic

approach acknowledges that SEBD may be the product of an individual's way of thinking, or it may be the product of the interactions an individual has with other people, or (and most importantly) it may reside entirely in the minds and actions of people other than 'the symptomatic individual' (i.e., the person assumed to 'have' the SEBD). On the one hand there is an obvious resonance between the systemic approach and the desire to avoid pathological labelling. A systemic approach demands that the individual should always be considered within his or her social contexts. This renders the systemic approach appealing from a social justice perspective. This approach brings with it an emphasis on avoiding the apportioning of blame in favour of the identification of solutions to dysfunctions that arise from an analysis of the ways in which individuals interact with one another. As a result, the systemic approach can be portrayed as providing a synthesis of the other approaches that we have referred to. In fact the interventions that flow from this approach often combine features of behaviourism, humanism and, most commonly, cognitive behaviourism. The distinctive intervention feature is the target for the application of the intervention.

A cautionary note

It is important to note that although behaviourism is often singled out for its openness to abuse, all forms of therapy (and education) are vulnerable to abuse. This draws attention to the fact that education and therapy must always be delivered within the context of an explicit ethical framework. This applies at every level: from policy makers, to the managers, to front-line practitioners. At its most basic level, this ethical approach demands answers to questions such as:

- Whose interests are being considered in and served by the selection of a particular intervention (or intervention approach)?
- Whose interests are being considered in and served by the identification of the intended outcome from this intervention?
- Who is the greatest beneficiary of this intervention?

The educational challenge

It is important to recognize that psychological therapies rest on often complex psychological theories. The effective implementation of psychological therapies, therefore, often depend, in part at least, on the therapist's background knowledge in the discipline of psychology as well their skills in the application of a particular therapeutic technique. This makes the adaptation of therapeutic techniques for use by teachers and other educators problematic. While there are some highly skilled teachers with degree level qualifications in psychology and specialist training in the use of therapeutic approaches, in English-speaking countries teachers are often required to have only rudimentary knowledge of psychological theory and therapeutic practice. As a result of this situation the growth in the perceived need for school-based interventions for SEBD in recent years (coupled with the drive towards seeking to cater for SEBD in mainstream schools) has been met with a proliferation of intervention 'packages' intended for use by teachers and other educational staff with minimal training. As subsequent chapters of this report will show, many of these packages exploit behavioural and cognitive be-havioural approaches. Many of these approaches are designed to be used on a 'whole school' (aka 'universal') basis, owing to the empirically supported assump-tion that consistency of approach across an institution enhances effectiveness in the achievement of goals (e.g., Cowie *et al.*, 2008b; Rutter *et al.*, 1979).

Understanding the Development of SEBD: A Bio-Psycho-Social Approach

We have shown that students with SEBD represent significant challenges on a variety of fronts in modern societies. Any effective exploration of successful intervention into these problems must start with an appraisal of some of the most important of these challenges.

First it is important to consider the pivotal position of education and schooling. In various ways the school setting is a key site for the expression of SEBD, as well as, in some cases, being a trigger or exacerbating influence. Furthermore, disaffection from school and educational failure are strongly associated with SEBD. In turn, a history of SEBD in the school years, coupled with educational failure are common features in the life histories of adult criminals (Patterson *et al.*, 1992) and adults presenting with a range of psycho-social disorders (Rutter and Smith, 1995). Conversely, 'attachment to schooling' and other resilience factors are protective against the development of SEBD and delinquency (Smith, 2006) as well being associated with the resolution of SEBD in children of school age (Cooper and Tiknaz, 2007). This means that interventions that centre on the aim of promoting the educational engagement of youngsters with SEBD are likely to have wide-ranging and long-lasting effects.

Second, the role of the family as a causal agent in the development of SEBD, through various mechanisms, while offering a significant site for effective inter-vention (e.g., Kazdin, 2002), can also be acted upon by influences that are brought via the child, including the sometimes negative impact of the school (Cooper and Tiknaz, 2007). This suggests that the family should be considered in relation to wider systemic factors, especially the school, when seeking to understand what makes for effective intervention (e.g., Bronfenbrenner, 1979; Cooper *et al.*, 1994).

Third, the supposed tension that is sometimes perceived to exist between 'within child' biological and/or psychological factors and social/environmental explanations for the nature and development of SEBD can be misleading if it results in a blanket 'in principle' rejection of one set of explanations in favour of the other (e.g., Skidmore, 2002; Slee, 1995). We illustrated this point in detail in Chapter 1 in relation to the phenomenon of Attention Deficit/Hyperactivity

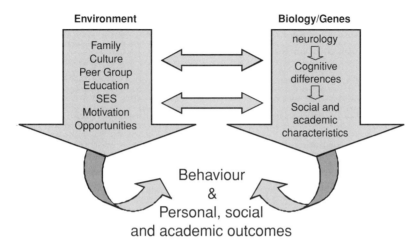

Figure 2.1   Biology and environment: bio-psycho-social interactions.

Disorder (AD/HD). It is important to start a search for effective interventions from a position that recognizes the validity of a 'bio-psycho-social' perspective (Cooper, 1997; Hernandez and Blazer, 2006; Norwich, 1990), whereby nature (genetic inheritance) and nurture (environmental influences) are seen as being in constant fluid and dynamic interaction (see Plomin, 1990; Frith, 1992).

Figure 2.1 offers a diagrammatic representation of a bio-psycho-social model. A central feature of the model is recognition of the fact that biological systems, such as neurology, are strongly influenced by genetic inheritance. However, from the earliest stages of life, the development of biological systems are affected by environmental factors, such as nutrition, and experiential factors, including parenting styles, peer influences and the kinds of stimuli to which the developing individual is exposed. For example, most relevant to the sphere of SEBD is the fact that it has been shown that the neurological development of children can be adversely affected by prolonged exposure to abuse, neglect or lack of stimulation, leading to cognitive and social impairments. Conversely, adjustments to the environment may, in certain circumstances help to reverse these effects. Furthermore, the 'plasticity' of the brain sometimes enables the brains of individuals who have experienced serious neurological insult, perhaps through injury or stroke, with concomitant loss of cognitive functioning (for example loss of language functions) to compensate for the loss of functioning in one area of the brain by transferring the functions to other brain areas leading to the restoration of cognitive functioning. In addition, a growing list of so-called 'smart drugs', many of which are psycho-stimulants of one kind and another (e.g., methylphenidate: 'Ritalin') and ampekines, are prescribed by physicians to augment, temporarily, neurological dysfunctions that are associated with specific cognitive deficits.

Other, perhaps more powerful forms of compensation and augmentation are of social and educational nature. These include the provision of compensatory skills for individuals, in the form of behavioural training, through the application of rewards and sanctions and the manipulation of behavioural antecedents; cognitive strategies (e.g., anger management training; mnemonic strategies) and various therapeutic interventions (e.g., counselling). Within the educational arena psycho-educational interventions, including specific pedagogical strategies (Purdie *et al.*, 2002), emotional literacy strategies (Mosely, 1993), and specific intervention packages such as Nurture Groups (Cooper and Whitebread, 2007), are claimed to make an important contribution to enabling the educational engagement of students with a wide range of social and psychological difficulties, some of which have a biological basis. Other educational interventions that have an augmenting/compensatory effect are of an institutional nature, and include 'school effectiveness' (e.g., Rutter *et al.*, 1979) and 'school improvement' (e.g., Fullan, 1992) interventions. More socially-focused interventions include systemic and multi-systemic interventions, as well as restorative justice and peer mediation strategies. It follows from a bio-psycho-social approach that the search for effective interventions should range widely across disciplines as diverse as education, psychology, sociology, medicine and psychiatry. For this reason multi-disciplinary and trans-disciplinary approaches are a focus of major interest in the SEBD area (see Chapter 6).

It should be acknowledge that the bio-psycho-social approach is closely related to the systemic approach, sharing a common origin in general systems theory (von Bertallanfy, 1968). The distinctive feature of this approach is to combine the psycho-social system with the individual biological system. Just as the systemic approach has the effect of synthesizing other, often individualized approaches to SEBD, while drawing attention to social environment influences, so the bio-psycho-social approach takes this synthesis a stage further, by integrating fully the internal biological and intrapsychic dimensions with the interpersonal and social dimensions. This makes the approach truly holistic and lends itself well to understanding the complexities of SEBD and its concomitant interventions.

The following chapters build on the themes developed here by focusing in detail on research evidence evaluating the effectiveness of specific educational and community interventions for SEBD in school students.

Summary

We began this chapter by defining Social, Emotional and Behavioural Difficulties (SEBD), highlighting some of the terms that are commonly used throughout the world to refer to this phenomenon. Emphasis was placed on the contextual nature of most SEBD and the unique challenges posed by SEBD in the school setting. When considering the causes of SEBD a variety of social and psychological models were referred to, illustrating the complexity of the phenomenon. Particular attention was given to the role of schooling as a causative or exacerbating factor, with reference being made to a long and wide ranging research tradition on this topic which reveals the toxicity of certain often taken for granted practices in schools and the historical tendency to neglect the social and personal needs of the most vulnerable students.

The remainder of the chapter was devoted to principles of intervention for SEBD. The educational significance of 'attachment to school' was emphasized, and cited as a major positive outcome of effective intervention. This construct was linked to seminal work of certain British educational 'pioneers' who, operating in the early and mid to late twentieth century, often in the special school sector, developed strategies for engaging 'maladjusted students' emotionally, socially and educationally. Modern equivalents of this early work were identified in relation to the concept of social and emotional resilience. A brief review of psychological principles underpinning therapeutic intervention for SEBD was then presented. The educational significance of these various approaches was emphasized. The chapter concluded with a discussion of the bio-psycho-social approach to understanding SEBD that, it was argued, highlights the interactive nature of environmental and individual factors, thus providing an excellent framework for combining interdisciplinary understandings of and approaches to SEBD.

3

The Teacher–Student Interface

Overview

The teacher–student relationship stands at the heart of the formal educational process. This view is evident in approaches to teaching and learning which stress the central importance of social interaction in the learning process. This chapter is concerned with research evidence on the professional qualities and attributes of teachers and their impact on the social, emotional and academic engagement of students.

Teachers' Characteristics and Skills

As noted in the previous chapter, there is a 'therapeutic' tradition in the SEBD field which emphasizes the importance of adult-initiated emotionally-supportive and stable relationships in the lives of young people with SEBD. The absence of such relationships is often associated with the onset of SEBD, while the resolution of these problems is often associated with their presence (Bridgeland, 1971; Cooper, 1993; Greenhaulgh, 1994).

Teachers who have a negative influence

Research showing the association between aversive relationships with teachers and negative student outcomes has a long tradition. Recently, Myers and Pianta (2008), for example, reported that there was a long-term intensification of problem behaviours in those children who experienced a negative relationship with a teacher. Something of the social psychological mechanisms at work here was shown two and a half decades earlier by Tattum (1982), who on the basis of informant style interviews that he conducted with disruptive students attending

From Inclusion to Engagement: Helping Students Engage with Schooling through Policy and Practice
By Paul Cooper and Barbara Jacobs © 2011 John Wiley & Sons, Ltd

an off-site unit in the United Kingdom, exposed five categories of motive that students gave for behaving in a disruptive manner. These were:

1. it was the teacher's fault;
2. being treated with disrespect (by the teacher);
3. inconsistency of rule application;
4. we were only messing about – having a laugh;
5. it's the fault of the school system.

Tattum's work echoes the findings of Rosser and Harre's (1976) symbolic interactionist study of disruptive students, who described the motives for their behaviour in terms of 'reciprocation' and 'retribution' for their treatment at the hands of teachers. More recently, similar views were expressed by secondary school students in a series of case studies in English schools which examined the different ways in which schools promoted and prevented student exclusion. Students contrasted their experience of exclusion-promoting schools, where they felt marginalized and anonymous and yet labelled as deviant, with exclusion-preventive schools where they felt known as persons and were treated with respect (Cooper *et al.*, 2000). These findings are echoed in recent studies by Pomeroy (2000) and Lodge and Lynch (2003) referred to in the previous chapter.

Interestingly, support for this view of the effects of teacher negativity on student conduct is also provided by research into teachers' views. Twemlow and Fonagy (2005) administered a questionnaire to a convenience sample of 214 teachers enquiring about their perceptions of teachers who bully. The study found that teachers who taught at schools with high levels of suspensions were more likely to report that they themselves had bullied students, had themselves been bullied at school and had worked with more bullying teachers over the past three years. The authors concluded that teachers who bully students may have some role to play in the etiology of behavioural problems in schoolchildren. These findings are in line with earlier case research carried out by Reynolds and Sullivan (1979) in secondary schools in South Wales. This study, located within the School Effectiveness paradigm found that teachers in the more effective schools adopted 'cooptive' as opposed to 'coercive' approaches to discipline, the latter being characterized by an emphasis on punishment, while the former favoured more humanistic approaches.

Teachers who have a positive influence

Although the previous section has emphasized the negative influence that aversive personal styles of teachers can have on student engagement, it was also noted that some of the evidence cited was based on the effects of contrasting teacher styles, and the general superiority of non-coercive and humanistic approaches. Various other studies have shown that teachers who are able to convey emotional warmth, and respect for students are often perceived to have a positive effect on the social and psychological engagement of students who present with SEBD. Buyse *et al.* (2008) in two studies of kindergarten teachers in Belgium, one involving 3798 children, the other involving 237, found that emotional warmth in a teacher helps children with both externalizing and internalizing behaviours to develop non-conflictual relationships in classrooms. LaRusso *et al.* (2008) used structural equation modelling on data from a nationally representative group of 476 14–18-year-old students in the United States and found that students who reported that their teachers were supportive were more likely to report a healthy school climate and lower drug use, greater social belonging and lower levels of depression than those who did not attribute these qualities to their teachers.

It is important to note that these qualities of personal warmth and supportiveness are also associated with desirable academic outcomes. McDonald *et al.* (2005), in a quantitative correlational study, showed that these positive characteristics of some teachers impacted strongly on academic outcomes, with warm and responsive teachers promoting stronger language skills in their students by the end of 1st grade. Cooper and McIntyre (1996), using a qualitative 'grounded theory' approach, studied 288 students and 13 teachers from five English comprehensive schools and found that 'a supportive social context designed by the teacher to help pupils feel accepted, cared for and valued' (p. 158) was among eight teacher qualities identified by both teachers and students as being associated with effective teaching leading to high levels of student engagement. An important finding of this study was that there appeared to be a strong relationship between students' self-declared sense of emotional security and their apparent levels of academic engagement. These factors were mediated by the social-emotional climate fostered by the teacher. Students were most socially and academically engaged when they felt supported and respected by their teachers, and when they expressed a sense of trust in their teachers.

The efficacy of social-constructivist approach to teaching, which was emphasized by the Cooper and McIntyre study is echoed in a study of seven teachers in an Australian school conducted by Gillies and Boyle (2008). They found that the teachers who showed the highest levels of ability to communicate, to ask metacognitive questions, and to mediate learning in a social-constructivist manner (such as through the use of scaffolding) were most successful in enabling students to achieve success in reflective thinking. The authors suggest that the mechanism by which this outcome was achieved involved students modelling teachers' communicative behaviour. Other small-scale qualitative studies have suggested the efficacy of the employment of reflexive techniques by teachers, whereby they record, examine and adjust their emotional responses to and communicative activities with their students. In one study in the United States, teachers were asked to keep a journal of their daily practice (Kreminitzer, 2005) in order to reflect critically on their own classroom management strategies, examine their emotional responses, and as a result reframe the strategies, where necessary. Similar small-scale studies have been carried out in Norway (Flem *et al.*, 2004), and Greece (Poulou, 2005).

Teachers' knowledge, understanding, beliefs attitudes and values

There is a widely held view that the adequate delivery of professional services depends upon certain minimum standards of training which are reflected in the sometimes legally-recognized credentials held by those people who present themselves as professionals. As a result of this view it is common, in the developed world, for state-funded education systems to require teachers to have a recognized professional qualification in teaching. Having said this, there is a sense in which the particular challenges posed by students with SEBD are often conspicuously absent from the compulsory initial training, tending to be available, if at all, only at the in-service, usually voluntary level (Maag and Katsiyannis, 1998). This is in spite of the fact that various authorities have cited the importance of knowledge and understanding of SEBD among teachers working in effective provision for students with SEBD (e.g., Charlton and David, 1990, and Daniels *et al.*, 1999).

Frölich *et al.* (2002), claimed that although ADHD provided teachers with many of their classroom problems, there was little teacher training in the foundations and principles of treatment of ADHD for teachers in regular classrooms, and poor coordination between parents, therapeutic institutions and teachers which militated against multi-modal treatments. His team of therapists, researchers and psychologists intervened in one Cologne elementary school, giving an intensive three-month teacher in-service training which provided information about the disorder, together with encouraging teachers to be a part of the 'treatment' process, and giving instruction about behavioural therapy in school. Outcomes of this case study indicated that the programme had a positive impact on teachers' effectiveness in managing difficulties that they encountered in relation to ADHD.

In an Israeli study (Shiff and BarGil, 2004), two workshops for a total of 42 elementary school teachers on the understanding and management of children with SEBD, were followed by improvements in teachers' confidence in coping with these children in their classes. Marzocchi *et al.* (2004) in an intervention study in Italy, trained teachers in behaviour modification strategies, resulting, at the end of the seven months intervention in significant improvements in the students' attention, levels of hyperactivity and oppositional behaviours, and improved teacher-student relationships. In another German study, in Hamburg (Rossbach and Probst, 2005), 18 advisory teachers were trained in ADHD theory, contingency management and antecedent training, together with the structured learning intervention TEACCH (Schopler *et al.*, 1971). A sub-group of 6 of these teachers then taught 10 classroom teachers the basic strategies, with 4 of these teachers receiving further training in contingency management. ADHD symptoms were significantly improved, in both treatment groups, with more maintenance in the group of those teachers who had received the additional training. A similar improvement in teacher skills, and confidence was produced in a larger-scale in-service intervention study, involving 49 teachers and 796 of their ADHD students, by Zentall and Javorsky (2007), in the United States.

These studies appear to suggest that training has an important role to play in the development of teachers' and other education professionals' knowledge, understanding and skills in relation to SEBD. This issue seems to be all the more pressing in an international climate that favours the inclusion of students with SEBD in mainstream schools. In these circumstances the knowledge, understanding and skills that mainstream school personnel have in relation to SEBD becomes of critical importance. This point is illustrated by questions about the extent to which the role of the teacher is now overlapping with that of the mental health professional. This is the subject of a recent UK qualitative study (Rothi *et al.*, 2008), in which 30 teachers, from primary, secondary and special schools, participated in semi-structured interviews to determine the extent to which they believed that it was their duty to identify mental health needs, and whether they thought that they had the necessary training to do this. Almost all agreed that their skills needed to be supplemented with additional skills relating to SEBD, but several pointed out the challenges posed by the fact that such training would inevitably compete with other training demands related to the curriculum and other government initiatives.

Before we turn to a consideration of some of the empirically-based programmes that might be made available through training materials to school personnel it is important to give consideration to the issue of teachers' beliefs, values and attitudes. This is an important issue, not least because there is a strong emphasis on the significance of these factors in contemporary scholarship in the field of inclusive education (e.g., Booth and Ainscow, 1997; Skidmore, 2004; Slee, 1995) (see Chapter 1). In keeping with the positive teacher qualities described earlier in this chapter the 'educational values hypothesis' (Becker *et al.*, 2003, p. 12) states that:

> The best teachers hold a particular set of values about education – typical examples include commitment to helping all kinds of children learn, valuing diversity and caring, and espousing patience and persistence (Metzger and Jia Wu, 2008).

One response to the evidence based contention that 'good' teachers display these qualities might be that we should select recruits to the teaching profession on the basis of the extent to which they portray these qualities. Metzger and Jia Wu (2009) carried out a meta-analysis of 24 studies on the efficacy of this approach to selection in relation to a number of outcome variables, including efficacy ratings provided by administrators (i.e., school managers), observers (i.e., researchers) and students. Student gain scores are also included in the analysis. The results indicate that there is a small positive effect ($r = .28$). Having said this, questions remain about the validity and reliability of these instruments. More serious questions relate to the assumed association between an individual's espoused beliefs, attitudes and values, and those they reveal in their actual classroom interactions. In any event, the over emphasis on values and beliefs identified by MacBeath *et al.* (2006), and illustrated with reference to some inclusion literature in Chapter 1 of this book, is rendered questionable by existing empirical evidence.

Managing the physical environment of the classroom

The impact of the physical environment on students' social and educational engagement is a relatively neglected topic in the research literature. Early school effectiveness researchers, for example, found, at best, only a limited association between the physical school environment and social and academic outcome measures (Rutter *et al.*, 1979). This view would appear counter-intuitive to many teachers, as Lowe (1990) found in an interview study with high performing teachers in the United States. When asked to describe aspects of the physical environment which affected their teaching, they referred to the availability and quality of classroom equipment and furnishings, as well as environmental factors such as climate control and acoustics as the most important environmental factors. They emphasized in particular the need to be able to control classroom temperature, and considered this to have a significant effect on the performance of both students and teachers. While this latter finding could be explained as relating to specific local climatic conditions which featured extreme temperatures, the study is consistent with the findings of similar studies that teachers commonly view the physical environment to have a significant influence on personal, social and educational performance.

In the United States there have been a number of substantial, retrospective correlational studies that have examined the relationship between the quality of the physical environment of the school and student outcomes. Several of these studies have highlighted the negative impact of poor environmental conditions in schools on student and staff morale. Studies which have controlled for socio-economic status have found students experiencing school environments characterized by dysfunctional toilets, poorly-maintained buildings and ineffective control of climatic conditions achieve significantly lower scores on standardized achievement tests than students attending schools with higher environmental standards (Uline and Tscannen-Moran, 2008).

Overcrowding in schools has been a serious problem in many school systems. A study of overcrowded schools in New York City found that students in such schools scored significantly lower on both mathematics and reading exams than similar students in schools that were not overcrowded.

There is also evidence, often from small scale qualitative studies, to suggest that the choices teachers make which affect the quality of the classroom environment can sometimes be interpreted to reflect to students and others what teachers value in behaviour and learning (Savage, 1999; Weinstein, 1992) as well as the extent to which the students themselves are valued as persons by the teacher (Cooper, 1993; Cooper and Tiknaz, 2007). This point is illustrated in Nurture Group provision (see Chapter 4) that imports features of a comfortable, homely residential environment into the classroom as part of a regime designed to promote feelings of emotional security in students. This echoes approaches adopted in therapeutic residential schools for students with SEBD (Bridgeland, 1971; Cooper, 1993) referred to earlier.

Studies of the spatial configuration of the classroom focus on such issues as patterns of student seating, the physical proximity of students to teachers, patterns of physical circulation in the classroom, and the overall sense of atmosphere and order. Drawing on a range of studies (Bettenhausen, 1998; Fullan, 1992; MacAulay, 1990; Quinn *et al.*, 2000; Rinehart, 1991; Shores *et al.*, 1993; Stewart and Evans, 1997; Walker *et al.*, 1995; Walker and Walker, 1991; Wannarka and Ruhl, 2008; Wolfgang, 1996) the following spatial concerns are highlighted for their significance in relation to student engagement in classrooms.

- The need for the teacher to define clearly spaces within the classroom for specific purposes and to ensure students know how to behave in each of these areas.
- Seating students in rows facilitates individual academic engagement, whereas more open arrangements (e.g., groups or semi-circles) facilitate social exchanges among students more suited to tasks requiring student interaction with one another.
- Classrooms need to be arranged to limit student contact in 'high-traffic' areas such as the space surround the pencil sharpener and wastebasket, and instructional areas; and to seat easily-distracted students farther away from 'high-traffic' areas.
- Students with special needs or behaviour problems will be easier to manage if placed in close proximity to the teacher's desk. This facilitates both monitoring of student behaviours and teacher delivery of positive statements when appropriate.
- As far as possible all students should have a clear view of the teacher and vice versa at all times.
- It is useful to limit visual and auditory stimulation which may distract students with attention and behaviour problems.
- It is advantageous to keep the classroom orderly and well-organized. For example, the classroom is safe, clean, free of distracting physical features; the furnishings are flexible and fit the people who use them; media equipment are available and operable; lighting, windows and blinds are operable; and there is adequate control over ventilation and temperature.

In conclusion to this section, it should be stressed that the topic of the impact of the physical environment and organization of schools and classrooms has not received a great deal of attention from researchers. The limited evidence that does exist is based in relatively low-powered studies and no Random Controlled Trials (RCTs). With these reservations in mind, however, it can be stated that there is evidence indicating that both students and teachers are influenced by the physical environment of schools, and that the choices that teachers make regarding the ways in which their classrooms are organized can affect student performance and engagement. An important implication of this research is that teachers' and students' achievements may be adversely affected by poor environmental conditions.

Peers as a Classroom Resource

The student peer group performs a powerful role influencing the quality of student behaviour in schools that if not harnessed effectively can have a negative impact.

In a study conducted by Barth *et al.* (2004), it was concluded that peers can serve as reinforcers and models, and that, in examining 65 classrooms in 17 schools with a high proportion of SEBD, disruptive students can serve to promote negative behaviours, and that the classroom environment can be counter-productive where these children serve as role models. Dishion *et al.* (1999) examined this negative influence on interventions designed to alleviate behavioural difficulties.

In a retrospective study of two peer-oriented interventions for high-risk boys, conducted by Gottfredson (1987) outcome measures appeared to point to the success of the interventions during their course. However, follow-up studies showed that both these interventions had been not only unsuccessful, but that the children who had taken part, in the short and long term, were more likely than those in the control groups to indulge in the very high-risk behaviours which the programme had been targeting. This was particularly evident in the earlier intervention, which showed no differences in improvement between treated and control group adolescents, but more worryingly, appeared to have harmful long-term effects, especially those who had been involved in the most intensive of the interventions when follow-up data about these participants were collected during their late middle-age. This effect, referred to as 'deviancy training', was most noticeable in the boys who had been older at the time of intervention, confounding the assumption that younger more vulnerable boys would be more likely to be negatively influenced by older peers. Gottfredson (1987) argues that this potentially 'toxic' peer influence effect must be taken into account in SEBD interventions.

Having said this, this study identified two additional encouraging and useful findings. One was that those boys with internalizing depressive symptoms appeared to benefit from peer training in the absence of peers with disruptive or externalizing disorders (Lewinsohn and Clark, 1990). This suggests that different interventions may be appropriate for different types of conduct problems, and that where the disorder involves 'acting-out', the intervention may not be successful with those who suffer from anxiety and depression, and vice versa.

It has also been observed that where parental training and involvement is added to the peer-group intervention, this appears to have a protective effect against the tendency of youth to cluster into deviant peer-groups (Dishion *et al.*, 1999). The authors qualify their findings by concluding that not all peer-group interventions have produced such negative effects (Feindler *et al.*, 1984, Wassef *et al.*, 1996), although most of these studies have been with students with internalizing disorders. This type of parental-inclusive intervention is explored further, in Chapter 5.

Positive Peer Reporting and 'Tootling'

Research also directs attention to the effect that student with SEBD may have on their typically-developing peers. For example, children who are the victims of disruption often socially-marginalize the disrupters (Lochman and Lampron,

1985). Skinner *et al.* (2002), points to the relationship between this pattern of rejection, and disciplinarian educational regimes which model rejecting and exclusionary behaviours against those perceived to be 'deviant'. Hamre and Pianta (2001) found that such rejection, when evident during students' earliest encounters with schooling, is likely to increase the manifestations of SEBD over time, and early evidence of difficult relationships between 1st grade children and their teachers can persist through to 8th grade (i.e., when students are approximately 13 years of age). In a recent study of teachers' attributions of misbehaviour conducted in the United Kingdom and Ireland, teachers acknowledged that their own interaction with the children they teach, including the rewards and sanctions they utilize, may contribute to misbehaviour in their students (Gibbs and Gardiner, 2008). Students' perceptions of unfairness in the application of discipline was seen as a major factor in causing this effect, which was further exacerbated in situations where teachers failed to give sufficient verbal praise and recognition of good work. In these circumstances the any prosocial behaviours displayed by the 'SEBD student' are overlooked by both staff and peers, resulting in what has been known for a long time as the 'self-fulfilling prophecy' whereby certain students are labelled with deviant identities from which it become increasingly difficult to escape (Hargreaves *et al.*, 1975). Peer 'grassing' and 'tattling' can become powerful components in this process (Skinner *et al.*, 2002).

Skinner *et al.* (2002) review two interventions which may alleviate this social rejection and discourage negative feedback from peers about what may be judged to be unacceptable behaviour. In one, Positive Peer Reporting (PPR) (Bowers *et al.*, 2000; Ervin *et al.*, 1996; Jones *et al.*, 2000; Moroz and Jones, 2002), children were told that they would be given the opportunity to earn tokens for noticing another child's positive behaviour, and reporting on it, aloud, in an end-of-day 10-minute session. A student was chosen as 'Star of The Week', and peers were trained to notice any prosocial behaviour of this 'star' each day, and to give their reports with the child and teacher present. PPR was introduced to the class as being the opposite of 'tattling' or 'grassing' on unacceptable behaviour. Data from all studies determined that PPR was effective in increasing positive peer interaction, and in increasing peer acceptance of children with SEBD. In the Ervin *et al.* (1996) study, rather than the students being rewarded individually for their input, each positive report earned a cotton-wool ball, and these were put into a jar. When the jar was full, the entire class was rewarded with a party. This group reward was found to be particularly effective.

The other intervention, 'Tootling' (Skinner *et al.*, 2002), does not target an individual child as the focus of peer support, but rather offers all children the opportunity to alter their behaviour from tattling negatively about other children's behaviour, to seeking to praise the rather less noticeable prosocial behaviour of all their peers. During the course of each school day, the pupils are encouraged to fill in report cards about all prosocial behaviours they encounter in their classmates. At the end of each day, these report cards are handed in to the teacher. As in the Ervin *et al.* (1996) study, the rewards gained by students are shared by the group. Tootling is flexible and progressive, in that as the classmates develop an awareness of what constitutes helpful behaviour, over time, changes are made in the criteria to be met for reinforcement, and the use of group reinforcements may be randomly selected to prioritize certain positive but overlooked behaviours. These two interventions have certain limitations, the most challenging of which is the fact that once reinforcers are withdrawn, behaviour reverts to baseline. Research continues, to discover whether fading (i.e., the gradual diminution of rewards), rather than withdrawal, may encourage maintenance.

Skinner *et al.*'s (2002, p. 199) paper concludes with a provocative observation:

> Proactive punishment systems may be needed to prevent incidental antisocial behaviour. The attention and energy placed into developing and implementing these systems may teach children that inappropriate behaviours are unaccept-able, but do little to suggest that society values incidental non-dramatic pro-social behaviours. Thus, future researchers should determine if implementing programs designed to encourage pro-social behaviours may help shape adults who value and respect incidental pro-social behaviours.

In relation to an earlier point, this reminds us of the importance of the values and attitudes that are revealed in teachers' actions (as opposed to those which they may espouse), and the influence these can have on student behaviour. As we have already noted, punitive and coercive teachers tend to promote, albeit unwittingly, coercive behaviour in their students. This is not to say that the reinforcement of behavioural boundaries through the application of proportional sanctions is undesirable, on the contrary, it is highly important that citizens in a civil society come to learn that selfish and uncivil behaviour bring negative consequences to the perpetrators of such behaviours. The central point being made here is that where punishment is the *only* or *main* means employed for the control of behaviour, there will be a tendency among those receiving the punishment to wish to avoid receiving punishment, but not necessarily through the adoption of prosocial behavioural strategies. If we want our students (and citizens) to engage in prosocial behaviour, rather than simply seeking ways of being deviant without receiving punishment, we must find ways of locating our sanction regimes within schemes which reward and reinforce prosocial behaviour.

Class-Wide Peer Tutoring (CWPT)

One of the most strongly-evidenced behavioural interventions for academic progress in children with SEBD is peer-assisted learning which in the main addresses academic outcomes for children at risk, through peer-assistance and increased opportunities to respond (Damon, 1984; Pigott *et al.*, 1986; Suther-land *et al.*, 2003; Topping, 2005). One of the best known of these strategies is Class Wide Peer Tutoring (CWPT) originally devised in the early 1980s in the Juniper Gardens Project (Delquadri *et al.*, 1986), which is a community-based instructional programme for children in a low-income urban area, overseen by the University of Kansas. It is based on a discovery by behavioural analysts that children with academic difficulties and those with attention problems (DuPaul and Henningson, 1993) can have their learning accelerated by being given more frequent opportunities to respond (Hall *et al.*, 1982). The researchers noted that one of the differences in what were then called Chapter One schools, those serving the most deprived areas, is that teaching staff engaged students in response far less, on average 11 minutes a day less, than schools serving areas of high socioeconomic status (Greenwood *et al.*, 1989). CWPT which twins each learner with another peer rather than a teacher to increase the reciprocal responses of each, can be adapted for use in all classrooms, is most effective in kindergarten and early grades of elementary school, and is now being trialled in middle schools (Kamps *et al.*, 2008; Veerkamp *et al.*, 2007).

In this intervention, after pretesting, and tutoring them in tutor skills, on Monday morning children are divided into dyads and each pair is then assigned to a team. Each student tests the other student on spelling, mathematics, reading and comprehension. The two take it in turns to test the other on the previous Friday's lessons. The tutee earns two points for every correct answer, and if an incorrect answer is given the tutor can then earn a point by writing the correct answer on the worksheet three times. After 10 minutes the tutee and tutor exchange places. At the end of the session points are entered up on a team point chart. This peer tutoring is held on every Monday to Thursday morning for half an hour in all. The team with the most points is announced daily, and the week's winning team is rewarded on Fridays, when all children are individually tested on the week's work. This intervention incorporates the two elements identified by Slavin (1990) as those conditions necessary for children to help each other learn: group goals (interdependence), and individual accountability.

The first large-scale trial to determine whether this intervention was reliable (Greenwood *et al.*, 1987), was a field replication of early pilot studies and was a single-subject design with baseline, reversal, and pretest probes conducted in four inner-city schools, involving 211 1st and 2nd grade pupils, in a socio-economically deprived area of Kansas City, over two years. Students were assigned to a high or low pretest group. The groups were assigned to either: (a) Teacher Regular Procedures; or (b) Class Wide Peer Tutoring. Results indicated that substantial improvements were made by students under direct teacher instructional procedures, but that significant additional improvements were made by both high and low groups during CWPT.

A further longitudinal study (Greenwood *et al.*, 1989) over four years, initially involving 416 students, compared the achievements of students in low socioeconomic status (SES) area schools, and those in high SES schools. Two groups, one a high SES area school were offered teacher instruction only (comparison), and one low SES group (control). One low SES group was offered CWPT (experimental). After four years a total of 877 students had entered the database. There was a high attrition rate (68.2%) in the experimental group because of population mobility, exacerbated by the closure of one of the schools. Post hoc tests indicated that the experimental group engaged in significantly more reading aloud, academic talk and question asking, but significantly less hand-raising, to request teacher assistance, than both comparison and control groups. The low

SES experimental group achieved significantly greater gains in language, reading and mathematics than did the equivalent low SES control group. However, there were no significant differences between the gains made by the experimental group compared with the high SES comparison group which received teacher instruction only, although effect sizes were higher in the high SES group. After four years the experimental group exceeded or approached the national norms in all academic domains, while the control group remained consistently below this level. Effect sizes ranged from .37 to .60.

Some of the subsequent trials, which produced similarly positive results, particularly in spelling improvement, involved low sample sizes. Kohler and Greenwood (1990) used only three students, Sideridis *et al.* (1997) only six, of whom three were typically-developing children and three had mild difficulties, and Mortweet *et al.* (1999) studied four students with mild mental retardation. Bownam-Perrott *et al.* (2007) investigated the use of CWPT in secondary level students with SEBD in two alternative school classrooms with a high teacher-student ratio, finding, in an ABAB single-subject design that CWPT had little effect in one of these classrooms on biology test scores, and only slightly improved in the second. On adding self-monitoring skills to the original design, and comparing this with instruction in a third classroom on spelling instruction, using an alternating treatment design, sizeable improvements in most but not all weeks of the study were obtained. More importantly, students in all three classrooms improved in on-task time, when using CWPT, as opposed to conventional instruction. Allsopp (1997) used CWPT with groups of 14 year olds to improve their understanding of algebra, comparing it with individual instruction, discovering that there was little significant difference within the two groups, although those most at risk for mathematics failure did show modest improvements.

CWPT has received the 'Proven' certification from the US Promising Practices Network (www.promisingpractices.net), which summarizes the findings of the studies. The various project evaluations found that:

- When students began CWPT in the 1st grade, by the end of the 4th grade they scored more than 11% higher than control groups on a nationally standardized test in both reading and mathematics (40% versus 29% in reading, and 49% versus 38% in mathematics), after test scores were adjusted for differences between the two groups that were determined in the first grade (for example, measured IQ).
- CWPT produced average gains of 12% on spelling tests among 3rd and 4th graders, with 80% of the students receiving grades in the A range (90% and higher).
- Children were 20–70% more likely to stay on-task, remain engaged with their lessons, and respond to the teacher during CWPT than they were before the programme.
- On average, 1st graders tested above the 2nd grade level on comprehension and vocabulary using the Gates-MacGinitie Reading Test, with a class average of 2nd grade, fourth month, in comprehension and 2nd grade, seventh month, in vocabulary after five months of CWPT.

• An experimental group of children in elementary schools in economically depressed areas performed almost as well as a comparison group of children from higher socioeconomic groups and performed significantly better than a control group of students from other elementary schools in economically depressed areas who did not receive CWPT.

Peer Assisted Learning Strategies

The core elements of CWPT have been incorporated into another programme which partially replicates the methodology of its predecessor, but adds certain other elements which have been shown to increase academic competence in children with reading and numeracy delay, in particular. This variant, Peer Assisted Learning Strategies (PALS) (Falk and Wehby, 2000; Fuchs *et al.*, 1999, 2000a, 2000b, 2002; Mathes *et al.*, 1998) has been tested for improving mathematics skills (Baker, 2004), but largely concentrates on language skills and reading for students at risk, and incorporates paragraph shrinking (summary and comprehension), and prediction relay, in which the students have to predict what might occur next in the text. There is sound cognitive research on both these elements. Practise in summarizing key ideas in a paragraph enhances reading comprehension (Baumann, 1984) and practise in formulating predictions is also associated with reading comprehension (Palincsar and Brown, 1984). The PALS scheme has been shown to be an effective reading intervention (US Department of Education Program Effectiveness Panel) across learning disabled, low-achieving and average-achieving children in elementary schools, and with children with SEBD (Wehby *et al.*, 2003) and its recommended use is for three 35-minute sessions each week, in which peers correct each other's reading, shrink paragraphs in turn into 10 words, and then, in turn predict what the next half page will say. Points are earned much in the same way as in CWPT.

In a study designed to examine whether the improvements produced by PALS could be carried over to high school students with serious reading problems (Fuchs *et al.*, 1999), the authors discovered that in this 16-week intervention carried out in nine classrooms with an average pupil size of 15, with a control group of a similar size, reading comprehension was increased in the PALS group with an effect size of .38. However reading fluency did not improve differentially as a result of the intervention, nor did the students in the intervention group increase their overall belief in their reading abilities. The adaptation of this programme to the needs of older reluctant readers continues, and further research will be needed.

The scheme was also used in a Canadian study to determine whether there would be an improvement, following peer tutoring in students' social preference and friendship making, but there were only modest positive effects, and those on the least popular and most isolated children, pretest (Dion *et al.*, 2005). A similar study on the social behaviours of six 3rd grade students with emotional and behavioural disorders using the PALS programme, discovered that reading improvement was not related to generalized changes in inappropriate behaviour (Barton-Arwood *et al.*, 2005).

In a meta-analysis of all peer-assisted learning schemes Rohrbeck *et al.* (2003) determined that this type of intervention was most successful with younger, low-income, and minority students, and that those that used interdependent reward systems, self-evaluation procedures, and provided students with most autonomy, had higher effect sizes.

A further meta-analysis by members of this same group of researchers (Ginsburg-Block *et al.*, 2006) examined the social, self-concept and behavioural effects of peer-assisted learning. This concluded that there were small to moderate effects on these three social-emotional outcomes and that there was a positive re-lationship between these outcomes and student achievement. The most effective procedures were those already noted in the previous meta-analysis, with the ad-dition, in these outcome measures, of structured student roles and same-gender grouping. Although causal relationships could not be established between these procedures and the outcomes, this, they felt, may be elucidated by further study. The authors conclude (Ginsburg-Block *et al.*, 2006, p. 749) 'PAL interventions may help address the affective needs of vulnerable student populations without sacrificing their academic needs'.

This conclusion is echoed by the findings of another meta-analysis (Roseth *et al.*, 2008) of 148 independent, international studies on the effect of early adolescents' achievement and peer relationships, and the effect on these of coop-erative, competitive and individualistic goal-setting. Positive peer relationships were predicted by cooperative goals, and these were associated with a positive association between achievement and successful peer relationships.

Conclusion

The evidence reviewed in this chapter has shown the enormous importance of the skills and qualities that effective teachers reveal in relation to the ways in which they manage their interactions with students at the classroom level. We have also noted, however, the damage that occurs when these interactions are badly handled, echoing the findings of the MacBeath *et al.* (2006) study which we reviewed in Chapter 1. The strongest message from this chapter is the importance of the knowledge and skills that teachers and paraprofessionals need to possess in order to be effective. They need to understand the importance of the relationships between social, emotional and pedagogical factors, and have command of the interpersonal, social and pedagogical skills that follow from this. The most surprising and frustrating conclusion to be drawn is that many of the research findings presented here are neither new nor antithetical to the education policies espoused by countries which claim to be pursing an inclusive education agenda. Furthermore, these findings offer active and positive support to such agendas. Yet they remain, to all intents and purposes absent from the compulsory initial and in-service training programmes of these same countries.

Until this anomaly is rectified the crippling problems with the implementation of inclusive education, which have been identified by various commentators, will remain potent.

Summary

This chapter has examined the kinds of understandings and skills that individual teachers, who are effective in promoting the educational engagement of students, possess particularly those presenting with SEBD. Teachers who demonstrate emotional warmth have been shown to improve the well-being of students, not only in engagement with school but also in enabling academic achievement. A number of research studies which show that in-service training about the nature of SEBD is of considerable assistance to classroom teachers. Effective approaches to managing the physical environment of the classroom in relation to SEBD are supported by a limited number of studies which tend to be small scale, often taking the form of prospective or retrospective case studies. There is some evidence, though of a relatively low power, to indicate that poor quality educational environments inhibit the effective performance of both students and teachers. Strategies for utilizing student peer influence are supported by promising empirical evidence. The chapter concludes by noting the lack of novelty in these findings coupled with surprise at the failure of policy makers to respond comprehensively to these findings through their pre- and in-service training programmes for teachers and paraprofessionals.

4

Interventions for Enhancing Teachers' Skills

Overview

In this chapter we examine a range of interventions designed to promote positive student engagement that can be employed by individual teachers in a school setting. Behavioural, cognitive behavioural and instructional strategies are explored. We review evidence for the efficacy of these approaches.

Behavioural Interventions

Behavioural approaches for dealing with SEBD are based on principles of contingency management and reinforcement that were developed initially on the basis of research with animals. It is to the work of Watson and Skinner that the widespread applications of behavioural theory to human subjects can be attributed (see Chapter 2). This history has sometimes led to behaviourism being attacked for its reductionist portrayal of humans as being on same behavioural plane as animals, and for its denial of the importance of 'mind' (e.g., Malik, 2000). Along with these views come concerns about the undeniable power of behavioural methods to shape and thus manipulate human behaviour. These are important criticisms that must not be ignored. Having said this, it is equally important to emphasize the way in which behavioural approaches require us to understand deviance in terms of objectively observable behaviour without reference to attitudinal or other personal factors (Cooper *et al.*, 1994). Such an approach can, for example, have the positive effect of removing feelings of hurt or blame which may serve to exacerbate a problem and direct attention to aspects of the educational environment which may be influential as antecedents to or consequences of the behaviour in focus. As with all SEBD interventions, it is the responsibility of the person carrying out the intervention to do so in an ethical manner.

The Good Behaviour Game (GBG)

In the research literature on interventions for improving student behaviour in school setting the Good Behaviour Game (Barrish *et al.*, 1969) stands out as one of the most powerful applications of behaviourist principles to this problem. This approach has been enjoying significant demonstrable success in Europe and North America since the 1960s. Its longevity has also enabled its effects to be measured longitudinally (e.g., Kellam and Anthony, 1998). Evidence indicates that it is particularly effective for a wide range of social, emotional and behavioural difficulties and in a wide range of educational settings with students from 4 to 18 years of age (Tingstrom, 2006).

The GBG is played between teams of students and is based on interdependent group contingencies in which each member of a team is rewarded for the aggregate behavioural performance of their team. This means that each group member must try to both regulate his or her own behaviour and help fellow team members to do the same in order to gain the reinforcing reward.

Usually, the GBG involves the teacher and pupils establishing a small set of classroom rules which deal with desired behaviour. These might include on-seat behaviour, and/or quiet working. These rules are then posted so that members of the class can familiarize themselves with them. In the following weeks, the class is divided into two or three teams at various times in the day. In the initial stages the Game is played over short periods of time, usually 10 minutes, although these sessions are increased over the course of the intervention both in terms of time and in terms of frequency. Within each team, pupils will receive a tick on the blackboard if one of the members of the team breaks one of the agreed rules. Teams with four or fewer ticks at the end of the Game session are awarded token reinforcements, perhaps small gifts like stickers, or an activity choice.

Research evidence suggests that in order to employ the GBG effectively, the game coordinator (usually a teacher or teaching assistant) must exercise skill in avoiding some of the pitfalls that can occur in interdependent contingency management situations. For example, children who exhibit strongly oppositional behaviour may attempt to sabotage the game, leading to their being ostracized by their peers in the team (Skinner *et al.*, 1996). The literature provides strategies for preventing and dealing with such occurrences, and the research evidence appears to demonstrate that the flexible application of the Game succeeds in overcoming these difficulties. As Kelshaw-Levering (2000) described, there could be a randomization procedure whereby at the end of certain sessions a lottery is held, the results of which determine whether the ticks of the group as a whole are counted, or whether one named member of each team, drawn in the lottery, is chosen to represent the whole team. Rewards are also the subject of a lottery and might range from the small scale, such as gold stars, to large rewards, such as a field trip. Another effective option for managing this type of sabotaging behaviour is to create a group composed of those students who find it most difficult to remain within the rules. These pupils are thus removed from the groups they were sabotaging, and required to work as a team in order to compete with the other teams (Kelshaw-Levering, 2000).

The largest random controlled trial on the GBG was conducted in Baltimore public schools between 1985 and 1988, as part of a large-scale epidemiological project, on two successive year groups of entrants to inner-city schools. In all, 2311 were involved in total, 1196 in the first intake, and 1115 in the second intake (Dolan *et al.*, 1993; Kellam *et al.*, 1994; Kellam and Anthony, 1998; Poduska *et al.*, 2008). The aim of this preventative intervention was to reduce risk behaviours associated with later-life substance abuse and social disorder. Both externalizing aggressive behaviour and anxious internalizing behaviours were targeted. The intervention was carried out over two years for each cohort of 808 boys and 796 girls, who were randomly assigned to three groups. The first group was the control group which received no additional intervention save those typically applied within the school management system. The second group was assigned to a cognitive intervention, Mastery Learning, and the third to the Good Behaviour Game. This cohort was been interviewed annually for 11 years, from the ages of 8/9, to the age of 19/20. The data were continually analyzed in relation to a variety of outcome measures. Some of the short and long-term findings follow.

- Teachers of those in the GBG group rated their pupils significantly lower for aggression and shyness following six months of intervention. The greatest reductions were for those who had exhibited the most aggression and disruption. Peer ratings agreed, but the reductions for girls were not significant (Dolan *et al.*, 1993).
- In adolescence, the GBG participants maintained their initial gains, particularly those most highly rated for aggression at the age of 6. However, some boys who had not displayed aggression at school intake had developed aggressive and disruptive behaviour by adolescence, despite having taken part in the game (Kellam *et al.*, 1994).
- The biggest improvements at adolescence involved those placed in classrooms for the most aggressive at 1st grade (Kelham and Anthony, 1998).
- Where the GBG was compared to a parental-training and support scheme, it was found that both sets of pupils had a lower likelihood than did control students of being diagnosed with Conduct Disorder in adolescence, or to have been suspended from school. Pupils who had engaged in the GBG were less likely than both controls and those in the parent-training group to have used mental health services by adolescence. This study suggested that even more positive results may be obtained from combining the two interventions (Ialongo *et al.*, 2001).
- Boys who had taken part in the GBG aged 5 and 6, were less likely to smoke than controls by the age of 14, and less aggressive boys in the initial intervention group were less likely to smoke than their more aggressive peers. This protective outcome did not apply to girls (Kellam and Anthony, 1998).

The effectiveness of the GBG has also been shown in a large-scale RCT (random-ized control trial) study carried out in the Netherlands (van Lier *et al.*, 2004), where 31 classes of children from inner-city schools, 744 in all, with mean age 6.9, were randomly allocated to classes using the GBG (16 classes) or to class-rooms where conventional classroom management approaches were employed (15 classes). The cohort contained a high proportion of students diagnosed with ADHD, and 31% of these children were from ethnic minority backgrounds. A key finding was that children in the GBG group showed a significant decrease in classroom symptoms of ADHD.

A small scale study of the GBG, carried out by Saigh and Umar (1983) on a rural Sudanese class of 20 students found very similar results to those produced in urban conditions in the Western countries, indicating that the intervention is not culturally-specific.

Advantages of the GBG are that it reinforces behavioural inhibition in an inclu-sive classroom, is cost-effective, and is simple to implement (Embry, 2002). It can be adapted as a behaviour-modification intervention over various social and aca-demic settings (Tingstrom *et al.*, 2006). It has also been used in non-classroom set-tings, for example, as an intervention for increasing prosocial behaviours in a series of volley-ball lessons (Patrick *et al.*, 1998), and to control disruptive behaviours in a library (Fishbein and Wasik, 1981). Most usefully it appears to reduce the future incidence of substance use and adverse social consequences for boys at risk (Poduska, 2008), although its protective value for girls appears to be less evident (Kellam and Anthony, 1998). It has been named as a 'best practice' intervention by Social Programs That Work (http://evidencebasedprograms.org/wordpress/), and by several other national assessment bodies in the United States.

General behavioural strategies: The value of 'kernels'

Recently, Embry (2004, 2008) and Embry and Biglan (2008) have identified and described 52 strongly evidence-based behavioural strategies which they term 'kernels'. These are specific strategies that are embedded in more elaborate schemes and interventions approaches. Analyses by Embry and Biglan appear to show that if used competently, frequently enough, and sometimes in conjunction with each other, these kernels can produce significant and lasting behavioural change.

Although the kernels are related to various institutional and community fo-cussed preventative interventions (Embry, 2008), for the purpose of this review we have selected those kernels which are most relevant to the school setting in relation to SEBD. All these kernels are supported by strong empirical evidence, and the authors of the papers comprehensively list those studies which support each behavioural intervention.

While we should be aware of the dangers appearing to reduce effective be-havioural intervention to series of simple strategies, it is important to note that these are strategies which are frequently used in many behavioural interventions to demonstrably positive effect (see Table 4.1).

Table 4.1   Evidence-based strategies ('kernels').

Intervention	Description of 'kernel'	Evidence from studies
Response cost	Non-emotional removal of a token or privilege for misbehaviour.	Foreman (1980), Kendall and Finch (1976), Little and Kelley (1989)
Verbal praise	This can be oral or written, and encourages cooperative acts between individuals. It encourages positive teacher-student relations, and reduces aggressive and disruptive behaviour.	Lowe and McLaughlin (1974), Marchant and Young (2001), Marchant *et al.* (2004), Martens *et al.* (1997), Matheson and Shriver (2005), Robinson and Robinson (1979), Scott *et al.* (2001)
Beat the timer	This is a strategy in which children are set a task to be completed in a given time, and are rewarded in some way if they succeed.	Wolfe *et al.* (1981), Adams and Drabman (1995), Drabman and Creedon (1979)
Mystery motivators	Students are invited to select from a jar or bowl a mystery prize for achieving a target.	Brown and Redmon (1989), Foxx and Schaeffer (1981), Moore *et al.* (1994)
Team competition	In which groups compete on a task, performance or game against each other.	Beersma *et al.* (2003), Hoigaard *et al.* (2006), Kivlighan and Granger (2006), Koffman *et al.* (1998)
Time out	Using a timer, withdraw child from the current environment, into another place, for one minute, plus one minute for each year of his/her age. The best results are obtained from shorter (5 minutes) than longer (15 minutes) time out.	Fabiano *et al.* (2004), Kazdin (1980), Wolf *et al.* (1967)
Premack principle	This principle is that children will adopt a behaviour which they may be resisting if they believe it will lead to something they want. This is the principle of 'work now, play later'.	Agathon and Granjus (1976), Andrews (1970), Browder *et al.* (1984), Ghosh and Chattopadhyay (1993), Gonzalez and Ribes (1975), Harrison and Schaeffer (1975), Homme *et al.* (1963), Hosie *et al.* (1974), Knapp (1976), Leclerc and Thurston (2003)

Table 4.1   (*Continued*)

Intervention	Description of 'kernel'	Evidence from studies
Low emotion 'private" reprimands	Corrective feedback given without threats or emotion. Short reprimands work better than long reprimands. Reprimands work better than encouragement on off-task behaviour.	Abramowitz *et al.* (1987), Acker and O'Leary (1987), Houghton *et al.* (1990), Merrett and Tang (1994), Ostrower and Ziv (1982), Pfiffner *et al.* (1985), Piazza *et al.* (1999)
Traffic light system	Using the traffic light colour system to indicate when a behaviour is becoming disruptive (red) or when the behaviour is desirable and safe (green).	Medland and Stachnik (1972), Wasserman (1977)
Non-verbal transition cues	This could be the playing of music, or the switching of lights on and off, the ringing of a bell, the change of tone of voice, or some other cue, to signal the end of one activity and the start of another.	Abbott *et al.* (1998), Embry *et al.* (1996), Krantz and Risley (1977), Rosenkoetter and Fowler (1986)
Meaningful roles	Providing meaningful roles to children to encourage responsibility.	Kahne and Bailey (1999), Rutter (1983)
Praise notes from peers	Peer approval notes, posted in a book, displayed on a wall, or read out loud, in which children are praised for their behaviour, strengths, achievements or cooperation by other children.	Abbott *et al.* (1998), Embry *et al.* (1996), Gottfredson (1986), Skinner *et al.* (2002)
Positive school - to-home notes	Sending notes home to the family when behaviour has been particularly desirable.	Gupta *et al.* (1990), Kelley *et al.* (1988), McCain and Kelley (1993), Taylor *et al.* (1984)

Functional Behavioural Analysis (FBA)

Functional Behavioural Analysis (Baer *et al.*, 1968) is a useful and exact tool which has been widely employed to evaluate the match between the needs of the child, and the support required. Its origins are as a tool applied to children who are developmentally delayed, although it is now being used with students who present with SEBD.

Currently, in the United States, as in many countries, an important outcome of educational assessment for students with SEBD is the Individual Behaviour Plan, the purpose of which is to provide a clearly defined set of objectives which can be used to inform educational interventions and provide a basis for evaluating progress. Such assessment is often carried out by teachers, and sometimes by behavioural support teams. Recently, researchers in the United States have examined whether teachers and others can be taught the skills required to conduct such assessments, and whether this might improve the quality of assessment for students with SEBD and other special educational needs (Barnhill, 2005). A Functional Analysis is an analysis of the child's relationship to the environment and makes note of rate and frequency of behaviours, how long they last, when they occur, and where they occur. FBA employs the behaviourist constructs of: **A**ntecedents (what happens just before a behaviour), **B**ehaviour (the behaviour of concern), and **C**onsequences (what is the result of that behaviour). In this way the approach eschews explanations of behaviour which appeal to the internal states of individuals (including psycho-medical accounts which might invoke diagnostic categories such ADHD, CD or ASD) in favour of a focus on the search for the stimuli which reinforce behaviours in a specific setting. The purpose of FBA, therefore, is to determine the fitness for purpose of specific interventions and assist selection from the wide array of options.

For example, Umbreit *et al.* (2004) provide an account of how expert FB analysis led to the conclusion that a disruptive student's behaviours occurred when he had finished an assignment, and usually gained him access to preferred activities. This led to an intervention which involved increasing the difficulty of tasks, thus ensuring that the student remained occupied for longer periods. This in turn resulted in reduced levels of disruption.

As this example illustrates, while FBA-published studies have produced some interesting results, the studies themselves tend to be small scale, sometimes carried out in individual schools and summer schools, and often with very small numbers of participants.

Another FBA study in a mainstream classroom (Lewis and Sugai, 1996) determined that in three cases, the children had peer group problems, and were trying to gain, inappropriately, the attention of peers who rejected them. In another study (Kamps *et al.*, 2006) an FBA conducted by a teacher (with guidance from an ABA practitioner) on the behaviour of two disruptive male students, concluded that more teacher praise, 'help' tickets, and some self-management enabled more on-task behaviour. Teacher praise appears to be an important element in modifying behaviour. A study of the behaviour of nine students with SEBD in a self-contained classroom showed that in a reversal ABAB withdrawal design (Sutherland *et al.*, 2000) teacher praise was an important factor in maintaining on-task behaviour.

Chandler *et al.* (1999) demonstrated that when a group of teachers of pre-school children were trained in behaviour modification techniques including FBA, the outcome was a significant modification of the children's undesirable behaviours. Grey *et al.* (2005) studied a 90-hour FBA training scheme for 11 teachers of autistic children in schools in Ireland. The results showed that the support plans they devised and implemented produced an average 80% change in targeted behaviours after training, to the satisfaction of parents, as well as the teachers themselves.

However, Scott *et al.* (2005) examined the work of 13 FBA teams and determined that there were still practical barriers to efficient use of these teams, and that school-based personnel were more likely to select negative and exclusionary strategies as a response to challenging behaviour. In the same year a state-wide critical analysis of completed FBAs and Behaviour Intervention Plans (BIPs) across Wisconsin (Van Acker *et al.*, 2005) noted serious flaws in the drawing up of BIPs, even after a training session. Many school teams did not link the function of the behaviours noted by the FPA in deciding on an intervention. Further and simplified teacher and team training, and the use of check-listed reviews were recommended by this study. Similar findings were produced in a study by Blood and Neel (2007) who examined behaviour intervention plans of children with EBD in a mid-sized district in eastern Washington State. The majority of these students did not have a BIP, and where they existed they did not include specific suggestions for replacement behaviours but contained generalized lists of responses to behaviour without reference to the particular needs of that student. Cook *et al.* (2007) also found inadequacies when checking the Positive Behaviour Support (PBS) plans for special education students drawn up by two different groups of educators. Plans drawn up by teams with insufficient training in PBS were found to be largely insufficiently-tailored to the child's needs. Benazzi *et al.* (2006) found that in teams that contained at least one trained BPS specialist produced the most effective behaviour plans.

Another shortcoming of BIPs/IEPs was investigated by Martin *et al.* (2006) who, in an observational study of 109 IEP meetings and a post-meeting survey, found that the student's voice was rarely listened to at these meetings: they spoke only 3% of the time. The discussion was dominated by special education teachers (51%), family members (15%), general teachers and administrators (9%) and support staff (6%). The researchers called for the teaching of participation skills so that the students could self-advocate in their own IEP.

Cognitive Behavioural Strategies

We outlined the principles underpinning Cognitive Behavioural (CB) approaches in Chapter 2. To summarize briefly: Cognitive Behavioural approaches are concerned with the ways in which the relationship between external stimuli and target behaviours can sometimes be influenced by thought processes. The aim of Cognitive Behavioural therapy is to encourage the development of functional ways of thinking by challenging and changing dysfunctional ways of thinking.

Previous reviews have shown that there is strong evidence to suggest the efficacy of CB approaches with problems as diverse as self-monitoring difficulties among children with ADHD (Shapiro and Cole, 1995), self-control among children with ODD and CD (Altepeter and Korger, 1999; Fonagy and Kurtz, 2002; Kazdin, 2002), anxiety disorders (Fonagy *et al.*, 2002; Kearney and Wadiak, 1999; Schoenfeld and Janney, 2008), and depressive disorders (Fonagy *et al.*, 2002)

It is important to stress that for the purposes of this review CB interventions are divided into two main categories on the basis of their scale and scope. On the one hand there are the large-scale whole-school, and sometimes district-wide 'universal' approaches which are often multi-dimensional and have the potential to affect very large cohorts of students. These approaches are dealt with in Chapter 5, which is concerned with interventions that that are outside the control of the individual practitioner. In this chapter we deal for the most part with the second category of CB approaches which take the form of specific intervention techniques that might be adopted by the lone practitioner working within the school.

Self-evaluation and self-regulation

Strayhorn (2002a) emphasizes the central importance of self-regulation in the social and emotional functioning of human beings, pointing out that deficits in self-control are central to a wide range of psychopathologies. He argues for the following key skills to be taught to children who have difficulties in this area:

- the art of self-instruction;
- the ability to remove oneself from tempting stimuli, physically and mentally; and
- self-monitoring

Strayhorn (2002b) then goes on to provide a set of guidelines for developing self control skills in children, including:

- that self-control is fostered most effectively through a long-term positive relationship with a dependable person who communicates the value of self-control;
- the need for self-control challenges set for the child to be carefully selected so that they are within the skill range of the child;
- the need for the child to be exposed to a wide range of positive models showing the successful exercise of self-control;
- the importance of intensive practice coupled with the rewards for effort;
- the use of 'fantasy rehearsal', whereby children are required to engage in simulations of situations involving self-control challenges; and
- the importance of developing a personal vocabulary in relation to self-control, thus promoting a sense of ownership;

It is essential to note that these general guidelines are consistent, highlighting important features that run through the empirical literature on the application of CB approaches.

Empirical support for the importance of self-regulation skills in children who display impulsive behaviour is provided by Elias and Berk (2002), who carried out a naturalistic longitudinal observational study of 51 children in a US kindergarten. The purpose of the study was to examine the effect of socio-dramatic play involving imaginative role-play on the development of self-regulation. They found that children who engaged in complex socio-dramatic (CSD) play with others exercised higher levels of self-regulation in 'clean-up' and circle time sessions than students who engaged in solitary play, and that the effect was particularly strong for impulsive children. The authors argue that these findings are consistent with Vygotsky's contention that CSD play in early childhood contributes importantly to the development of self-regulation, and that CSD activities are, therefore, an important aid in the development of self-regulation, particularly among impulsive children.

An important component of self-regulatory behaviour is self-monitoring, whereby the individual observes his or her performance and evaluates it against compliance criteria. There are various empirically-supported techniques for promoting self-monitoring by students with SEBD in classrooms. Davies and Witte (2000) focus on 'interdependent group contingency' techniques, that is, approaches to promoting self- monitoring that teachers can use with whole classes. They cite the Good Behaviour Game (discussed previously) as a well-known example among a number of examples of this technique. They then go on to describe an evaluation of an intervention in a 3rd grade US mainstream classroom (n = 30) in which a teacher employed an 'interdependent group contingency' technique aimed at reducing the 'talking out of turn' behaviour of four students with ADHD.

The technique involved students being instructed to monitor their own performance in relation to the target behaviour on a chart with three coloured zones. Each group began with five counters in the green zone. In the event of a group member breaking the rule he or she was required to move a counter from the green to the blue zone. If 10 seconds after a rule infringement the group had not done this, then the teacher moved a token into the red zone. Each student also was required to maintain a tally of his/her personal performance in terms of the number of times they had moved the token themselves against the number of times it was moved by the teacher when they broke the rule.

The study employed an ABAB reversal design, with a first intervention period of 12 days and a second intervention period of 10 days, separated by one week when the intervention did not take place. The four target students were each matched to a non-ADHD control. Baseline data (A) was taken on the target students' and the controls' level of talking out of turn behaviour before the intervention and the same measures were repeated during the intervention period (B). This procedure was then repeated.

The findings showed that the intervention had a dramatic and positive effect on the talking out of turn behaviour of the students with ADHD. The first set of baseline data showed that the students with ADHD exhibited much higher levels of target behaviour than the controls. This difference was found to be statistically significant. Measures taken during the first intervention period showed a dramatic decrease in the incidence of target behaviours performed both by the students with ADHD and the controls. The second set of baseline data revealed lower levels of target behaviour for both groups than the time 1 baseline data, with no statistically significant difference between target students and controls, though there was a statistically significant improvement in baseline 1 and 2 scores of the students with ADHD. During the second intervention levels of target behaviour these were again dramatically reduced. The researchers also noted that there was no significant statistical relationship between talking out of turn behaviour and whether the students had self-identified their rule-breaking or whether it had been teacher-identified. This was taken to suggest that although students had not entirely adopted a self-monitoring approach, self-monitoring plays a role in leading to the positive outcomes.

While the study by Davies and White is small scale and, in itself, is indicative of the potential efficacy of the approach described, rather than offering generalizable findings, it is worthy of attention as much for its form as its content. Crucially, it illustrates how behavioural and cognitive behavioural approaches lend themselves to accurate and rigorous evaluation.

Similar small-scale studies have shown that a range self-monitoring techniques have been associated with improvements in behavioural functioning:

- Amato-Zech *et al.*, (2006) showed the efficacy of pager-type electronic 'beepers' in reducing noncompliant behaviour in 3 elementary age students with SEBD.
- In a more complex multiple baseline study by Gureasko-Moore *et al.* (2007) 6 boys (aged 11–12) diagnosed with ADHD attending a mainstream school were trained to use a log book and self-management checklist as aids to self-management. Data from systematic observation revealed significant improvements in the students' classroom-preparedness behaviours and homework-related behaviours. An interesting and valuable adjunct to these quantitative data were quantitative and qualitative 'social validation data' which indicated that the target students' improved behaviours were comparable to levels achieved by their classroom peers, and that teachers, parents and the students themselves expressed satisfaction with the programme and its effects.
- Rhode *et al.* (1983) carried out a multiple baseline repeated measures study of the use of self-evaluation strategies with 'behaviourally handicapped' elementary school students (n = 6) who were initially placed in a short-term special provision ('resource room'). Two particularly interesting features of the study – generalization and maintenance – are the results of the complex, 14 stage self-evaluation programme described, and the persuasive evidence of its efficacy in securing behavioural improvements that were generalized and maintained when the students returned to full-time placement in a mainstream classroom. The programme was divided into two phases, the first of which consisted of seven stages which were designed to introduce the students to self-evaluation techniques, first through direct instruction by the teacher. Students were then required to adopt the techniques that were being applied by the teacher, and a process of comparison and discussion was entered into with the intention of encouraging convergence between teacher and student evaluations. Initially students were given reinforcement in the form of points.

Over time these reinforcers were withdrawn and students were reinforced through verbal praise and self-reinforcement as they achieved the goals of the programme. Once convergence was achieved and the students were able to demonstrate accurate self-monitoring that revealed at least 80% compliance with behavioural goals, over a 4 day period, the students were able to enter phase two of the programme. This involved returning to the mainstream class on a full time basis. The remaining seven stages of the intervention involved a less intensive version of the strategy-reinforcement that had occupied phase one. The findings indicate four of the six students maintained a level of compliant behaviour that was consistent with their mainstream peers after the intervention period had ended.

A particularly interesting feature of several of these and other similar studies (e.g., Hoff and DuPaul, 1998) is the apparent success that they are able to achieve with students diagnosed with ADHD, a condition that is commonly treated with stimulant medication in the United States (Greenhill and Ford, 2002), though less commonly in Europe (NICE, 2008). In the studies cited here students diagnosed with ADHD were often being prescribed medication *before* the onset of CB intervention. This suggests that CB may have a significant value-added effect when combined with medication (Kazdin, 2002). Having said this, it should be emphasized that the CB studies so far reviewed are often very small scale and lack the power of large-scale RCTs.

Self-regulation for anxiety disorders

As we noted in Chapter 2, there is a strong tendency for educational approaches to SEBD to focus on acting-out/disruptive behaviours to the neglect of withdrawn/acting-in behaviours. This is in spite of the widespread prevalence of acting-in disorders as well as evidence of their impact on educational functioning. For this reason it is important to give attention to the fact that an important specific application of CB self-regulation techniques is with anxiety disorders.

   Schoenfeld and Janney (2008, p. 598) recently completed a research review of school-based CBT interventions for anxiety disorders and concluded that:

> The results of this intervention research are unequivocal: school-based intervention for anxiety disorders is effective. Students with anxiety disorders who participate in cognitive-behavioural intervention at school emerge with fewer anxious symptoms than non-participants, and show similar effects to school-based cognitive-behavioural therapy as do peers who participate in off-campus interventions.

An illustration of the efficacy of clinic based CB interventions for children with anxiety disorders is provided by Kendall (1994) who carried out a RCT of the application of a CB intervention on children aged 9–13 (n = 47). The interventions were carried out on a one-to-one basis over 16 sessions by clinical psychology doctoral students, and included the following (Kendall, 1994, p. 103):

[Measures to assist] the child in (a) recognizing anxious feelings and somatic reactions to anxiety; (b) clarifying cognition in anxiety-provoking situations (i.e., unrealistic or negative attributions and expectations); (c) developing a plan to help cope with the situation (i.e., modifying anxious self-talk into coping self-talk as well as determining what coping actions might be effective); and (d) evaluating performance and administering self-reinforcement as appropriate.

Intervention included behavioural training strategies such as modelling, in vivo exposure, role-playing, relaxation training, and contingent reinforcement. The therapists also used social reinforcement with the children, and encouraged them to verbally reinforce their successful coping behaviour. Outside the therapeutic sessions the children practised using the coping skills when anxiety-provoking situations arose at home or in school. The duration of the intervention was 8 weeks.

The findings from the study indicated that children who underwent the intervention showed significantly better performance than controls on a battery of standardized tests which measured various dimensions, including children's self-reported depressive symptoms, negative affectivity, and ability to cope with stressful situations. Systematic observation data were gathered by therapists, and parents and teachers completed standardized measures of students' social, emotional and behavioural functioning in classroom and home settings. These improvements were found to be maintained at follow-up after one year.

A much smaller scale and less complex study was carried out by McCraty *et al.* (1996) in which CBT practitioners introduced an emotional self-management skills training programme into a US middle school. In this study, students volunteered for a course which taught them techniques designed to intercept stressful responses during emotionally-challenging situations. Behavioural outcomes were assessed using a standardized instrument, and autonomic function was measured by heart rate variability (HRV) analysis during and after stressful events. Outcomes of the study showed that students who had followed the programme exhibited significant improvements in areas including stress- and anger-management, risky behaviour, work-management and focus, and relationships with family, peers and teachers when compared to controls. These improvements were maintained over a six-month period.

These studies are of course clinic-based and, as such do not conform to the other interventions described in this chapter, which are by and large school-based and intended to illustrate the kinds of skills that individual teachers and other professionals in schools might adopt. The point being illustrated here is that techniques, many of which have been shown to be accessible to school-based personnel, and which have been shown to work well with acting-out behaviour are also efficacious for acting-in problems. In the following chapter we examine evidence of the effectiveness of universal whole-school approaches adopting a CB approach to acting-in problems.

Social problem-solving

Other important school-based applications of CB approaches are in the related areas of social problem-solving and anger-management. Social problem-solving is directed at providing students who exhibit difficulties in engaging in harmonious social relationships with their peers and others, with the skills necessary to identify the ways in which they might contribute to these problems and strategies for overcoming them. Anger-management involves enabling students to identify triggers to aggressive outbursts and strategies for controlling these.

Battistich *et al.* (1989) studied the effects of a classroom-based social problem-solving programme on students (n = 342) from kindergarten through to 4th grade in three US elementary schools over five years. Students from three similar schools where the programme was not followed were used as comparators. The intervention, which set out to promote 'a caring environment' in classrooms, involved a range of teacher-led components outlined below.

- *Cooperative activities*, where small groups of children work together toward common goals on academic and non-academic tasks. Emphasis was placed on fairness, consideration, and social responsibility. Students were trained in group interaction skills and engaged in reflection and discussion in relation to these.
- *Developmental discipline*, whereby the internalization of prosocial norms and values and the development of self-control were fostered through the building of positive interpersonal relationships. This involved children in class rule-setting and decision-making.
- *Activities promoting social understanding*, such as discussion of classroom events where issues of social cooperation were relevant.
- *Highlighting prosocial values*, through discussion of everyday events.
- *Helping activities*, whereby students were encouraged to help each other in various ways, participate in peer tutoring and 'buddying' activities, and engage in community-based charitable activities and helping activities in the school at large.

The students were annually assessed through structured interviews and systematic observation. Findings showed that the treatment group became significantly better at cognitive problem-solving skills (i.e., interpersonal sensitivity; consideration of others' needs, and means-ends thinking), and used resolution strategies which were significantly more prosocial than comparison children. They were also more competent in applying these skills to hypothetical situations. The findings were replicated with a second cohort.

Kazdin *et al.* (1989) carried out a RCT in the United States comparing the effects of person-centred relationship therapy (RT) and CB training in problem-solving skills (PSS) on the levels of anti-social behaviour among students (aged 7–13) with severe anti-social behavioural disorders with (n = 112). The students assigned to the PSS treatment showed significantly greater reductions in anti-social behaviour and overall behaviour problems, and greater increases in prosocial behaviour than RT children. Students who were allocated to a third condition, in which PSS training was combined with parent-training achieved even better outcomes than the PSS-only trained group. A follow-up study carried out a year later found that PSS had maintained their gains, though the enhanced effect of the parent training appeared to have faded.

A Type 1 RCT carried out in the Netherlands (De Castro *et al.*, 2003) in a primary special school focused on severely aggressive boys (n = 32) who were taught the CB 'stop and think' strategy, which is designed to enable impulsive individuals with aggressive behaviour problems to regulate their behaviour in provocative situations. There were three strategies taught: (1) to pause to monitor their own feelings; (2) to consider the feelings of others; and (3) to delay their response when in a provocative situations. The target pupils and controls (n = 31) were presented with vignettes concerning provocation by a peer and given specific cognitive assignments which involved applying one or other of the three strategies. It was found that monitoring and regulation of participants' own emotions reduced aggressiveness in the aggressive group to a significant degree, while the other two strategies tended to increased aggressiveness in this group. While this study indicates the importance of discriminating between different strategies, the absence of systematic in vivo observational data or other data on students' behaviour in everyday interactions limits the robustness of these findings.

Another study which set out to differentiate between two school-based CB interventions for students with ADHD was carried out in the United States by Bloomquist *et al.* (1991). The study followed an RCT design in which students were assigned to one of two conditions, the first of which was a multi-component condition that provided coordinated training programmes for parents, teachers, and children, and the second offered training for classroom teachers only. A control group was composed of students on a waiting list. Post-intervention performance measures were compared with baseline data and repeated after 6 weeks in a follow-up study. Measures included classroom behaviour observations, teacher ratings of child behaviour, child self-report, and teacher ratings of adjustment. Although the multi-component CBT condition was found to be significantly more effective than the teacher-only condition initially, differences between these two conditions faded after 6 weeks. On the one hand this study offers support for the teacher-only version of the CB intervention. There are, however, important limitations created by the relatively short duration of the intervention and the lack of data in the comparability of the control group to the experimental group.

Another study which emphasizes the value of school-based CB interventions delivered by teachers was carried out by Jordan and Métais (1997). This case study of 26 children (aged 10–12) involved them in a 10-week programme of cooperative learning to develop their social and academic skills. Classroom activities provided training in specific social skills. Students were also trained in sharing, persuading and managing time, as well as being positive, valuing others and conflict resolution. Outcomes of the study indicated that the programme was effective in promoting more effective prosocial behaviour.

Anger management

Anger management is an application of the CB self-regulation strategies already discussed, to the problem of dysfunctional anger. The approach is illustrated in a case study by Kellner *et al.* (2001) which was carried out in a repeated measures design control group study in a US special day school with a class of early adolescents with serious emotional and/or behavioural problems. The 10-session intervention programme employed a whole-class format which involved introducing students to self-monitoring (including logs), and self-regulatory techniques specifically focused on anger. Booster sessions were employed to help students maintain positive gains. Findings indicated that after participation in the programme, students were less likely to engage in fighting with peers, more likely to engage in talking problem situations through with a counsellor when angry, and more likely to use anger logs. At the 4-month follow-up, students who received booster sessions continued to make more use of the log than controls.

An RCT carried out by Feindler *et al.* (1984) in the United States focused on severely aggressive boys (n = 100) in a junior high school. The Anger Control Training programme was delivered in a group format fortnightly. Students were randomly assigned to one of three treatment groups, or to a control group. Students were taught both general self-control strategies and strategies specific to aggressive/disruptive incidents. Findings showed significant changes among members of the treatment groups on dependent measures of problem-solving ability and self-control. Members of the treatment groups were also less likely to incur fines or be expelled for disruptive behaviour and for severe aggression after engaging in the programme. This last finding is of particular interest, illustrating, as it does, the superiority of the cognitive ('therapeutic') intervention over punitive interventions.

Instructional Strategies

Instructional strategies are pedagogical techniques employed by teachers in order to promote students' academic engagement. Unfortunately, when we examined the research literature in search of evidence of the efficacy of such approaches for students with SEBD, we find an array of mainly small-scale low-power studies. One of the most useful studies of this topic is a meta-analysis by Pierce *et al.* (2004).

The authors present their analysis in the context of serious reservations about the small sample sizes of many of the studies. The findings of this meta-analysis in public school classrooms in the United States are summarized here with the exception of interventions that were set in single classrooms, and non-educational settings. The sample size for each study is bracketed after the name of the study, to give some guidance as to the weight of the evidence.

- Previewing reading material gave an effect size of 1.93 on accuracy of scores (n = 3) (Rose, 1984).
- Sequential prompting in a secondary school setting resulted in an effect size of 2.04 for written sentence production (n = 3) (Schloss *et al.*, 1985).
- A programme designed to teach test-taking skills resulted in an effect size of 1.03 (n = 34) (Scruggs and Marsing, 1987).
- Personalized instruction increased the number of spelling tests passed, in children between 10 and 12 years old, with a mean effect size of .92 for the class (n = 10) (McLaughlin, 1991).
- A structured instructional system which involved teaching school survival skills to children with a mean age of 12.9 increased task completion, with an effect size of .38 (n = 14) (Foley and Epstein, 1993).
- Incorporating the student's interest in lesson content in the curriculum delivered to children aged between 5 and 11 increased their productivity on words written and colours identified with an effect size of 1.47 (n = 4) (Clarke *et al.*, 1995).
- A study of the effects of story mapping on students aged 10 and 11 in order to increase reading comprehension of text produced an effect size of 2.68 (n = 4) Babyak *et al.*, (2000).
- Individual curricular modifications designed to promote reading skills, increased academic productivity as measured by the number of words read, with a mean effect size of 1.62 (n = 2) (Kern *et al.*, 2001).

These findings offer some interesting suggestions as to some of the pedagogical strategies that might be worth pursuing with students with SEBD, but the overwhelming impression created by this study is that there is a dearth of significant research in this important area.

Conclusion

The evidence reviewed in this chapter complements the findings of Chapter 3, in emphasizing the value and nature of specific competence based interventions that can be delivered by teachers and paraprofessionals in schools. It is clearly the case that the impressive evidence for the effectiveness of behavioural and cognitive behavioural strategies suggests that they should occupy a vital place in the knowledge base and repertoires of professionals working with all students, and particularly those presenting with SEBD. Clearly, there is an important role here for specialist support from sources such as educational psychology, and child psychiatric and clinical psychology services to be made available to staff in schools.

For such support to be utilized most effectively, it remains essential that staff in schools should have basic knowledge and a sense of ownership of in relation to the implementation of strategies.

The evidence for the effectiveness of instructional strategies in relation to SEBD, while offering extremely interesting lines for future enquiry, is disappointing, largely owing to the small scale nature of many of the published studies. This suggests that pedagogical strategies for students presenting with SEBD is a relatively neglected research topic. This is a matter of deep concern given the central challenge posed by SEBD to the inclusive education enterprise. Having said this, there is sufficient existing evidence to provide adventurous staff in schools with hypotheses to test and build on in their pedagogic practice.

Clearly, the obvious value of knowing about and being able to use approaches and strategies of the type discussed in this and the previous chapter resides in their ability to enable staffing schools to achieve positive outcomes through the application of these specific techniques. Equally important, however, is the knowledge of students' social and psychological functioning which emerges as a by-product of learning about these techniques and applying them. Such knowledge is likely to feed into the wider professional knowledge of teachers and paraprofessionals, allowing them to adapt their general approaches to teaching and learning and to innovate in accordance with their developing knowledge and skill base. This emphasizes the importance of incorporating such knowledge and skills into the pre- and in-service training programmes of teachers and paraprofessionals working in schools.

Summary

This chapter has explored evidence a variety of interventions for enhancing teachers' skills. It was noted that behavioural strategies receive support from a large body of research evidence including some well-conducted RCTs. The Good Behaviour Game (GBG) was found to be a well-studied and adaptable intervention that can be employed in a wide variety of educational settings to significant positive effect. Other general behavioural strategies, in the form of 'kernels' were seen to be likely to contribute to the effective management of students with SEBD. In addition functional behavioural analysis was shown to be a powerful and demonstrably-effective assessment and intervention tool, gaining support from many well-conducted RCTs, though the complexities of this approach indicate the need for expert support in its use in schools.

Cognitive Behavioural (CB) strategies were identified as a second major category of intervention which was found to receive support from a large body of research evidence including RCTs. The CB strategies most applicable to schools and supported by RCTs are self-evaluation and self-regulation interventions. Many of these interventions can be employed by teachers, but they tend to be mainly directed at acting-out problems. There are effective CB strategies for self-regulation for anxiety disorders which have RCT evidential support but the most persuasive studies of this are either clinic-based or involve clinicians rather than school-based personnel in their implementation. There was also found to be significant empirical support for CB approaches to *social* problem-solving and anger management in schools, including RCTs.

Finally, instructional strategies, involving particular pedagogical strategies and adaptations, while being found to show promise lacked the evidential robustness of the behavioural and CB approaches.

5

Whole-school Approaches and Support Systems

Overview

In the previous chapters emphasis was given to an evaluation of empirical evidence on the skills and approaches that teachers, and other personnel, working with students in schools and other settings draw on when working with students with SEBD. This was with the intention of emphasizing the importance of the choices that individual teachers and other school personnel make when deciding how to intervene with SEBD in schools, and the need for such choices to be informed by evidence based training and education. The current chapter is concerned with what might be termed 'whole-school' or 'universal' intervention programmes. These share many common features with interventions discussed in the previous chapter, and in some cases incorporate identical strategies. In particular these approaches rely upon the same knowledge and skill base that were discussed previously.

What is distinctive about the interventions explored in the current chapter is the scale on which they are intended to operate and, therefore, the extent to which they reflect local and or national social policy priorities and commitments. It should be borne in mind that universal programmes work on a number of different levels, usually for the entire student population of a school, and often in areas of rural and urban deprivation.

National and Local Support Systems

In most developed countries of the world the SEN work of schools is embedded within a support network of services and provisions. Although these vary to some extent from country to country there are certain common features (see Booth and Ainscow, 1997; EADSNE, 2003; and Appendix II), including:

- support from psychological services;
- support from other therapeutic services, such as speech therapists; and
- support from teachers or advisors from specialist centres, such as behaviour support teams or special schools.

In the case of SEBD, schools may receive support from specialist mental health services and social work departments (Cooper, 2006; Waller, 2006). In the United Kingdom this approach is supported by a system of integrated children's services at Local Authority level, which combine children's education, social work and health service provision under a single administrative umbrella in an attempt to maximize coordination between the different services.

External agencies tend to link with schools in a variety of ways, including provision of:

- advice and consultancy services to school staff;
- direct intervention support for students and/or their families;
- assessment of students' needs; and
- training for staff.

In many countries committed to a policy of inclusive education, mainstream schools employ designated, and sometimes specially trained staff to coordinate, manage and contribute to the delivery of SEN services within the school (e.g., Booth and Ainscow, 1997). In the case of SEBD these may include special educational needs coordinators, behaviour support teachers, teaching assistants, mentors, and counsellors (Cajkler *et al.*, 2007).

The importance of such services should be neither under-estimated nor over-estimated. As we noted in the previous chapter, there is an important role for specialist services in supporting the work of staff in schools in relation to the challenges posed by SEBD. While it appears to be the case that some of the dysfunctions of inclusive education identified by some researchers (e.g., Blatchford *et al.*, 2009; Curcic, 2009; MacBeath *et al.*, 2006; Shevlin, 2008) are clearly attributable to a lack of knowledge and skills among teachers and paraprofessionals in schools, it may also be the case that this problem is exacerbated by the perception that the key expertise for dealing with SEBD resides in external support services. This is not the case. The evidence examined throughout this book points to the crucial significance of the knowledge, skills and actions of *staff in schools*. Experts who are external to schools can for the most part only have an indirect influence on what goes on in schools. They can help staff in schools to develop necessary knowledge and expertise, but they cannot exercise those skills for them. It is a dangerous managerial assumption (bordering on the delusional) that the aims of inclusive education can be served by centralized specialist services occasionally interacting with inadequately trained teachers and, often, untrained teaching assistants in schools.

Whole-school Academic Interventions

The association between academic failure and SEBD has been the subject of longstanding concern and debate (Landrum *et al.*, 2003). In a meta-analysis, Reid *et al.* (2004) reported that the overall academic status of these students produced a mean average of -.64, indicating significant deficits in academic achievement and that an examination of moderators indicated that students with SEBD performed at a significantly lower level than children without SEBD across a wide range of academic subjects and settings. Trout *et al.* (2003) describe a small scale study of a direct instruction reading intervention which addressed the effect of the intervention on students presenting with SEBD (n = 18). Six students with SEBD received the intervention and six were assigned to a waiting list, with six other control group children assessed as being not presenting SEBD or be otherwise 'at risk'. The children in the direct instruction programme out-performed or equalled both the other students with SEBD, and those deemed to be not at risk. This led the authors to conclude that some of the educational failure experienced by students presenting with SEBD can be accounted for by literacy levels and could be in part remediated by interventions targeted at improving reading skills.

However, few reading programmes addressing the needs of these children have employed the extensive research base of *Success For All*, (SFA), a whole-school reform model originating in the United States (Borman *et al.*, 2005a, 2005b, 2007; Borman and Hewes, 2002; Chambers *et al.*, 2006, 2008; Datnow and Castellano, 2000; Hurley *et al.*, 2001; Park and Datnow, 2008; Ross *et al.*, 1997, 1999; Slavin, 2002, 2004; Slavin *et al.*, 2001, 2006, 2007, 2008). In all, there have been 74 studies of SFA, of which, the Borman *et al.* cluster RCTs (2005a, 2005b, 2007) fully met the criteria laid out by the What Works Clearinghouse (http://ies.ed.gov/ncee/wwc/) and six further quasi-experimental studies met the evidence standards with reservations. SFA on this basis, is now regarded as having moderate to large effects on alphabetics, comprehension and general reading achievement, although no studies show that the programme is effective for reading fluency. It is the most robustly-evidenced reading programme in the United States, with 1200 Title One schools, those of low socio-economic status and entitled to further federal funding, in high risk areas employing the programme in 46 states, and has been used also in Israel, Mexico, Canada, Australia, and the United Kingdom.

In this programme, specifically designed for at risk students, classroom in-struction in reading is given each day in a 90-minute session in which children are regrouped out of their regular classrooms and into smaller groups containing children grouped on reading ability only. In the early years of the programme, kindergarten and pre-kindergarten emphasis is placed on phonemic and phonics awareness and reading-preparation. Peers read to each other, encourage compre-hension and summarizing, much in the same way as in the Peer Assisted Learning programmes, and all learning is collaborative and fast-paced, employing not only printed text, but multi-media technology. Some students who make little progress are targeted for additional tutorials. The scheme is highly organized with an in-school facilitator, carrying a .5 contact timetable, overseeing all aspects of the scheme. There is also a Solutions Team designated from members of staff in all schools, who liaise with other members of staff, and students, to give instant response to any problems which might arise during implementation, and work with parental issues, absenteeism, and behaviour problems as and when these occur. Teachers have at least 19 days of intensive training in the first year, reducing to 15 in year 3. Assessment tests are carried out quarterly throughout the school year to determine group designation. An unusual facet of this programme is that it is only implemented in schools where the staff have held a secret ballot as to whether they would like to join it, and where 80% of staff have approved. This ensures enthusiasm and commitment, which may contribute towards programme fidelity in implementation, although it has been argued that this commitment contributes bias to outcomes (Borman *et al.*, 2007). Having observed this, it seems appropriate to suggest that an educationally literate approach would have to identify staff enthusiasm and commitment as an independent variable in research studies of this kind.

The RCT which reported final outcomes in 2007, (Borman *et al.*, 2007) with interim reports in 2005 (Borman *et al.*, 2005a, 2005b) involved 41 schools across 11 states. There were two main conditions to which schools were randomly allocated: (1) the SFA 'treatment' schools which used the SFA programme with students in kindergarten and 1st grades, and (2) 'control' schools where the SFA programme would be used in Grades 3–5 only. A second sample of the longitudinal group of 3290 students, and 890 in-movers who had joined treatment, or intent-to-treat control group schools, after baseline assessments, were also used in the study at the time of Year 2 post-tests.

In the 2007 assessments all children were assessed, including those who had received the full three-year SFA intervention. Approximately 72% of these students received free school meals. The 18 experimental schools and the 17 control schools were well-matched on demographics. There were some weaknesses in that teachers in some schools in which SFA was offered in Grades 3 to 5 were found to be using the SFA materials in lessons with the younger (control) groups. There were also variations in the duration of SFA sessions, ranging from 30 minutes to 2 hours. Assessments for research purposes were made through the Peabody Picture Vocabulary Test, and the Woodcock Reading Mastery Test (Revised), by graduate student trainers blind to the control or experiment condition.

Effect sizes for the intervention were, as hypothesized by the researchers, significantly improved from the outcomes at the end of Year One, to the outcomes at the end of Year Three. Final effect sizes on outcomes from the longitudinal studies ranged from .22 to .33 on the sub-groups of the Woodcock Tests. In its own evaluation of these results, the What Works Clearinghouse (http://ies.ed.gov/ncee/wwc/), using its own stringent 'improvement' index, concluded that SFA had a 'potentially positive results' on the improvement of alphabetics; 'mixed effects results' on comprehension, and 'potentially positive results' on general reading achievement.

There has been considerable interest in SFA in the United Kingdom, as in many ways it echoes and addresses many of England's National Literacy Strategy requirements, although in a small-scale qualitative comparison of students studying under the NLS guidelines (2 schools), and those following the SFA programme (2 schools) Joliffe (2006) concluded that the SFA programme, although costly, transmitted a genuine understanding of the underlying pedagogy of literacy teaching to the schools involved, and also included all children in effective learning, partly by its use of cooperative interactive strategies which enabled all students to contribute, and encouraged listening and oral skills in addition to pure textual reading skills.

An evaluative two-year pilot scheme in SFA was initiated in Nottingham, in five primary and one secondary school in an area of considerable deprivation, in 1997, (Hopkins *et al.*, 1998). In years 1–3 SFA students performed considerably better than expected, although there were less impressive gains in each of the following three years. Teachers reported that they had more confidence in and understanding of, the teaching of reading, and there were noted behavioural improvements in the intervention schools, although variations due to implementation differences. A further two small scale studies in the United Kingdom, Tymms and Merrell in four Durham schools (2000), and Russ and Harris (2005), on SFA in two schools in London and two in Leeds. While the evidence that SFA was effective, especially in the early years and especially in literacy, was persuasive in these studies it must be borne in mind that these were limited in scope and in design, and randomized controlled trials have not been carried out. However, the organizational structure of SFA, and its relative success in encouraging verbal skills and in engaging parental support have made it a strongly-supported intervention (e.g., Wood and Caulier-Grice, 2006).

Success For All, however, is not without its critics. For example, Pogrow (2000a; 2000b; 2002) argues that programmes such as this are too costly and too prescriptive. Walberg and Greenberg (1999) and Jones *et al.*, (1997), on the other hand, challenge the evidence base, methodology and outcomes of SFA. Kozol (2006) is a more recent critic of the general principle of attempting to remediate the racial disadvantage of many US urban schools by intervening with a strict literacy programme which dominates the curriculum and could be thought to limit creativity.

In spite of the critics, other more recent independent comparative studies (Correnti *et al.*, 2007) are more forgiving and supportive. The programme appears to have addressed some of the basic implementation problems (Bifulco *et al.*, 2005) and the latest RCT (Borman *et al.*, 2007) has shown improvements in terms of the outcome measures used.

Perhaps of greatest significance, from the point of view of the current book, are the socio-emotional components which are built into the SFA. As Wood and Caulier-Grice (2006) point out, such features are rare in universal literacy programmes but are particularly important for promoting the social and academic engagement of students with SEBD. These components include:

- the emphasis on *cooperative learning* which involves working with students to develop their social interactional skills;
- the use of intensive *one-to-one mentoring* for pupils who may have difficulty in keeping up with the programme; and
- the use of a *family support team* to encourage parental involvement in the programme and in the school as a whole.

These components address directly some of the key barriers to educational engagement experienced by students with SEBD.

Whole-School Interventions for Social-Emotional Learning

As referenced in previous chapters, various therapeutic interventions have in recent years been encouraged and supported by the contention that sound relationships within a school setting may promote the resilience of vulnerable children with SEBD. There has been an emphasis on the part played by emotional literacy, as an essential adjunct to learning processes. Some researchers use the term 'socio-emotional learning' (Elias, 2004; Elias *et al.*, 2000, 2003; Zins and Elias, 2007) in order to stress the educational dimension of the concept. The following sections refer to school based interventions that relate to this concept of emotional literacy.

Circle Time

One of the most widely used socio-emotional interventions, worldwide, is Circle Time (CT) (Ballard, 1982; Mosley, 1993). This intervention seeks to promote unconditional positive regard (see Chapter 2) in which children feel that their views are heard, valued, and supported by teaching staff. Essentially the intervention involves children sitting in a circle with the teacher or facilitator without the barriers of desks and tables, sometimes using a 'talking object' to hold while they take turns to speak, and, after an opening game, discussing the issue of the week which they can all offer their thoughts and feelings about. There can be a ritual similar to PPR (see Chapter 3) in which children say positive things about each other. The session closes with another game. For younger children CT can involve chanting, action songs and rhymes. The CT session can also involve reading stories. The primary objective of this intervention is to foster the development of students' skills and confidence in identifying, understanding and expressing their emotions, and both giving and receiving validation of each others' rights to their emotions. In addition, the formal procedures associated with CT are claimed to encourage social skills such as turn-taking, conflict resolution, improved listening and speaking, and can increase self-esteem, and tolerance, although there is no research evidence available.

However, CT does offer some challenges to the class teacher or facilitator. Cremin (2002) cites some of the major challenges to the success of Circle Time to be lack of time owing to pressure from other curriculum areas, incongruence between the intervention and some teachers' negative beliefs about the empowerment of children, a failure to implement the CT philosophies within a whole-school approach, lack of teacher/facilitator training, and paucity of resources. She advocates a whole-school approach to Circle Time, requiring that before Circle Time is adopted, questions should be asked of all school staff about the involvement of children in formulating behaviour policies, about the role of the lunchtime supervisors in dealing with disruptive behaviour, and in the degree of recognition and support which teaching assistants and other paraprofessionals have from teaching staff to ensure that CT is not a bolt-on intervention but is a product of whole-school commitment to its theoretical position. These views are entirely consistent with the advice of the leading Circle Time exponents (e.g., Mosely, 1993).

The apparent simplicity of CT may be deceptive and create problems for some staff, especially those without formal training in its implementation. Taylor (2003) on the basis of interviews with 57 school staff in 14 schools identified serious shortcomings with the ways in which Circle Time was sometimes implemented. In certain cases staff behaved in ways which completely subverted the intentions of the intervention. This emphasizes the importance of proper training and careful monitoring of interventions of this kind. This insight is supported by other studies, such as that by Wiltz and Klein, (2001) which found students citing CT as an aversive classroom experience.

In this way CT could be said to illustrate the importance of staff training. It also suggests the importance of locating interventions such as this within a broad understanding of SEBD. In this case the role that developmental status might play in SEBD is highlighted. The emphasis which CT places on both unconditional positive regard and empathy is likely to render it unsuitable for students with serious communication difficulties (e.g., Autistic Spectrum Conditions) which can be characterized by a delay in, or absence of, Theory of Mind thus making empathy an extremely difficult skill to master (Baron-Cohen *et al.*, 1985). Additionally, children with attentional, impulse control and/or motor control problems (e.g., ADHD) may find it difficult to inhibit behaviours which disrupt CT sessions (Lougy *et al.*, 2007).

Although CT appears to be a very widely-used intervention that has a strong theoretical rationale, there is currently a paucity of empirical evidence to support its efficacy. There is clearly a case for this intervention to be subjected to rigorous empirical evaluation.

Social and Emotional Aspects of Learning (SEAL)

The UK-based Social and Emotional Aspects of Learning programme (SEAL) (Weare and Gray, 2003) is another universal programme worthy of consideration not least because it is has been adopted as a government-sponsored nationwide strategy. SEAL adopts a tiered approach with small group work being offered as additional assistance to children with SEBD. It is based in part on the PATHS intervention, (see Chapter 6) and on the Child Development Project. There is also a debt to CASEL (Collaborative for Academic, Social, and Emotional Learning), the international consortium (Greenberg *et al.*, 2003) which works to advance 'the science and evidence-based practice of Social and Emotional Learning (SEL)'. Though, having said this, SEAL has no discernable, explicitly-stated, coherent underlying theoretical framework.

SEAL's purpose is to add to the school-wide curriculum an additional element which includes five broad social and emotional issues:

- self-awareness;
- managing feelings;
- motivation;
- empathy; and
- social skills.

The SEAL programme includes staff-development modules, parent activities, resource files, and is intended to be employed by schools either as a supplement to the current National Curriculum areas dealing with Personal, Social and Health Education (PSHE) and citizenship, or as a stand-alone framework into which other similar interventions can be slotted. It is a highly organized programme, incorporating Circle Time, with the curriculum not only divided into year groups, but also into specific delivery months. The Guidance document details the following factors essential to its successful implementation:

- senior management commitment to the principles and understanding of the implications;
- school or setting systems which make sure that all individuals feel valued and listened to;
- positive relationships in the school or setting: adult–child, child–child, adult–adult;
- teacher (or practitioner) insight and knowledge into the emotional factors that affect learning;
- clear and consistently implemented policies on behaviour, bullying, race equality and inclusion;
- high professional standards;
- skilful teaching which arouses pupil interest and motivates;
- proactive work with parents; and
- the active involvement of children themselves.

Details on the operationalization of these imperatives is conspicuously lacking, as is information on how these 'essential' factors might be evaluated.

Unlike many of the whole-school programmes developed in the United States, SEAL is not a data-driven, nor a data-gathering programme, and there does not appear to be a rigorous built-in evaluation element.

A pilot evaluation scheme of the Primary School SEAL intervention (Hallam *et al.*, 2006) covered various outcome measures with an emphasis on behaviour and attendance. The purpose of this pilot evaluation was to determine the effectiveness of a range of measures proposed by the DfES, singly and in combination which involved:

- improvements in behaviour, attendance and attainment for individual children (the small group strand, enabled by the use of a health worker attached to schools);

- teacher skills and confidence in presenting the material (the Continuing Professional Development, CPD, strand, enabled by the use of 'leading teachers' to visit schools, observe, and coordinate CPD); and
- the promotion of whole-school approaches to positive behaviour, attendance and achievement (the school improvement strand, enabled by the use of a 'teacher coach' to work with existing services).

Some schools had employed all strands in this programme, some had employed only one or two, posing difficulties for comparative evaluation. The research design, which involved an examination of SEAL dissemination in 25 local authorities in the United Kingdom between 2003 and 2005 included an analysis of all the Local Authority plans for the scheme, telephone and email interviews with all Local Authority SEAL coordinators, questionnaires for teaching staff in 10 of these Local Authorities' schools, observational visits to 16 of 'best practice schools', questionnaires relating to small group interventions, case studies, and an analysis of attainment and attendance data in all SEAL primary schools. Data were compared with attainment and attendance in the SEAL pilot schools, to all other primary schools in the United Kingdom.

Data were collected from a wide range of stakeholders. 156 teachers and teaching assistants completed questionnaires, 23 non-teaching staff, 26 parents, and 22 parents whose children had been involved in the small-group initiative. Questionnaire data was available for 4247 children at Key Stage 1, pre-test, and 2163 post-test

Findings indicate no significant effects in relation to unauthorized absences. There were small gains in academic achievement, but no significant gains in relation to social development.

All pilot groups reported difficulties in engaging parents. Recommendations highlighted problems with the management of the scheme, with poor communication cited as one of the main difficulties. Poor attendance at SEAL training events for school staff (only 50%–60% of staff attended overall, and in some schools nil attendance was recorded) was a source of concern, as were issues around implementation of the SEAL materials. Failures in addressing cultural diversity were also noted, and poor understanding of SEBD was found among staff implementing the programme. There was limited support by teachers of small-group work, and difficulties in securing follow-up support from other agencies to support children whose particular needs had been identified through the small-group work sessions. This study was seriously undermined by difficulties experienced by the researchers in extricating useful data. On the positive side, the SEAL scheme overall was judged to be most effective where it had the commitment of the senior management team, where it adopted a whole-school approach, where teaching staff were given sufficient time to understand the materials and built on previous experience, and where a designated coordinator had been appointed within the school.

A further evaluation of the small-group work interventions was carried out for those considered to need additional support within the second wave of the SEAL programme (Humphrey *et al.*, 2008). The small-group work involved the withdrawal of targeted children (n = 461) together with comparison group children who were deemed to be positive role models (n = 163) in groups of up to six, for 35 minutes per week over seven weeks. In each school, a target group was assessed in comparison with a waiting list group. Data were gathered on students' performance on SEAL assessment protocols. Quantitative data were also collected from staff, pupils and parents at three different times during the evaluation. Finally, case studies of six lead practice schools were presented.

Findings overall were disappointing. Attrition levels were high, particularly in the parent group, at more than 53 %, and with staff (35% average) and students (over 40% average). Parent data showed they believed that none of the subject topics had any effect on pupil performance. For the topic *New Beginnings*, which deals with transitions and the students' understanding and acceptance of these, staff ratings showed no effect, while pupils' own ratings showed a small to moderate effect size of .44. For *Going For Goals*, a motivational topic, staff rating showed an improvement in self-regulation and a lowering of peer problems, while pupils indicated an increase in empathy skills, self-regulation and overall emotional literacy with a small effect size of .35. The other two topics, *Getting On and Falling Out* on conflict resolution and *Good To be Me* concerned with self-awareness and self-efficacy, had no statistical impact. However, staff reported, unexpectedly, a lowering of empathy levels during intervention. Skills and knowledge and experience of the facilitators, the majority of whom were teaching assistants and learning mentors, were seen as crucial to any possible success of the intervention.

The SEAL evaluators made a series of recommendations which appear to be based on the assumption that a more intensive application of the programme may produce better results. This remains to be seen. Questions remain about the extent to which a programme such as this can succeed without being more fully embedded in the life of the school through, for example, direct association with the formal curriculum. Explicit measures for the direct involvement of teaching staff in the delivery and/or reinforcement of the programme would also seem to be a desirable feature which is missing.

Second step

It is useful to compare SEAL with the US-based Second Step programme, which, like SEAL, is a curriculum modification intervention, used throughout a school. It engages students in a variety of theoretically-modelled interventions, to enhance social, emotional and behavioural skills. Second Step is primarily directed towards students in the first and second years of secondary school education. Another factor which differentiates it from SEAL is that it is typically embedded in the school curriculum, delivered usually by teachers but sometimes by psychologists and counsellors, within relevant subjects such as English, Social Studies and Health Studies. It is, therefore, at the heart of the formal curriculum rather than being an 'add on'. This is an important feature, because it promotes the view that success in the programme can contribute directly to academic success. This is an important consideration for both staff and students in schools where academic outcomes are highly (and sometimes disproportionately) valued.

Second Step is essentially as wide-ranging as SEAL, inclusive of a number of strategies which may be loosely said to fall into the socio-emotional learning category. The components most frequently embedded in similar universal programmes are anger management, social problem-solving, perspective-taking and behavioural social skills training.

Results from a pilot study of Second Step (Van Schoiack-Edstrom *et al.*, 2002) offers important points for comparison with Humphrey *et al.*'s (2008) findings in relation to SEAL. The pilot study involved 714 students from five schools in the United States and Canada. First year results were similar in effect size to those of the SEAL study, and with some effect sizes being negative. In the second year of implementation, however, there were more significant positive results. The authors concluded that the reasons the second year of intervention showed more positive outcomes is that the programme had been intensified. The effect of lesson concentration on Year 1 students was all-important: those who had received at least 2.5 lessons each week were most successful in developing relational skills. However, the authors admit to certain limitations in their study, notably the difficulties in establishing valid and reliable measures of lesson intensity, and the fact that participating schools were not randomly assigned to the conditions of the study. This latter flaw opens up the possibility that differences found between control and experimental groups may have been due the keenness of the teachers in the experimental group to involve themselves in the project and a dissimilarity in general teaching practices between themselves and those teaching the control groups. The researchers also suggested that a multi-method, multi-informant approach, which collected different kinds of data from a number of sources, including that from peers, may be more useful than the methodology used in this study which relied completely on confidential student self-reporting.

A further relevant study into the *Second Step* intervention programme was undertaken in Norway (Holsen *et al.*, 2008). A major question here was whether the intervention would work effectively when adapted to a European real-world context in which externally-directed training was not widely and intensively available, as opposed to the US model in which an intensive one-day training course was given to all teachers involved in the research. Schools in the Norwegian study were largely left to their own devices to train staff as they thought fit, as Steg for Steg (Second Step) had been included as a curriculum element in Norwegian schools for many years, although not in the schools used in this study. These features make this adapted version of Second Step closer to the implementation pattern used in SEAL.

This research project (known as the Social Competence Early Adolescence Study), took the form of a three stage quasi-experimental age cohort design study that was carried out in 11 elementary schools, involving 1153 students. The absence of a control group, limits the validity of the results. Baseline data were taken from a Year 7 group who were moving on to high school, without participating in the programme, and therefore could be used as a comparison group. Nine of the 11 schools adopted a whole-school policy, in which all classes used the Steg for Steg programme, but only modest positive outcomes were identified. However, when comparing these outcomes to those achieved by other universal competence programmes with similar sample size, the authors noted that average effect size in those studies were around 0.20, whereas those in this study were 0.18, 0.27 and 0.32. The authors in this case also cited differences in implementation as some teachers did not find time to deliver the programme twice each week, but sometimes ignored the intervention for several weeks due to the pressures involved in national testing for academic outcomes. This contrasts strongly with the US study which had a 99% rate of programme completion. Thus, frequency and intensity of intervention does appear to have some effect on outcomes, a factor noted in a report for the Center for Evaluation Research and Methodology in a meta-analysis of the effects of school-based universal social information processing interventions on aggressive behaviour. The authors (Wilson and Lipsey, 2006 p. 22) concluded:

> Finally, programs with more frequent treatment sessions per week tended to be more effective at producing reductions in aggressive and disruptive behaviour. The cognitive skills emphasized by social information processing programs are difficult to master and the more frequent programs may involve more opportunities for practice and reinforcement. The frequent programs may also allow children to pick up the various cognitive skills more quickly, because concepts from previous lessons are fresher or more salient.

A similar adaptation of Second Step in Germany, renamed Faustlos, produced similar modest effect sizes in the differences between the experimental and control groups (Schick and Cierpka, 2005, 2006) on internalizing disorders, but no effect on externalizing disorders. This was a randomized controlled trial with pre- and post-test data collected involving 14 elementary schools randomly assigned to the intervention (experimental) condition, and 7 schools assigned to the non-intervention (control) condition. However, the authors noted an additional issue which should always be considered in the case of universally delivered programmes of this nature: that where very few of the children in the study are within clinical limits for internalizing or externalizing disorders, effect sizes will be modest on all outcome measures, overall, because mean scores of social-emotional functioning will tend towards the statistically normal since the majority of participants do not exhibit deficits. It is interesting to note that the Faustlos studies have had a similarly very high attrition rate to the SEAL studies, with only 47% of parent questionnaires returned, 64% of the children attending interview, and 66% of teacher questionnaires returned. Reasons given by the authors for these poor returns included: family relocation, and students repeating a class or moving to a different class. The authors argue that these problems did not affect the validity of their results.

A recent study of Second Step (Cooke *et al.*, 2007) attempted to rectify the major implementation fidelity problems which had arisen in previous studies by extending training, and by incorporating training for parents and community members, and attempting to mediate self-report bias by adding two further outcome measures: behavioural observations and referral-to-office disciplinary data. Results were similarly mixed, and at times unexpected. This study was, again, a quasi-experimental design without a control group and was a city-wide intervention involving five of the eight elementary schools in Meriden, Connecticut. A total of 741 children, all 3rd and 4th graders, took part in the study. The training, in this intervention was intensive, with full-day training for all teachers, three one-hour training sessions for support staff, four one-hour workshops for parents, and a three-and-a-half day training of trainers adapted to the needs of community organizations. Self-report student assessment measures were administered by trained research assistants for two two-week periods at the start and end of the school year, and the disciplinary referral checklists were collated by a research assistant. Behavioural observations were carried out within two weeks of baseline testing and within two weeks of follow-up, using the Social Interaction Observational System.

Results from self-report follow-up at the end of the intervention showed very little change for most students, who scored high on the positive behaviours and low on negative behaviours both on baseline and follow-up. Of the students 41% reported changes in a negative direction and 33% of students reported a lower score at follow-up on at least one measure of positive functioning. Students who showed specific positive changes were significantly more likely than other students to show a major decline in bullying and aggression. Less encouraging was that 5% of students reported increases in anger and conflict, despite the intervention. On behavioural observation, there were no significant differences in pre- and post-test scores. Disciplinary referrals increased. However, anecdotally, teachers and staff reported that the intervention had made them more aware of the need for referrals to address disruptive behaviour. The authors conclude that targeted interventions, in addition to universal programmes like Second Step may be necessary to address some students' more serious and persistent behavioural and attitudinal problems. Teachers, school staff, parents and community members were very positive in their response to the intervention, with training provision scoring 3.73 out of 5 for satisfaction. The authors reported limitations to the study in that it did not have a control group.

Limitations in design and implementation of the studies of Second Step in the United States and in Europe and the fact that only one randomized controlled trial has been carried out (Grossman *et al.*, 1997) mean that claims for the efficacy of the programme need to be treated with caution while we wait for more reliable data. Having said this, the programme has received endorsements from a number of national organizations in the United States (CASEL, 2002; US Department of Education, 2001). Also, the findings that are extant are interesting because they show (albeit by negative example sometimes) the importance of systematic training and the careful programming of implementation strategies. It has to be noted that the North American implementations are often relatively more successful than the European ones probably because of the more systemic approach adopted in the former. This observation suggests important implications for the UK SEAL programme which appears poorly focused and chaotic by comparison.

School-Wide Positive Behavioural Support (SWPBS)

School-wide Positive Behavioural Support (Lewis *et al.*, 1998; Sugai and Horner, 2002, 2006; Walker *et al.*, 1996) is a whole-school (i.e., 'universal') intervention which is grounded in behavioural theory and the application of behavioural analysis. Originally researched as an intervention in special and residential schools for those with the most severe challenging behaviour, and informed by preventative mental health initiatives, it has now been adopted in many states of the United States as a response to IDEA legislation (1997) which mandates some degree of functional behavioural analysis for those students who may present the most challenging behaviours (Cheney *et al.*, 2008). It has extended its remit to resystematizing whole-school initiatives in the United States, based on the primary principles of Applied Behaviour Analysis that is data-driven and data-providing. It is now available in 20 of the states in the United States (Doolittle *et al.*, 2007). It is 'a proactive systems approach to school-wide discipline and is designed to be responsive to current social and educational challenges' (Sugai *et al.*; 2003).

As is common with many universal programmes in the United States it is a three tier whole-school intervention strategy which is divided into 'primary level' (i.e., universal level, relating to all pupils), 'secondary level' (i.e., targeting students who present specific challenges that can be managed within the school's regular resources) and 'tertiary level' (i.e., targeting students who present specific challenges that can be managed within the school with support from external agencies). At primary level, which accounts for 80% of school students, basic SWPBS (positive behaviour support) is provided for all students. This consists of a few very simple rules of referring to personal and social responsibilities, positively expressed, which emphasize positive aspects of behaviour. Typically, these are, 'I am respectful; I am responsible; I am safe'. In contrast to more punitive approaches to behaviour management, such as Assertive Discipline (Canter and Canter, 1976) which focus on 'problem' behaviour and seek to correct it through the application of sanctions (Amos, 2004), positive behavioural support seeks to replace school-wide undesired behaviour with new prosocial behaviours and skills (Anderson and Kincaid, 2005). It achieves this by removing the environmental factors which might reinforce undesired behaviour (Barth *et al.*, 2004), and introducing explicit systems for rewarding (i.e., reinforcing) appropriate behaviour (Barrett *et al.*, 2008).

There are nine steps towards implementing school-wide positive behavioural skills. These are:

1. define three to five school-wide behavioural expectations;
2. provide a 'defining rule' for each expectation;
3. build a culture of competence by teaching the school-wide skills to *all* students;
4. teach behavioural expectations in a variety of school settings;
5. teach specific social behaviours that are examples of these behavioural expectations;
6. teach behavioural expectations with 'negative' examples;

7. give students the opportunity to practice appropriate behaviours;
8. reward appropriate behaviour; and
9. acknowledge appropriate behaviour on a regular basis after the skill is learned.
    (Walker *et al.*, 2004, p. 137)

It can be seen that its basic tenets have much in common with the principles underlying the Good Behaviour Game (Barrish *et al.*, 1969), except that it moves much further into the use of behavioural analysis in environmental modifications (Dunlap *et al.*, 2006) and into the area of social-skills training. In order to define the environmental factors which produce behavioural responses, the school staff collect data on 'office referrals' (i.e., whereby students are reported to the school Principal for disciplinary infringements) in a highly systematic way (Sugai and Horner, 2002; Sugai *et al.*, 2000). Data are produced on the rate of referral, type of behaviour, time of referral (date and time of day), the place of referral (Oswald *et al.*, 2005), and identity of referred pupil (in to identify repeat referrals). These data are analyzed by means of a web-based school-wide information system (SWIS) which allows antecedents and consequences for behaviour to be monitored and analyzed. This analysis helps to identify intervention targets and strategies as well a means for evaluating the effectiveness of these when they are subsequently implemented.

The SWIS methodology was empirically evaluated by Irvin *et al.* (2006), using Messick's (1995) construct validity approach as a conceptual framework. The study included 22 elementary schools and 10 middle schools. The important finding from this study was that office referral data were found to be efficient and effective for purpose. In a study by Lassen *et al.* (2006) data from an urban school in the Midwest was gathered over three years and revealed that improvements in school behaviour were reflected in academic performance, with specific reductions in office referrals and significantly-related increases in mathematics and reading scores.

These positive results were echoed in a longitudinal study of SWPBS in Canada (McIntosh *et al.*, 2006) with data collected over five years from a cohort of children who entered kindergarten in 1998. Luiselli *et al.* (2005) in another longitudinal study in a Massachusetts urban elementary school produced similar findings. McIntosh *et al.* (2008) tracked the academic records of students transitioning between middle and high school and found that discipline referrals in 8th Grade were significantly correlated with positive academic achievement in 9th Grade, indicating academic benefits from SWBS.

Sailor *et al.* (2007) also noted the relationship between academic standards and behavioural support and appealed for the integration of the SWPBS social-behavioural development pedagogy into curricular and instructional efforts to produce higher academic achievement for all students. This finding had been the subject of an earlier study (Fleming *et al.*, 2005) which arrived at a similar conclusion in analyzing longitudinal data from 7th to 10th grade students (n = 576) in the Washington State Raising Healthy Children project. The findings supported the conclusion that school-based social-development interventions which address specific risk factors are likely to improve school engagement and academic achievement.

However, it is in the second and third tiers of the SWPBS intervention that it becomes more multi-modal. Within the second tier are those students who may need additional support. In this way it reflects the UK model in which basic mainstream education is supplemented, first by Behavioural Support Teams and other experts who implement School Action and School Action Plus (equivalent to SWPBS second tier) and finally a Statement of Special Educational Needs (equivalent to third tier or tertiary intervention). The model generated by the positive behaviour support researchers shows that 15% of students are likely to need intervention at second tier level, for students with at-risk behaviour, and that 5% of students will need intervention at third tier level, for high-risk students. These figures are again roughly equivalent to the statistics in the United Kingdom.

In second tier intervention the student is usually provided with a group intervention targeted to support a small group of students in areas such as social skills training or additional mentoring or classroom aide support. Some of the group contingencies may be carried out in a group-within-a-school setting. One of these programmes used in tandem with SWPBS is Check In/Check Out (CICO), which is a behaviour report card system which employs additional parental involvement in monitoring the student's progress (Todd *et al.*, 2008). The purpose of using this programme is to bring in a secondary level of support for the student. In a quasi-experimental study by Filter *et al.* (2007) into the fidelity of implementation of the CICO programme an administrative team (n = 17) from each of three schools, monitored the progress of a total of 19 students. Outcomes were generally positive, indicating that two-thirds of all students (13 out of 19) made good progress, according to the perceptions of teachers and administrators. However, a source of concern in this study is that only 7 of the 17 respondents reported that a family member had signed the report card daily, an issue which was not adequately foregrounded in the discussion of results.

The involvement of parents of children with SEBD is a difficult issue to address (Zellman and Waterman, 1998), even in schemes such as SWPBS (Harvey *et al.*, 2003) which cites parental involvement as being crucial (Epstein and Sheldon, 2002). In an opinion paper which asked the question, 'The Wave of SWPBS – who is left behind?', Vaughn (2006) highlights what he sees as the neglect of the parental dimension in some of the published work on SWPBS for students with 'Severe Disabilities'(Harvey *et al.*, 2003; Martin and Martin 2007; Murray *et al.*, 2008). At the tertiary stage, which caters for students with the most challenging behaviour, two options have been proposed for promoting parental involvement (Freeman *et al.*, 2006). The first is a wraparound system, where representatives of the community, parents, teachers, health workers (Rief, 2003) and other services, are called together to monthly meetings to decide on the most effective interventions that may help the student who may have problems in multiple life domains (Lewis and Newcomer, 2002). The second proposed option involves a Person Centred Planning (PCP) strategy worked out for the child, if s/he has developmental difficulties or serious emotional difficulties (Artesani and Mallar,

1998). Functional Behaviour Assessments are used to determine the efficacy of these strategies.

One of the strengths of SWPBS is the emphasis that is placed on constant monitoring, and the variety of data evaluation instruments that have been devised, such as the School Wide Information System (SWIS), already described above. Another tool, the School-wide Evaluation Tool (SET) (Sugai *et al.*, 2001) has been put in place to monitor each school's performance and fidelity to the scheme. This is a 28-item scale, administered annually by an onsite observer who reviews documentation and interviews staff and students. The scale is used to analyze a range of issues, including: the ways in which behavioural expectations are defined and taught; the rewards that are provided for following behavioural expectations, and the continuum of consequences in place for responding to problem behaviour. Findings from data analysis are used to inform decision-making. The administrative support required to implement this approach is not insignificant, however, the rewards appear to be substantial given the positive effects achieved by the programme along with the ownership that school staff inevitably develop owing to the way in which the intervention is designed to be embedded in the fabric of daily school life. Such is the potency of SWPBS approach that it is reported that SWPBS data is sometimes used in US school districts to contribute to external assessments of school performance (Horner *et al.*, 2004). This is regrettable and may detract from its practical utility by encouraging a temptation among some school managers to maximize outcome scores by any means, rather than using the data to improve the quality of actual behaviour in schools.

A further strength of SWPBS is its process of delivery. Rather than requiring sudden changes to an established school regime, the initial stage is scheduled to take a year during which representative teams of staff led by a 'trainer', gather data about the current school functioning, build an action plan, and implement only the first tier. This involves teacher training to produce consistency of response to behavioural issues, and the selection of 'coaches' who will take a leadership role. One of the purposes of SWPBS is to 'teach natural leaders within schools and districts to facilitate the implementation of SWPBS, thereby decreasing reliance on outside "experts" and avoiding traditional "workshop" approaches' (Freeman *et al.*, 2006).

Understandably perhaps, SWPBS has been a subject of international interest, being adapted for use in Australia and several European countries. A notable non-US study of an adaptation of SWPBS was carried out in Norway in a quasi-experimental design intervention named Peer Assisted Learning Strategies (PALS) in four elementary schools involving 735 children in grades three to seven, with 363 in the intervention group (Sørlie and Ogden, 2007). The control group in this study involved four similar elementary schools. A cognitive-behavioural element – the Stop Now And Plan (SNAP) strategy – has been added. This study deviated from those in the United States in that it did not take as its barometer of success the numbers of office-based referrals, but chose, instead, to base its methodology on teacher/student observations. While teacher reported reductions in disruptive classroom behaviour in the first two years after implementation ranged from moderate to large, and while teacher efficacy was significantly related to the better outcomes, the results based on student ratings of social competence and on classroom climate were statistically not significant. However, those schools with the highest levels of disruptive student behaviour at baseline were those which reported greatest decreases.

Many behavioural support interventions are in use worldwide which share common features with SWPBS, being universal, school-wide programmes based primarily on behavioural principles. These are not based on SWPBS but share a common ancestry that owes much to the seminal work of Kounin (1970), which in turn is rooted in the work of the pioneers of behavioural psychology (see Chapter 2). The incorporation of this into a tiered approach is borrowed from community medicine models, with more personalized approaches being introduced in the second tier, and a third tier involving direct intervention from support teams outside the school. One such similar scheme is the Birmingham *Framework for Intervention* (Ali *et al.*, 1997). However, apart from initial, small scale evaluations, such as those carried out on the Birmingham framework (Cole *et al.*, 2000; Williams *et al.*, 1997), there is little robust research evidence to support these schemes, which is why the strongly evidenced SWPBS intervention has been foregrounded in this book. Having said this, the ubiquity of generic versions of SWPBS testify to the robustness of this approach. This probably owes a great deal to the fact that SWPBS employs tried and tested behavioural interventions, such as contingency management (see Chapter 4), and combines them with empirically supported humanistic and cognitive interventions, such as teacher involvement, social skills training, peer mentoring, and parental involvement. This respect for evidence based practice, however, is combined with what might be termed 'educational literacy'. That is, a detailed awareness of the practical functioning of schools and the day to day circumstances in which teachers operate. As we have noted, SWBP operates in harmony with the rhythms of the school year and has a simplifying and systematizing rather than an elaborating effect on school practices and procedures. In other words, SWPBS helps school staff to be more effective in doing what most of them are trying to do already, and, by and large through the use of methods with which they are familiar or with which they can be familiarized with relative ease.

Restorative practices

Restorative practices, or measures, sometimes employed in the United States (Casella, 2003; Haft, 2000; Heydenberk and Heydenberk, 2005; Karp, 2001; Stinchcomb *et al.*, 2006) but more usually in Australia, New Zealand and Europe (Ahmed and Braithwaite, 2006; Burssens and Vettenburg, 2006; Drewery, 2004; Morrison *et al.*, 2005; Shaw, 2007) are informed by principles of restorative justice, a concept derived from innovations within the criminal justice system in which conversation, dialogue and conferencing can be used as a vehicle for reparation and conflict resolution. At the root of this approach is the realization that any form of disciplinary punishment tends to treat the perpetrator as a passive object, who has no real agency in relation to externally-imposed sanctions. Restorative practices emphasize the role of individual agency, and therefore personal responsibility of all stakeholders in the conflict situation (Sherman and Strang, 2007). A key dynamic of this approach is the stimulation of inter and intrapersonal reflection among stakeholders. Restorative practices have been related to Maori traditions (Wearmouth *et al.*, 2007), in which the community as a whole can be gathered to examine the part all have played in the creation of the crime or the problem and all parties, including the perpetrator, are encouraged to be active in repairing the damage caused (Wearmouth *et al.*, 2007). There is also evidence to suggest that such approaches were being used with 'maladjusted' students in England in the 'pioneer' schools described by Bridgeland (1971) without any reference to Maori traditions. David Wills (1960) provides a first-hand account of the system of 'shared responsibility' which he pioneered at Bodenham Manor School in the 1950s.

As a school-based intervention, restorative practices are similar in purpose to the SWPBS ethos, contesting a zero-tolerance approach to disciplinary problems by attempting to create a school-wide climate of community-shared values for all students, and reduce levels of aggressive or bullying behaviour, although in this case there appears to be a heavier reliance on humanist relational ethics (Morrison *et al.*, 2005) rather than the strong evidence-based practice, pre-planned procedure, and manual-guided implementation evident in SWPBS. At this point in time there is 'insufficient evidence [...] about its effectiveness' (Sherman and Strang, 2007). Further research is clearly required.

In practical terms, the intervention consists of eliciting responses to several questions from participants involved in aggressive or disruptive behaviour.

- What has happened?
- Who has been affected?
- How can we involve everyone who has been affected in finding a way forward?
- How can everyone do things differently in the future?

The dialogue can take place informally in 'corridor conferences', or more formally in mini-conferences, sometimes adopting problem-solving circles similar to those used in Circle Time. Teachers are encouraged to use Circle Time, and to employ restorative pedagogy in which teachers themselves model the skills and values represented by the ethos, and create opportunities for their development throughout all class lessons. This intervention is universal rather than targeted, although the conferences are more likely to be used only in cases of more severe disruption and aggression (Drewery, 2004; Karp, 2001; McCluskey *et al.*, 2008), and can be employed in order to avert exclusions or suspensions. Peer support strategies (Cowie and Hutson, 2005; Cowie and Olafsson, 2000; Cowie, *et al.*, 2002, 2008a, 2008b) are sometimes employed in restorative practice initiatives, emphasizing the importance that this initiative places on interpersonal relationships within schools.

There is little robust evidence, as yet, about the value of restorative practices to SEBD populations in schools. One study in Flemish Belgium discussed

non-statistical findings from a two-year (2002–2004) employment of group conferencing to address serious disciplinary issues in 14 schools in 9 school areas,
concluding with various focus points that emerged from the experiment, including the time-consuming nature of organizing such conferences, and the difficulty
of organizing the conferences in schools which were not fully committed to the
ethos of restorative practices (Burssens and Vettenberg, 2006). Another (Kane
et al., 2008) was an evaluation of the first two years of a 30-month long pilot study
in Scotland into the use of restorative practices in 18 schools in 3 local authorities:
Highlands, Fife, and North Lanarkshire. However, the use of restorative practices
was only one of a number of programmes adopted by these schools under the
Scottish Executive's 'Better Behaviour, Better Learning' initiative, also simulta-
neously evaluated by questionnaires, surveys, observations of meetings activities
and lessons, documentary analysis of schools' policies and of national and school
statistical data, focus groups and interviews. The interim (McCluskey *et al.*, 2006)
and final report (Kane *et al.*, 2008) show that the intervention was more likely to
be considered useful by Primary rather than Secondary schools, although each
school adopted its own different version of restorative practices and this flexibility
was seen as a strength of the intervention. The report states (Kane *et al.*, 2008,
p. 14):

> When introduced in schools with at least a number of receptive staff and
> when the initiative was supported by commitment, enthusiasm, leadership and
> significant staff development, there was a clear positive impact on relationships
> in school. This was identifiable through the views and actions of staff and pupils,
> as well as evident in measurable reduction in playground incidents, discipline
> referrals, exclusion and use of external behaviour support.

The report concludes that restorative practices are not (nor indeed is there ever
likely to be) 'the one right answer' to issues of discipline and control, given the
complex range of pressures on and within education. Nonetheless, the evaluation
indicates strong and clear benefits for both staff and pupils (Kane *et al.*, 2008,
p. 380).

This conclusion is very similar to the one reached by the largest evaluation
in the United Kingdom, on restorative justice in 26 schools, six primary and 20
secondary, in England and Wales commissioned by the Youth Justice Board (2004,
p. 68) which ended with the statement that Restorative Justice was 'not a panacea
for problems in schools', but 'if implemented correctly [could] . . . improve the
school environment and enhance the learning and development of young people'.

Recently a Restorative Practices (RP) pilot scheme was evaluated in seven post-
primary schools in Co Donegal and Co Sligo, Ireland (McGarrigle, 2006). The
largest of the schools had 700 students and the smallest less than 100. In this initiative the authors envision RP as an intervention to ensure that more 'at risk' young
people remain in school and have an increased opportunity to lead a healthy and
successful life. This interpretation of the intervention also includes mediation.
Data collected from the 7 schools taking part comprised interviews, questionnaires, incident report forms and observations. School profiles were determined

using the School Ethos Questionnaire (Byrne and Barry, 2003). Although this was a very small-scale study, there were some interesting findings which replicated findings in larger studies, for instance that the most common barriers to implementing the intervention were said to be an overcrowded curriculum, lack of resources, and lack of training for teachers. There was a very clear change in disciplinary measures in all schools. Where reported incidents would have resulted in detention (57%), suspension (40%), a visit to the Principal's office (25%), after the intervention the results were: holding an impromptu (corridor) conference (62.5%), and restorative questions (62.5%). Of the incidents 10% were resolved by holding a large conference and another 10% by organizing class Circle Time and talking through the incident. No students were sent to the Principal's office, only 15% resulted in detention, and only 10% resulted in suspension. The report recommended that for future evaluation, validated outcome measures should be used, and that data on detentions should be collected more effectively. It should be strongly emphasized that this study was lacking in scientific rigour, and that the data analysis and presentation of findings were not of a high standard. However, there was some merit both in the undertaking, and in the possibility of further, better-designed and evaluated investigation into this intervention.

Cognitive Behavioural Programmes

In Chapter 4 we discussed evidence for cognitive behavioural approaches to SEBD emphasizing the underlying theory and specific approaches associated with this intervention. In particular we focused on the impact of CB interventions when carried out with individual students, small groups or single classes. In this chapter we focus on CB approaches that are designed for use at the whole-school level and further. These are known as 'universal' programmes, meaning that they are offered to entire populations, such as whole class groups, year groups or entire school populations. The intention behind such large-scale interventions are to (1) capture all students who may benefit personally from the intervention, (2) mobilize all students in supporting one another, and (3) promote resilience and have a preventive effect for all participants.

FRIENDS

A particularly promising example is the FRIENDS programme, which has been pioneered in Australia (Barrett *et al.*. 1999). The acronym FRIENDS stands for the following skill related factors:

- F = feeling worried (i.e., self-monitoring skills);
- R = relax and feel good (i.e., self-control skills);
- I = inner helpful thoughts (i.e., self-management skills);
- E = explore plans (i.e., skills for identifying options and making choices);

- N = nice work, reward yourself (i.e., self-reinforcement skills);
- D = don't forget to practice (i.e., maintenance skills);
- S = stay calm for life (i.e., extended maintenance skills).

Barrett *et al.* (2006, p. 406) succinctly describe the FRIENDS programme as:

> a brief cognitive-behavioural intervention designed and validated as an in-dividual or group-based treatment for clinically anxious children . . ... The programme assists children and youth in learning important skills and tech-niques that help them to cope with and manage anxiety and emotional distress through the application of learned coping and problem-solving skills.

Barrett *et al.*'s (2006) paper describes a randomized control trial of a FRIENDS intervention which, as is standard practice in this programme, consisted of 10 weekly sessions of approximately 70 minutes each, plus two 'booster' sessions in the following term. In this study there were two 'developmentally-tailored versions' of the programme FRIENDS for Children, for 6th Grade students, and FRIENDS for Youth for 9th Grade students (n = 669). The programme was deliv-ered by teachers who had undergone a one-day training programme. To retain the integrity of the universalist approach the evaluation strategy involved allocating schools (n = 6: 3 intervention schools and 3 controls) rather than individual students to intervention and control conditions. The main findings of the study indicated significant reductions in anxiety symptoms that were maintained at 12, 24 and 36 month follow-ups. Initially the effects on girls were significantly higher than for boys, though this difference disappeared after 36 months.

The study by Barrett *et al.* (1999) is one of a number of large-scale Type 1 RCTs carried out on this intervention in Australia. Lowrey-Webster *et al.* (2001) studied students (aged 10–13) attending seven secondary schools in Brisbane. Stu-dents (n = 594) were randomly-allocated by class group to either the FRIENDS programme, which was embedded in the school curriculum, or a no intervention condition in which students did not have exposure to the FRIENDS programme. Results revealed that children receiving the FRIENDS intervention reported fewer anxiety symptoms, regardless of their risk status, when compared to the compar-ison group.

Similar positive findings are reported by Bernstein *et al.* (2005) in a Type 1 RCT carried out with 7–11 year old students (n = 453) from three schools who undertook the FRIENDS programme in the United States. Students who had undergone the FRIENDS intervention programme showed significantly decreased anxiety levels than controls, while students who underwent an enhanced version of FRIENDS that included a parent training component showed the best outcomes.

A recent study carried out in the United Kingdom (Stallard *et al.*, 2007) focussed on the application of the FRIENDS programme in three primary schools, with children aged between nine and 10 (n = 106). The children were assessed on three occasions during the study: prior to commencing the training; during the training; and three months after completing the training. On each occasion they were assessed through the application of two standardized instruments: the

Spence Children's Anxiety Scale and the Culture-Free Self-Esteem Questionnaire Form B. At the three month follow-up, anxiety levels had significantly decreased and self-esteem increased. Children with the most severe emotional problems appeared to benefit most from the programme. Unfortunately, this study did not utilize a non-intervention comparison group. Also, the programme was delivered by school nurses as opposed to teaching staff. Having said this, evidence reported by Barrett and Turner (2001) found that there was no differential effect on student outcomes for students who received the FRIENDS intervention led by teachers compared with those who received the intervention led by psychologists.

The findings from these robust studies indicate that the FRIENDS intervention is an extremely effective intervention for students with anxiety problems between the ages of 7 and 13. The intervention is particularly effective for children with clinically- significant anxiety problems and low self-esteem, but has also been shown to be effective in improving the emotional coping skills of children and young people in the general population. In this sense FRIENDS can be seen as combining the best qualities of a therapeutic programme with a general life skills intervention that can be incorporated into the regular curriculum for all students. One of the many advantages of this is that it allows for vulnerable students to receive direct support without their having to be singled out and possibly stigmatized (Lowery-Webster *et al.*, 2001).

The fact also that there is evidence to suggest that FRIENDS appears to be as effective when delivered by a teacher as it is when delivered by a psychologist is also significant. Such an advantage, if generalizable, would facilitate the incorporation of the programme into schools and might well account for its apparent superiority over the SEAL programme. It should also be noted that the manualized one day training appears to indicate that a relatively modest financial outlay is likely to accrue significant benefits.

Coping Power

Coping Power (CP) is a cognitive behavioural strategy for use with aggressive children. It is derived from an earlier validated programme for anger management, Anger Coping, which is incorporated into its multi-component design. Many of the strategies in the Coping Power programme are also present in Fast Track (see Chapter 7). It is a short-term (15 months) intervention for both children in school, between the ages of 6 and 11, and their parents. The school-based programme is delivered to students in groups of 4 to 6 over 33 sessions and is led by a postgraduate psychologist or by the school's counsellor. Programme content includes training in cognitive-behavioural skills as well as problem-solving and study skills training. Emphasis is placed on training in refusal skills and in resisting peer pressure. These interventions are mirrored in a concurrent parent training programme, which is delivered over 16 sessions at the children's schools by school staff to groups of between four and six parents. The parent training component of Coping Power is based on a social-learning theory approach which involves modelling and the mobilization of social influence in a group setting.

Lochman and Wells (2002a, 2002b) carried out an RCT of the Coping Power programme involving186 boys in 5th and 6th grades in Durham, North Carolina who were identified as presenting with significant levels of aggression. These were randomly assigned to one of three groups: child intervention alone, child and parent intervention, or a control group. Three outcomes were measured: child-reported substance abuse, covert delinquency and overt delinquency. These participants were also subject to a one-year follow-up study which assessed parent-reported substance abuse and school behaviour (Lochman and Wells, 2003, 2004). The Coping Power programme was found to have significant impact on three of the five measures: covert delinquency (but only for those children who had been on the combined child/parent intervention), parent-reported substance abuse (6% of intervention children as against 17% of the control group), and school behaviour, an improvement which was maintained at follow-up, a year after the intervention had ended.

This RCT has some limitations the most obvious of which is that the sample base was small, and all male, but it gave backing to the initial hypothesis that the prevention of anti-social behaviours was enhanced when parent-training was incorporated in the programme. It was noted that there was no evidence of cultural differences in the results in that the programme worked as efficiently for ethnic minority families as it did for Caucasian families. Two further small-scale case-studies have been published showing the effective application of the Coping Power intervention. Boxmeyer *et al.* (2007) described the positive effects of the programme on an 11-year-old boy and his father, and Lochman *et al.* (2007) described the effects of Coping Power on the disruptive behaviour of a 10-year-old girl.

The manualized version of this intervention was also successfully trialled in the Netherlands in a clinical setting (Van de Weil *et al.*, 2003) and was then followed up, five years later. Differences were revealed in comparison with the a clinic-based group which had not undergone the intervention, with drug, tobacco and alcohol use lower in the intervention group and similar to the levels of healthy controls. Both the clinically-treated adolescents and the CP intervention adolescents were equivalent to healthy controls in outcome measures for delinquency. This study also endorsed the cost effectiveness of the intervention (Zonnevylle-Bender *et al.*, 2007).

Conclusion

The messages from evidence reviewed here are clear: whole school approaches, particularly those which address the common needs of all students can make a vital contribution to improving the behaviour and emotional well being of all students. By implication the adults in schools where such approaches are applied effectively are also bound to benefit. There is a need, however, for important conditions to be in place if such approaches are to achieve their optimal effectiveness. There needs to be clarity and precision in terms of the content of the programme, its aims, and methods of implementation. Furthermore, the most impressive programmes have built-in evaluation components. It is also important that whole school SEBD interventions are embedded in the main fabric of school life. This means that, where possible they should be incorporated into the formal curriculum and echoed consistently in the 'hidden curriculum' by which the social and emotional climate of the school is regulated. The findings relating to universal programmes (i.e., those which are applied to all students regardless of status) offer powerful support to the idea that all schools which focus on promoting the social and emotional competence for all students produce benefits not only for students with SEBD but also foster the social and emotional coping skills required by all students. Findings from school based programmes which incorporate parents, such as Success for All and Coping Power, are also indicative of the enormous potential that schools have for promoting improvements in social and emotional functioning of their students beyond the boundaries of the school.

It is a long held educational truism that when members of a school staff work together towards shared goals in a consistent way they add power to the efforts of individuals. The skills based, educative nature of many of the approaches reviewed in this chapter also mean that when the interventions are effective the students in the school are in effect coopted to work with staff in realizing and maintaining the interventions.

As in previous chapters an emphasis has to be placed on the importance of training and evaluation. Where training is overly complex or poorly attended, and evaluation strategies are not incorporated, implementation and outcomes are weak, as is illustrated by the disappointing evaluation findings relating to the SEAL project. Where training is tightly focused and delivered to whole staff groups and implementation is supported by a clear evaluation strategy, outcomes tend to be impressive. These qualities are illustrated by the impressive results achieved by SWPBS and FRIENDS programmes.

As we noted at the beginning of this chapter, external support services can have an important role supporting whole school interventions. They can provide training, support with monitoring implementation and evaluation. They also have important roles to play at second and third tier levels where specialist interventions are required that go beyond the resources and skills held within schools. However, the effective and efficient use of such support services depends on the proactive, competent and willing engagement of school staff with the kinds of approaches explored in this and the previous two chapters, which represent the basic tools that school staff need to be confident and effective in situations where the threat of SEBD looms large.

Summary

This chapter has dealt with whole-school support systems for students with SEBD and the wider range of educational provision and intervention that can be made available to such students. It was shown that whole school academic interventions incorporate strategies which can be adopted by management teams to enhance the academic potential of students with SEBD. The Success for All (SFA) programme was singled out as a well-evidenced approach to raising attainment in literacy that has a number of specific components that address directly some of the key barriers to educational engagement experienced by students with SEBD.

A second category of interventions explored were whole-school interventions for social-emotional learning. These are promoted as being able to promote an increase in social-emotional literacy for SEBD students. Several of these interventions were examined. Circle Time, although widely used throughout the world, was found to have little by way of firm empirical support. Concerns were raised about the quality of its implementation and potential problems relating to inadequate training of staff employing the approach. Social and Emotional Aspects of Learning (SEAL) is a social and emotional learning programme, intended to enable students to develop self regulatory and social problem solving skills. Although implemented on a large-scale in England and Wales it has achieved relatively poor outcomes and appears to suffer from implementation problems. We identified the Second Step programme as being, in principle, very similar to the SEAL programme in terms of its emphasis on developing students' self-management and social engagement skills. However, it differs in important respects, particularly in its implementation design which has the programme embedded in the formal curriculum and delivered by teachers. While the evaluation evidence for Second Step is more encouraging than that for SEAL, there remain questions about the efficacy of this programme.

We also identified whole-school behavioural management programmes which can act as a universal programme for all students, but can also enhance the abilities of students with SEBD to engage with learning in a safe environment. School-Wide Positive Behavioural Support (SWPBS) is a behaviourally-orientated programme which involves the development of a whole-school approach in devising and reinforcing rules for positive behaviour. There is strong evidence for its efficacy when implemented correctly. Restorative Practices is an approach to conflict resolution that is based on the principles of restorative justice involving students in an active engagement with problem issues within the context of the school community. This approach has many positive features, including a model of social engagement which emphasizes mutual respect and tolerance of difference. However, to date, the programme has not undergone significant evaluation and, therefore, there is little evidence of its efficacy in relation to SEBD in schools.

Finally, we considered two cognitive behavioural programmes that can be universal and whole-school in their approach in supporting all students, but may be particularly effective for students with SEBD. The FRIENDS programme stands out as one of the most robustly-supported programmes for internalizing disorders, and has the backing of the World Health Organization. A number of large-scale RCTs have been carried out in several countries showing that this 10-session CB programme (often delivered by teachers) is a highly effective curriculum-embedded intervention that is particularly successful in helping all students, regardless of risk status, to develop strategies for managing anxiety. Coping Power (CP) is a CB intervention that addresses aggressive/acting-out behaviour. An interesting feature of this programme is the incorporation of a school-based parent training component. Like FRIENDS it has strong empirical support based on RCTs.

The chapter concluded by emphasizing the importance of clarity and precision in the aims and implementation strategies, as well as the importance of built-in evaluation tools and procedures. The central significance of rigorous training and implementation fidelity were also discussed, as was the role of external services in supporting whole school approaches.

6

Small-Scale On- and Off-Site Provision

Overview

In this chapter we deal with various interventions which focus on the structure of the educational setting. Some of these approaches involve dividing large schools into smaller units, and some involve altering the nature of what is conventionally thought to be a 'school'. We also consider targeted interventions within a school which involve utilizing settings other than mainstream classrooms as venues for the education of students with SEBD. The chapter also deals with off-site day and residential provision.

Up to now this book has been concerned primarily with interventions for promoting the educational engagement of students with SEBD in what might be termed 'standard mainstream' schools. Although, as should be evident from much of the discussion in Chapter 1, we are critical of assumptions that 'mainstream' and 'neighbourhood' schools somehow equate with mainstream society (whatever that is) and that to have access to such schools amounts to having access to the widest range of social and educational opportunities available. On the contrary, we argue that some so called mainstream schools represent all of the features of marginalization, stigmatization and educational failure that some authors attribute to what they see as the discredited system of special schools and non-mainstream provision of the past. Some are in fact worse in the quality of the social-educational experience that they offer to their most vulnerable students than the very special schools some seek to abolish. As we have shown there are important, evidence-based skills and approaches that staff in mainstream schools can utilize in order to promote the educational engagement and attachment to schooling that are basic rights of every child. We have argued that at least some of these skills and approaches, although relatively new to 'mainstream' education have their precursors in certain pioneering special schools of the last century.

From Inclusion to Engagement: Helping Students Engage with Schooling through Policy and Practice
By Paul Cooper and Barbara Jacobs   © 2011 John Wiley & Sons, Ltd

In this chapter we consider evidence of the effectiveness of approaches to SEBD which bear more obvious similarities with what might be seen as more traditional approaches to meeting the needs of vulnerable students through the creation of diversity in provision.

Small-Scale Provision

There has been considerable recent interest, in the United States, in dividing large high schools into smaller units (Ancess and Allen, 2006; Felner *et al.*, 2007). It is claimed that Small Learning Communities (SLCs) provide safer schools, with a more personalized pedagogy (Cotton, 2001; Darling-Hammond, 2002; Kahne *et al.* 2008; Lee and Friedrich, 2007). With regard to children with SEBD (Dukes and Lamar-Dukes, 2007) it has been noted that 'there is overwhelming evidence that violence is much less likely to occur in small schools than in large ones' (Raywid and Oshiyama, 2000, p. 444). There is also a lower rate of drug use, vandalism, bullying, suspensions and expulsions (Gladden, 1998). However, it is important to eschew simplistic assumptions about the effects of school or class size alone on educational and behavioural outcomes. A national study of children with SEBD in the Netherlands (Mooij and Smeets, 2006, 2008) found that more violence occurred in small schools. The explanation is that in the Netherlands pupils with more social and emotional problems are educated together in special schools with a small number of students. Similarly, a recent study of mainstream schools in Malta found that levels of SEBD were inversely correlated with class size, meaning that the greatest level of difficulty was found in the smallest classes. As in the Dutch study, the authors were able to explain this finding by showing that the academically least successful and most challenging students tended to be placed in smaller classes than their peers (Cefai *et al.*, 2008). These important qualifying observations draw attention to the need for an understanding of the ways in which social and pedagogical opportunities that are created by small school and class sizes are exploited in well-designed interventions.

Of the various models of SLCs, some are historical, like Alternative schools, small rural schools, and autonomous schools, or schools that use the House System as many British Public Schools do, but of the more recent developments, the most pertinent to our current concerns are those which are schools-within-schools, and smaller learning communities within larger schools. We will consider the research on two of these: Career Academies in the United States, and Nurture Groups in schools in the United Kingdom, both of which specifically target students with SEBD. Before doing this, however, we will consider an example of an alternative to mainstream provision: the Outreach School.

Outreach schools

Outreach schools were first established in Alberta, Canada, in 1974 for 'at risk' high school students, and have been funded by the province since 1995. We were able to identify only one empirical study of Alberta Outreach schools. However, there are many interesting features of this model which are pertinent to the central concerns of this book, justifying its inclusion.

Outreach schools operate in a very similar way to distance learning centres, yet they also provide a stand-alone school building and facilities, and teaching staff who maintain the opening of the 'storefront school' during the typical school day, and sometimes for an extended day. Most of the high-school grade students attending Outreach schools have social, emotional and or behavioural difficulties and are primarily those who feel themselves overwhelmed by a larger school, or a full curriculum. As the schools provide education to young adults of up to 20 years of age, some of their students may be in work, or may be young parents. Some may be school drop-outs. The curriculum is delivered through modules which the student takes at her or his own pace, with school attendance requirements ranging from one to two hours each week, until the requisite grades have been obtained to achieve a high school diploma. Each student has an individual timetable, agreed with a member of staff, and staff/student ratios are particularly low. The staff are able to work on a one-to-one basis with students as mentors as well as teachers. Housego (1999) analyzed the responses from 13 teachers and staff, and 213 students from four of the schools and found positive attitudes towards the provision among these stakeholders. Key features of the provision that were highlighted included the maturity and flexibility of the staff, who tended to more years of experience than was the mean for mainstream colleagues; an emphasis on incorporative non-authoritarian teacher styles, and higher mean attendance rates than were achieved by comparable mainstream high schools. The current authors note important similarities between Outreach Schools and the 'pioneer schools' referred to in Chapter 2. However we also note the paucity of supportive evidence owing to the dearth of published studies on this topic.

Career academies

The Career Academy project (Stern *et al.*, 1992) has been cited as an evidence-based and research-validated nationwide intervention in 2500 inner-city schools in the United States, with the bulk of evidence from Philadelphia and from the University of California, Berkeley, under the leadership of David Stern and the Career Academy Support Network. Although originally designed as a drop-out prevention programme in 1969, the Career Academy intervention has developed and expanded and in 1993 research into its effectiveness and into how well the students engaged with learning was funded by Manpower Demonstration Research Corporation, a non-profit education and social policy organization. RCTs began in 1993, (Kemple and Rock, 1996) on 10 sites, one of which later dropped out, and involved 1953 students in all. In each of these schools, up to 40 students, each year, in Grades 9–12 applied to, and were either selected for or put on to a waiting list for the within-school intervention.

This consists of the group of 'at risk' students taking a more vocational curriculum linked to a career theme, such as business, computing or health care, together with core academic subjects. Each group of students remains together throughout their school years, and stays with the same small group of teachers for that time. Over the following 10 years data were collected on these students and their progress, and then over the years following school leaving to assess the extent to which gains were maintained. One of the unusual pedagogic features of this approach is that the teaching staff work as a team, across subjects, employing a team-teaching methodology. Another key feature is that academy members have continual access to employer partnerships, both in and out of the classroom. The non-selected students, who did not differ in any fundamental way from the selected group, became the control group for the RCTs.

Data were collected from school transcript records, student surveys, standardized mathematics and literacy tests and continual qualitative field research. Initial results (Kemple and Snipes, 2000) showed that:

- students at *high risk* of school failure in comparison with control group significantly cut drop-out rates, increased attendance rates, and 40% of them earned enough credits to graduate (a 50% increase on their control group counterparts). However, while the Academies did not produce a statistically significant reduction in risk-taking behaviour they were able to show some evidence of improvement in this area.
- students at *low risk* of school failure were more likely to graduate on time than their counterparts, and increased their career-related courses in addition to completing academic courses. Additionally, like the high risk group, there was no significant reduction in risk-taking behaviours.

These results appear to be rather disappointing, but the advantage of longitudinal studies such as this is that we can see the longer-term effects of intervention which may be different from those identified through initial evaluation. In 2004, follow-up studies (Kemple and Scott-Clayton, 2004) revealed that although the Career Academy system had little effect on the girls who had been involved in the intervention (a result which may be attributable to the fact that many of them had parental responsibilities), the young men on follow-up earned over 18% more than those in the control group over the four year period, and more than half the sample had achieved some further education qualification, or were working towards one. Four years later (Kemple and Wilner, 2008) the Academy graduates were earning 11% more, on average, per year, than the control-group. Academy graduates also had a significant gain over control group in terms of living independently, with children and a spouse or partner.

The Manpower Demonstration Research Corporation RCTs engage rather different outcome measures from those normally used on evaluations of educational interventions, as they concentrate on employment issues and economic measures. However, David Stern (Stern and Wing, 2004) summarizes his own evaluation of the Career Academy RCT studies by pointing to differential outcomes. Career Academy graduates, in a selection of data from the MDRC, felt they had more personal support, and more career guidance. Stern himself, however, points to some important factors that might be influential in the success of Career Academies, but are difficult to measure. Chief among these is the fact that students are required to apply for their place at a career academy. This might be taken to suggest that students who attend career academies have to be more highly motivated than their peers, or have other advantages, such as parental support. If these qualities are present, they may also influence the likelihood of students achieving success in the academy.

This may well be a weakness of the studies which provides a useful hypothesis that should be tested. It is possible, for example, that if motivation were found to be a significant independent variable then this would suggest that the CA approach might be usefully combined with some of the cognitive behavioural approaches directed at promoting the psychological qualities which are necessary underpinnings of motivation, such as a sense of personal agency (see Chapters 4 and 5).

Nurture groups

While Nurture Group (NG) provision in the United Kingdom is a different type of intervention, the notion of a 'learning community-within-a-school' is retained, although in this case the group selected is not completely self-contained, nor is that the purpose. The purpose is to take some students, usually those with SEBD characteristics, out of their mainstream classes for part of the day for an intensive and supportive adjunct to their social and emotional nurturing, with the intention of enabling their return to the full-time mainstream classes as soon as is feasible (Bennathan and Boxall, 1996). Children are selected on recommendations from social workers, health workers, from pre-school educators, and observations within the first term of the child's schooling. The balance of the group is important, and teachers are careful not to overwhelm the group with too high a proportion of those who act out or those who act in. The children's parents are consulted throughout the process, as parental agreement is seen as being primary and crucial. It is essentially a short-term strategy devised by Marjorie Boxall, an Inner London Education Authority educational psychologist working in Hackney, London, in the 1960s. The instrumentation used both at pre- and post-test are The Boxall Profile (later published as Bennathan and Boxall, 1996) a norm-referenced assessment instrument, devised by Marjorie Boxall specifically for use in NGs, and the Goodman Strengths and Difficulties Questionnaire. The profiles enable staff to monitor and assess individual pupils', social and emotional functioning and to chart changes over time After some years of comparative neglect as an intervention it is currently the subject of a number of studies, none of them a randomized controlled trial.

A classic Boxall type NG reflects the following principles (Cooper and Whitebread, 2007).

- They are located on the site of a mainstream primary or infant school, but can be located in a secondary school.
- They cater for 10–12 children who are already on the roll of the host school.
- They are staffed by 2 adults: a teacher and a full-time Learning Support Assistant.
- They operate for 9 out of 10 half day sessions in the school week.

- NG pupils remain on the roll of a mainstream class; register with this class daily, and spend curriculum time in this class when not attending the NG.
- Full-time placement in a mainstream class is the main object of NG placement.
- The NG provides an holistic curriculum, incorporating the UK National Curriculum with a curriculum designed to address social, emotional and behavioural factors underpinning academic learning.

In a study of 308 children placed in NGs between 1984 and 1998 in one London borough (Iszatt and Wasilewska, 1997), 87% were able to return to the mainstream after a placement duration of less than one year. In 1995 this group was revisited, and it was found that a very high proportion (83%) of the original cohort were still in mainstream placements with only 4% requiring SEN support beyond the schools' standard range of provision. Of the original cohort 13% were granted Statements of Special Educational Need, and 11% were referred to special school provision. This finding was contrasted with data on a non-matched group of 20 mainstream pupils who had been designated as requiring NG placement but for whom places had not been found. Of these 35% were placed in special schools and only 55% were found, by 1995, to be coping in mainstream classrooms without additional support.

In the absence of adequate matching measures it is difficult to interpret the significance of differences in outcomes for the two groups. However, the positive performance of the majority of NG cohort was consistent with studies of staff perceptions of the effects of NG placement assessed in other studies which point to improvements in pupils' self-management behaviours, social skills, self awareness and confidence, skills for learning and approaches to learning (Boorn, 2002; Cooper and Lovey, 1999; Doyle, 2001). O'Connor and Colwell (2003) assessed the performance of 68 five-year-old children placed in three NGs for a mean period of 3.1 terms. Using Boxall Profile data, they found statistically significant mean improvements in terms of cognitive and emotional development, social engagement and behaviours indicative of secure attachment. Boxall data was also reported on an opportunity sample (n = 12) of the original cohort after two years. Findings suggest that many of the improvements had been maintained, though there was evidence of relapse in some areas of emotional and social functioning.

An extensive longitudinal study over two years by Cooper *et al.* (2001) investigated the effectiveness of NGs within 25 schools, in eight LEAs. In this study, the effectiveness of NGs were judged on the basis of comparing pupils with two different control groups, one consisting of pupils matched according to age, gender, educational attainment and level of SEBD in mainstream classrooms and the other of pupils matched for age and gender with the NG children but without emotional and behavioural problems. On the basis of variations among different NGs in the sample, the authors did not report any statistically different outcomes, however positive perceptions towards to NGs were noted. In particular, mainstream teacher interviews reported a strong positive impact of NGs in terms of children's progress in their educational attainment as well as the development of a 'nurturing' environment in many aspects of school life.

In a subsequent publication, Cooper and Whitebread (2007) explored the effects of Nurture Groups on children (n = 356) enrolled in nurture groups (n = 27) compared to four groups of children matched to members of the enrolled groups on various dimensions but who were not enrolled in nurture groups (n = 190). The study followed the student participants over two years. The Boxall Profiles and SDQ measures provided the quantitative evidence, which indicated greater improvements for the NG children's social, emotional and behavioural functioning than the pupils who did not attend NGs. This study also found that the groups which had been in existence for two years or more achieved statistically significant improvements in pupils' social, emotional and behavioural functioning after two terms, when compared with the progress of pupils with SEBD in mainstream classrooms. A particularly striking finding was that students with SEBD who attended schools which had nurture groups, but who did not attend the nurture groups improved in their functioning to a statistically significant degree when compared to students with SEBD who attended schools that did not have nurture group provision. This was interpreted to indicate that nurture groups have the potential to have a whole school effect, a view supported by qualitative data gathered from staff in the participating schools. In line with the previous studies, the parents of NG pupils reported positive perceptions, and offered the possibility that NGs could have a positive effect on parent–child relationships.

Another substantial naturalistic prospective control group (type 3) study was carried out in the city of Glasgow (Reynolds *et al.*, 2009). The study focussed on pupils (n = 221) aged between 5 and 7 years with SEBD attending primary schools in Glasgow (n = 32). The intervention group (n = 117) attended nurture groups in 16 schools, while the remainder (n = 104) attended matched schools (n = 16) without nurture groups. NG pupils made significant improvements in self-esteem, self-image, emotional maturity and attainment in literacy when compared to the group of pupils attending the schools without NG provision.

Among other smaller-scale studies, those of Bishop and Swain (2000a, 2000b) explored the effectiveness of a NG in an inner city area of severe deprivation which consisted of children between Years 1 to 3. The researchers also reported a parent–school partnership model and explained this in consideration of a 'transplant model' which imply that the skills and expertise of teachers are passed to parents through their engagement to the NG (Cunningham and Davis, 1985; Dale, 1996, cited in Bishop and Swain, 2000a, p. 22). Howes *et al.* (2003) questions the potential of nurture groups in facilitating inclusive practice. Having reviewed three varying case studies, the authors identified that the size of group, the age of children and the mixture of emotional and behavioural difficulties that they exhibit as critical in relation to effective running of the nurture group, and also questions the opportunity cost of the nurture group, asking what those children lost when they separated from their peer groups in the mainstream settings.

Doyle (2001) reported that setting up a Nurture Group in her school, however, had the result of spreading nurturing practices into the whole school, a finding consistent with that of Binnie and Allen (2008) thereby offering an alternative to the question of opportunity costs. This supports the view that the most successful NGs operate as an integral part of the intercommunicating mainstream school in which the school as a whole community is committed to maximizing the social and educational engagement of all pupils (Cooper and Tiknaz, 2005; Cooper and Whitebread, 2007). There is recent (unpublished) research on the viability of NG provision in secondary schools, a possibility currently being tested by some Local Authorities within the United Kingdom in collaboration with the Nurture Groups Network.

Special units and classrooms/Pupil referral units

Not all schools-within-schools, or groups-within-schools, have the flexibility of arrangement which allows for students to remain for some of the day with their mainstream peers, as in the nurture group model. In a study of a 'special unit' in a Cypriot school, Angelides and Michailidou (2007) noted that the effect of educating students with special needs in such a unit can lead to marginalization.

This finding was also applicable to out-of-school settings, according to a study by Panacek and Dunlap (2003) into the social life of students with emotional and behavioural difficulties who were educated in a segregated classroom. Interviewing 14 of these children, and comparing their social lives to those of a matched group of 14 educated in regular classrooms, the authors discovered that the children in the segregated classroom had little opportunity to mix with their peers, and their lives within school were dominated by children and adults involved in special education. These children in segregated classrooms identified as important friends those who were in their home network, which were similar in size and constellation to their matched counterparts in general education classrooms, whereas those typically-educated children identified as their important friends others within their class or school.

In two US studies comparing EBD children educated in self-contained classrooms with those educated in specialist separate schools, Lane *et al.* (2005) discovered that there was little to distinguish EBD children in special schools from EBD children educated within a self-contained classroom in a mainstream schools. There was limited academic improvement in either setting, and limited progress in social or behavioural domains. The only observed difference was that those in special schools, referred as having more 'severe' difficulties were more likely to have externalizing disorders than internalizing disorders. Although the intention of the study was to question why some children were referred for education in more restrictive settings, that is, special schools, the results were taken to suggest that there is little social and emotional advantage in being placed in a segregated classroom within a mainstream school.

Soloman and Rogers (2001), in a small-scale study of 92 children in the North West of England aged between 13 and 16 registered in Pupil Referral Units (PRU), administered questionnaires to these students covering their perceptions of this placement, and included questions from the Patterns of Adaptive Learning Survey, enabling their motivations to be assessed. Findings revealed that, while the students engaged effectively with the formal curriculum, they did not appear to have developed the social and emotional coping strategies that the placement was intend to promote. The researchers conclude by favouring mainstream provision over the off-site PRU.

A case-study (Frankham *et al.*, 2007) of school exclusion, involving 6 children from two very successful PRUs, their families and their teachers, stressed that the quality of staff–student relationships can support or interfere with student attachment to school, and that warm relationships can be fostered through mentoring in the specialist settings of the PRU. In some ways this study reflects the findings of a previous case study by Hanafin and Lynch (2002) that involved focus group interviews in a primary school in a disadvantaged area of Cork. This study found that parents' views were rarely taken into account either by class teachers or by school management. In the case of 'hard to reach' families, such as the mixed-race families of some of the children in the Frankham *et al.* (2007) study, the authors emphasized the importance of working holistically and flexibly with families rather than by bureaucratic formulae. They concluded that the work of some PRUs might be reconceived as a form of respite from mainstream schools for some students. The authors also emphasized that in the case of exclusion from mainstream school, the students and their families should be consulted as to their preferences on educational provision.

The principle of flexibility and clarity underlying the nurture group philosophy, where children are withdrawn part-time, and short-term, from their mainstream peers, with the clear intention of returning them to full-time classroom inclusion is a principle underlying the Swedish system of day-school education which was introduced over 40 years ago, and stands in contrast to the use of the self-contained classroom or unit, and the self-contained placement, from which the child is unlikely to return. In this Swedish intervention, which could be regarded perhaps as a similar intervention to PRUs, children showing signs of significant disturbance, and children thought to be at risk, are withdrawn from regular education to spend some time in a special day school, in which their emotional and mental health is monitored, and in which classes are small, and children receive some social skills training. This is much in line with the respite recommendations from the Frankham *et al.* (2007) study. Svedin and Wadsby (2000) conducted a follow-up study of 104 children, most with disruptive behaviour, who had been referred to Swedish special day schools at some time in their school career. Of the children 88% had returned to mainstream schooling, after an average special day school placement of two years. There were significant improvements in their mental health, and 60% were symptom-free, or had only mild symptoms. However, their academic progress remained slow, and they were considered to be, even after placement, more disturbed than typical children. Most of the children (53%) had been diagnosed with oppositional defiant disorder, and 21% with conduct disorder, and it was this group who still displayed the most obvious problem behaviours.

Residential provision

Residential schools for students with SEBD were once described as the 'dinosaurs' of special educational provision (Cole, 1986). It is certainly the case that residential schools have played an important role in the history of educational provision for students with SEBD (e.g., Bridgeland, 1971; Cooper, 1989; Dawson, 1981) as we pointed out in Chapter 2. Unlike dinosaurs, however, residential schools for SEBD have shown remarkable resilience in the face of sometimes intense efforts to kill them off (e.g., Booth and Ainscow, 1997).

In a world where inclusive education is a dominant ideology the residential school might appear to epitomize the discredited segregationist practices of a by-gone era. In spite of the fact that residential schools for children and young people with SEBD continue to be employed in education systems throughout the world, they have been neglected by researchers, particularly in recent years. Nevertheless, the limited research evidence that exists on this topic offers important food for thought.

As we reported in Chapter 2, there are important strands in what might be termed the residential tradition that reflect what to this day might be regarded as *avant garde* approaches to the education and care of vulnerable young people (Bridgeland, 1971). The influence of the psychodynamic tradition, for example, is reflected in residential regimes which emphasize the child's needs for oppor-tunities for free expression and self-discovery in an environment of social and emotional safety (Reeves, 2001), such as exist in the present day in the Mulberry Bush School in the United Kingdom. Although many modern residential schools in the United Kingdom have long abandoned explicit allegiance to psychody-namic principles (Dawson, 1981), there is a legacy from this in the emphasis that such schools continue to place on the importance of adult–child relationships as the major tool for promoting emotional growth and social development (Cooper, 1989, 1993; Cole *et al.*, 1998) and in the democratic practices common to many such schools (Bridgeland, 1971).

Such evidence as does exist, much of which comes from small-scale observa-tional and interview studies, points to the residential experience being character-ized, at its best, by its restorative qualities. Cooper (1989, 1993), in a qualitative study of two residential special schools for boys (aged 9–17) with EBD (n = 77), found three consistent themes in the accounts given by these boys of the resi-dential experience. The first theme was that of *respite* from negative influences and unsatisfactory relationships in their home settings and former schools and the sense of safety and emotional security afforded by the residential setting. Sec-ond was their experience of positive, warm and supportive *relationships* that they shared with the residential staff. Third was their experience of *re-signification*, whereby, as a result of the positive experiences and relationships provided in the residential setting the boys were able to forge more positive self-identities in place of the negative and deviant identities that they often held on entry to the schools.

Grimshaw and Berridge (1994), in a study of children (n = 67) attending four contrasting residential schools, found the children and their families reflected the findings of Cooper's study. Though, unlike the essentially 'therapeutic' orientation reflected in the schools studied by Cooper, Berridge and Grimshaw found evidence of more directive and behaviourally oriented approaches in one of their schools. Even here, however, families and pupils spoke in positive terms about the effect that residential placement had on pupils' emotional and social development, and as a result, the quality of family relationships. A wide-ranging observational study of various types of provision for SEBD, including residential schools, carried out by Cole *et al.* (1998) endorsed these findings.

In a recent study carried out in Germany, Harriss *et al.* (2008) interviewed students between the ages of 8 and 12 (n = 13) who had attended a residential school for children with SEBD for an average of three years. The students attributed the following positive effects to the residential experience:

- improved ability to trust others;
- improved ability to cope with 'difficult feelings';
- improved classroom engagement and ability to remain in classrooms during lessons; and
- improved behaviour and relationships at home.

These findings were echoed by parents and residential staff, though while teachers observed positive developments in pupils' academic engagement and progress, parents expressed concerns that academic progress was often unsatisfactory.

It is a longstanding fact that SEBD correlates positively with poor educational performance (Cefai *et al.*, 2008; Landrum *et al.*, 2003). It is also the case that the few published follow-up studies that exist tend to reveal poor social and personal outcomes. Farrell and Polat (2003) were able to track down only 26 out of 172 former pupils from a residential SEBD school. They were aged between 17 and 25 and had spent, on average, 4 years and 3 months in the school. They were all under-qualified educationally, and only 13 had full-time, largely menial jobs. They expressed concerns about their lack of financial security and tended to have negative expectations for the future. In a similar study carried out in New Zealand by Hornby and Witte (2008) a group of former residential SEBD school students (n = 29) who had attended the school between 10 and 14 years prior to the study, were interviewed. Outcomes for this group were worse than those in the UK study. Only nine interviewees were in full-time work, mostly earning only marginally above the statutory minimum wage. Four ex-pupils were in prison. The researchers assessed the ex-students' 'community adjustment' on the basis of information about their interpersonal relationships, living conditions and engagement in community activities, and found comparatively low levels of performance in these areas.

It must be noted that these follow up studies do not offer the benefit of comparative data that would be possible if control groups composed of students with similar SEBD characteristics had been studied alongside the residential groups. In short we have no way of knowing if these outcomes would have been likely to be better or worse had these participants not attended residential schools. This makes it extremely difficult to assess the significance of the findings from these studies in determining the value of the residential experience. What can be said is that studies that have looked at the actual experience of students and related stakeholders while they are attending the schools paint a largely positive picture of this form of provision, particularly when these experiences are related to earlier exposure to unsatisfactory mainstream school placements. These studies suggest that residential provision can have the effect of promoting social adjustment and attachment to school for students who have experienced only failure and rejection in mainstream education. The disappointing life outcomes that are associated with residential SEBD placement, therefore, might be taken to suggest that the positive achievements of residential placements are often wasted when there is a lack of continuity in support and care for individuals after they leave residential provision.

It is important to reiterate that residential provision for SEBD, often a last resort for the most vulnerable members of this population has been poorly served by researchers in terms of the amount of attention that has been given to this area and in terms of the range and scope of studies, all of which have been very small scale. It is perhaps symptomatic of the problems surrounding this form of provision that the limited number of studies that have been carried out in recent years have been hampered by the fact that researchers often find it extremely difficult to locate former pupils, while the prevailing ideology which demonizes non-mainstream provision may encourage researchers in the misguided belief that there is likely to be little of worth to be gained from studying this area.

Conclusion

There are many possible reasons why students may find themselves in situations where they need access to specialist provision of the types explored in this chapter. As we have noted at various points in this book schools can provide remedies for the problems that pupils may experience, but they can also exacerbate or even cause the very same problems. A central message of the book has been to highlight the challenges that schools face and the understanding and skills that school staff need to meet these challenges. It is not the fault of schools and teachers that those most in need of such knowledge and skills do not find it easy to access them. For these reasons alone it is vital that suitable non-mainstream forms of provision should be understood and made available. This is not to say that we should accept exclusionary practices or make simplistic assumptions about those students who can and cannot be educated in mainstream classrooms and/or schools. In common with the conclusions drawn in previous chapters, we have found that the most promising forms of provision reviewed in this chapter can be distinguished from the least promising by the fact that they have clearly defined purposes and methods and that their effectiveness can be measured. With the exception of nurture groups these provisions do not have dedicated training programmes attached to them. This is a source of concern, particularly with such provisions as PRUs, which lack any discernable theoretical or operational identity. Clearly, the quality and effectiveness of these provisions will probably be enhanced when staff have appropriate training of either a specialized nature (such as that associated with nurture groups) or of the type referred to in previous chapters.

Summary

In this chapter evidence was reviewed for the efficacy of a range of small-scale provisions for students with SEBD. We noted that Outreach Schools are a form of provision for students who have been excluded from mainstream schools prevalent in Canada. They operate on student-centred lines and emphasize student choice and voluntary attendance. The limited qualitative and quantitative evidence that exists indicates that they are popular with students and contribute to improvements in educational engagement. In the United States Career Academies are small-scale vocationally-oriented programmes in some high schools. There is good evidence that they achieve positive social and academic outcomes for at risk students. In the United Kingdom *Nurture Groups* are a form of transitional provision most often located in mainstream schools. Although no RCT evidence has yet been gathered there is correlational evidence from a number of sources supporting their efficacy, especially for primary-aged students with SEBD, in promoting significant social, emotional and academic improvement. There is some limited evidence to support the use of Special units and classrooms/PRUs, though the nature and diversity of this range of provision is such that it is difficult to make meaningful generalizations about overall effectiveness. Where useful case study evidence exists, this has not been followed up by further larger scale studies. Although residential provision for SEBD is probably the longest standing form of specialist educational provision for students with SEBD it has been subject to only limited interest from educational researchers. Small-scale evidence indicates the effectiveness of residential provision in giving students respite from stress and helping them develop coping skills and improved social skills. However, maintenance effects appear to be weak. The chapter concludes with an affirmation of the continuing need for such provision as an adjunct or alternative to standard mainstream provision.

7

Working with Parents

Overview

This chapter shifts the focus to beyond the realm of schools and teachers to examine the contribution that parents can make in combating SEBD and promoting educational engagement. Three empirically tested parent-targeted programmes are examined. These programmes are delivered usually by psychologists or therapists, though there are examples of teachers being involved in the delivery of programmes and the school setting is sometimes cited as an important site for delivery.

Although this book is primarily concerned with educational interventions, mostly in schools and involving education professionals, it would be wrong to leave the reader with the impression that we are unaware of the importance of the family in supporting educational engagement and combating SEBD in schools. The role of the family in both the generation and remediation of SEBD is well known, and was briefly discussed in Chapter 2. Families and carers provide role models and reinforcement for children's ways of feeling and behaving. It is not surprising, therefore, that the incorporation of families and carers into intervention programmes for SEBD has been shown to be of enormous value. We showed in Chapter 5 some of the ways in which parental involvement (i.e., Success for All and Coping Power) can support the success of school-based schemes. This chapter reviews some of the research on the ways in which programmes that are dedicated to the training of parents and carers can help promote positive outcomes for school students with SEBD.

Parent Management Training

Parent Management Training (PMT), is one of the most strongly-supported preventative interventions for children with SEBD. The main purpose of PMT is to break the cycle of coercion between parent and child which has been shown to

---

From Inclusion to Engagement: Helping Students Engage with Schooling through Policy and Practice
By Paul Cooper and Barbara Jacobs © 2011 John Wiley & Sons, Ltd

contribute to the development of delinquency as the child grows older (Forehand and Long, 1988; Kazdin 1997; Patterson and Stouthamer-Loeber, 1984, Patterson *et al.*, 1989, 1998). In practice, PMT usually involves the teaching of behavioural strategies to the parents of at-risk children which concentrate on the transmission of knowledge about antecedents (prompts) and consequences (reinforcement and time-out techniques for example), by a therapist, to parents. The social learning thus instigated is then relayed through parental understanding and application of the principles, to the child.

In PMT, the therapist teaches parents to observe and identify child behaviours which could be defined as problematic, and to reframe them in ways which may lend insight and ultimately solutions to the reasons that may underlie those behaviours, such as the basic questions as to what caused that behaviour at that time, and what were the consequences of the behaviour (Graziano and Diament, 1992). Essentially, PMT involves the dissemination of information through social learning to families who might be confused about the best way in which to deal with the daily behavioural issues which their child might present (Kazdin, 1997). Negative/ineffective disciplinary parenting is thought to be a major contributory factor in conduct problems in children at school (Greenbaum *et al,*. 1996; Patterson *et al.*, 1989; Patterson and Stouthamer-Loeber, 1984). In this context ineffective parenting is characterized in terms of, on the one hand harsh parental discipline, and on the other, lax discipline, both of which have been found to be equally counter-productive (Hinshaw *et al.*, 2000; Snyder *et al.*, 2005).

In PMT parents are taught behavioural strategies for promoting prosocial behaviour. These include positive reinforcement and extinction strategies involving negotiation, contingency contracting, and punishments (e.g., time out and the loss of certain privileges). The best strategies are those which are used contingently, immediately and frequently; that employ varied and powerful reinforcers, and utilize prompting and shaping (Cooper *et al.*, 1987). Parents are provided with opportunities to see how these strategies can work, and with opportunities to reflect on the changes they produce. This observation can then lead to further developments in which parents begin to analyze and address the more complex issues of how their children can be encouraged to respond to these strategies in other environments, at school, for example, and are encouraged to see how they can intervene to enable their child to deal with issues like homework and support for learning (Callaghan *et al.*, 1998). Teachers at the child's school, meanwhile, monitor these interventions, as they apply to the school context.

PMT is acknowledged as one of the most robustly-evidenced interventions for children with conduct problems (Brestan and Eyberg, 1998; Cunningham *et al.* 1995; Eyberg *et al.*, 1995; Farrington and Welsh, 2003; Kazdin, 2008). Between 50 and 60 sessions of training appear to produce optimal results (Kazdin, 2002; McConaughy *et al.*, 2000; Strayhorn and Weidman, 1989), and the most successful maintenance effects (DeGarmo *et al.*, 2004; Eyberg *et al.*, 1998), although a long-term follow-up study shows that positive outcomes are maintained in some cases well into adulthood (Long *et al.*, 1994).

The issue of greatest significance in producing optimal results is the skill of the therapist who delivers the training, and the length and scope of the behavioural training the therapist has (Kazdin, 1997). These skills may not be very easily transmitted to others, such as teachers, who may be willing to engage parents in training sessions. This is also a problem which affects the performance of teachers when attempting to carry out Functional Behavioural Analysis (see Chapter 4). Similarly, PMT has been demonstrated to be less successful when delivered by non-specialist nurses to the parents of pre-school children (Sonuga-Barke *et al.*, 2004). However, it has been noted that when teachers join parents as participants in the intervention, the benefits of the training are strengthened in both home and school settings (Corkum *et al.*, 2005).

A limitation of many of the studies, from the perspective of this review, is that most of them are clinic based, rather than school-based. Also there is a dearth of good quality studies on this topic (Valdez *et al.*, 2005). Only three studies out of the 24 in the Valdez review show PMT to be effective in modifying the child's behaviour at school, and one of those (Kazdin *et al.*, 1987) was conducted on in-patients in a hospital setting. It should be noted that none of the studies was specifically designed with educational outcomes in mind.

A more recent meta-analytic review into the effective components of successful parent training schemes for children younger than 8 years old (Kaminski *et al.*, 2008), demonstrated that the three most effective components for predicting successful parenting behaviour were instruction in positive interactions with their child, encouragement of emotional communication, and practicing with their own child. Least effective were programme components involving problem-solving skills training, promoting their child's academic success, and the use of ancillary services. Four components were significantly positively correlated with reduction in childhood aggression. These were positive interaction, time out, consistent responding, and practicing with their own child. The mean effect size for parenting outcomes appeared larger than the mean effects for child outcomes, and for the children. Those with internalizing disorders appeared to benefit more from the interventions than those with externalizing disorders. Confounding existing beliefs about effective programmes, the researchers discovered that whether or not the programme was manualized was irrelevant to the success or otherwise of the intervention. Another meta-analysis, this time into moderators and follow-up effects, concluded that follow-up effects were small in magnitude for behaviourally-based programmes, and that parenting programmes were least effective with economically-disadvantaged families (Lundahl *et al.*, 2006). This last point is supported by Dumas and Wahler (1983).

The relatively poor outcomes for economically disadvantaged families is a source of concern, given that parent training is a technique most often offered to the most disadvantaged parents, for example through the Head Start programme in the United States and the Sure Start programme in the United Kingdom (Gray and Francis, 2007). These programmes specialize in providing services to low-income families with school age children. Sure Start (Glass, 1999) originally envisaged as serving the needs of children up to age 7 and their families, was redesigned to concentrate heavily on the first three years of the child's life. Its remit, rolled-out to local groups from 1999 and community-driven, involves the delivery of a range of services to ensure early years' support to vulnerable families, including:

- outreach services and home visiting;
- support for families and parents;
- good quality play, learning and child care;
- primary and community healthcare and advice about child health and development; and
- support for those with special needs.

It has been the subject of ongoing evaluation from its commencement, and the National Evaluations of Sure Start (NESS) ensure that this is a continually-monitored and data-producing scheme which could give some clear insights into the remediation of some of the problems facing at risk children from their birth.

In its most recent evaluation of the Sure Start Local Centres (SSLC) initiative (NESS, 2008) which reassessed those families whose children had been seen when they were nine months old, concluded that at three years of age follow-up, parents showed less negative parenting in Sure Start Local Programmes (SSLP) areas than those in non-SSLC areas, and provided their children with a better home learning environment. The children demonstrated higher levels of social development than those outside SSLC areas, and higher levels of self-regulation and independence. Results showed that the SSLC initiative appeared more effective over time and less inconsistent than the earlier report (NESS, 2005) had shown, although this could have been accounted for by differences in the research design.

Forehand and Kotchick (2002) suggest that the difficulties of reaching these at-risk families can be overcome when training interventions are delivered within the community, using community centres or schools in the neighbourhood and when they are delivered by agencies trusted by the parents so that the intervention is not seen in a negative authoritarian light. Furthermore they argue that the success of parent-training programmes will be strengthened by additional support systems. They suggest:

> Parents cannot fully engage in parent training until their other basic needs have been adequately addressed; thus, working with the socially isolated or highly disadvantaged families that present for assistance in managing their children's behavior may require much more than parent training in order to be successful (p. 380).

The most successful and evidence-based programmes claim to be sufficiently flexible and data-rich to recognize and address this problem. The Fast Track multi-systemic programmes, now being further analyzed over four sites in the United States (see Chapter 8) have confronted many of the challenges to the success of parent-training by siting the intervention at the child's own school, and having school staff as cofacilitators of aspects of the programme, as well as adding further components to the programme. The SWPB interventions, among others (see Chapter 5), utilize a wrap-around tertiary intervention in which community resources are fully called-upon to address an individual child's failure to engage with education, and both Webster-Stratton's *Incredible Years* parent-training programme in the United States and worldwide, and Markie-Dadds' *Triple P Parenting* programme in Australia and worldwide, have taken into account the need for refinement and flexibility to ensure their interventions reach the widest possible demographic.

Incredible Years

The Incredible Years (IY) programme is essentially a PMT scheme for parents of high risk children aged 2–7, its BASIC (early childhood) programme being delivered by a therapist or leader to groups of parents. The programme involves 12–14 two- hour weekly sessions. A unique component of IY is the use of short videotaped vignettes of child behaviour which are used both to illustrate situations which may arise, and also to act as stimulus to group discussion of strategies. Discussion and brainstorming sessions are seen as key to IY's success as a group intervention (Webster-Stratton *et al.*, 1988). The videotaped vignettes can also be used by individuals (Webster-Stratton, 1992).

The core of the theoretical basis of IY differs very little from Kazdin's PMT scheme, and its strategies are the same. There is a BASIC programme and an ADVANCE add-on programme for parents of school-age children to the age of 10 which, in a study of its efficacy showed little advantage (Webster-Stratton, 1994). It has an add-on programme for parents supporting their child's schoolwork. There is also a classroom programme, the Dina Dinosaur curriculum, with over 60 lesson plans for all age ranges of children (Webster Stratton and Reid, 2004), and a Dinosaur Treatment cognitive-behavioural programme for small groups of children with conduct problems (Webster-Stratton and Reid, 2003). Additionally there is a teacher-training programme for teachers who may be interested in the classroom management of children with externalizing and internalizing problems which operates in a manner very similar to that of the parent-training programme (Webster-Stratton *et al.*, 2001).

Every element of the programme has been the subject of RCTs, using children on waiting lists as controls, although this methodology precludes to a large extent the collection of longitudinal follow-up data, as control children also receive the programme after a waiting period, and therefore cannot be tested as follow-up controls (Reid *et al.*, 2003; Webster-Stratton, 1990; Webster-Stratton *et al.*, 1989). The programme has been trialled extensively with children on the Head Start scheme (Reid and Webster-Stratton, 2001; Webster Stratton *et al.*, 2001) with particular concentration on the programme generalizing across ethnic minority cultures (Reid *et al.*, 2002). Positive data have also been generated by fathers taking part in the programme (Webster-Stratton *et al.*, 2004). There have been additional RCTs in the UK, (Gardner *et al.*, 2006) which have produced similar positive results. The add-on programmes have not been empirically validated to date, but this may have been because of methodological issues which conflated the add-ons with the original programme making effects difficult to determine.

The programme has received endorsements of its efficacy for children with SEBD in all available published reviews (Eyberg *et al.*, 2008; Nixon, 2002; Weisz *et al.*, 2004). Interestingly, according to research by Reid *et al.* (2004) the programme was as efficacious for parents of the most disadvantaged children, as well as those parents with a higher socio-economic demographic. Although it may be difficult to unpick the reasons for this deviation from the overwhelming evidence to the contrary from other apparently similar parent-training schemes, the difference may lie in its use of videotape, and its ease of delivery (Forehand and Kotchick, 2002). In the most recent research study, Webster-Stratton, the originator of the IY intervention, has again considered the question of socio-economic disadvantage in certain high-risk families, and has concluded that her teacher-training programme may enable teachers to understand, and take on some form of mentoring role, fostering the development of social and emotional skills in the disadvantaged children they teach (Webster-Stratton *et al.*, 2008). Further research may be necessary to determine whether this is so.

The IY programme has been adopted successfully in England, Wales (Jones *et al.*, 2007), and Norway (Mørch *et al.*, 2004). An evaluation of a 2-year pilot scheme carried out in Norway, showed that 65% of children with conduct problems were helped by the programme, and currently 60 mental health agencies in Norway are offering this intervention (Mørch *et al.*, 2004). As a result of these positive findings the scheme has been adopted for use in Denmark, Sweden and Russia.

In Ireland, a pilot study into the efficacy of the Incredible Years, under the auspices of the Clondalkin Partnership in Dublin, and supported by researchers at NUI Maynooth, was set up in 2004. An overview of the programme, and of the study, is reported by the Clondalkin Partnership (2006). Analyses of both qualitative and quantitative data from parents (n = 32) and children (n =28) showed that the programme led to improvements in children's conduct, relations with peers and emotional status. The one area in which improvement was not observed was in children's levels of hyperactivity (as measured by the Goodman Strengths and Difficulties Questionnaire (SDQ)).

Some parents reported that they had difficulties in attending the scheme because of the constraints of childcare, and suggested changes to the timing of the programme sessions to overcome this problem. A number of parents mentioned that they felt it would be beneficial for the facilitators to meet their children, and this was accommodated. This same adjustment was made in the parent-training component in the Fast Track programme. Most felt that the earlier the intervention took place, the better, and although this is a view associated with programmes, research into parent training shows that it can be effective at any age (Kazdin, 2002). A serious concern of many of the parents who took part was that the school the child attended was not involved in the programme, and may not have been aware that the parent was attending such a programme. They stated the belief that their children's teachers would have benefited from the instruction they themselves received. There were also issues related to the attendance of fathers and male carers, with one female carer feeling that her efforts were diminished because her partner did not attend sessions with her. The involvement of fathers, as already mentioned, can be an important factor in the success of such programmes.

There were limitations in this pilot study, not least of which was the failure to include a control group. Another was the small number of parents who took part, with 90% of them being mothers and 60% being single parents, with little male participation. The small proportion of parents who offered feedback at completion (25%) was also a limitation as was the decision to use only one outcome measure, the Goodman's SDQ. Another problem was that the Partnership had not been able to gather detailed data about the children, to facilitate further study. However despite the limitations of the study, the research group decided to implement a three year national evaluation of the Incredible Years programme which began in January 2008 over 11 sites: four parent groups in Dublin/Kildare, and several teacher groups in and around Limerick, making this one of the largest evaluations to be mounted outside the United States.

Triple P

The Triple P-Positive Parenting and intervention, originating from the University of Queensland, Australia, is a clinic-based or self-administered programme which can be adapted for use in group settings (Sanders, 1999). There are no published RCTs reporting its use in classrooms. It is, however, an internationally validated intervention for conduct disordered children, using parent-training as its principle component. It has five levels, the first usefully a community-wide dissemination of parenting fact sheets, tips and basic advice, and the second recommended for mild or specific conduct problems which also involves help-sheets, but with the addition of videotaped vignettes and advice. The third level offers an additional four sessions of personal or group advice and help, but for more severe conduct problems level four which includes 8 to 10 sessions delivered by a mental health professional to groups or individually, is advised. The level five intervention is an enhanced service and is advised for families where there are additional problems: divorce, transitions and mental health issues. However, this enhanced programme appears to offer little more efficacy than the level four programme which produced an 80% behaviour improvement from pre- to post-test and follow-up (Bor *et al.*, 2002), although a previous study (Hoath and Sanders, 2002) that compared the enhanced intervention to control group outcomes established that there was a significant decrease in intensive child disruption problems. Triple P has been extended as a mental health preventative intervention in Canada, New Zealand, Singapore and the United Kingdom, and has been the subject of an RCT in Hong Kong (Leung *et al.*, 2003).

Unlike Incredible Years, which has extended and harnessed its intervention increasingly to educational needs and outcomes, and has redesigned and added to its components so as to extend its efficacy into schools and pre-schools, the Triple P programme remains firmly established as a community-wide parent-training intervention. It is delivered by mental health professionals, as an evidence-based, effective practice which is available to parents of school-age children with SEBD, and can be part of multi-agency provision to those children. Both Triple P and Incredible Years take as their benchmark the work of Kazdin and PMT, and of Patterson with his initial developmental work on coercion, which was to form the basis of the OSLC (Oregon Social Learning Center). Neither of these has, so far, redeveloped their interventions to accommodate direct delivery in educational settings. However, the seminal work on the value of parent-training has enabled and informed educational practice within the preventative and resilience framework.

Conclusion

The evidence briefly reviewed here indicates that effective parent training is a very potent intervention for SEBD. We have repeatedly noted in preceding chapters the importance of understanding and skills for teachers. The evidence presented here suggests that the same is true for parents. Of particular interest here, in the context of the book as a whole, is the importance that is attached to the interface between parents and teachers. While the idea that teachers might be involved in delivering parent training is not surprising, the suggestion that parents and teachers might attend training events as fellow students is more innovative; it suggests, in particular, the importance of teachers and parents sharing each others' perspectives.

Summary

This chapter has explored the vital issue of parent training and has identified three empirically validated programmes. All three programmes are based primarily on behavioural principles (see previous chapters) whereby parents are taught strategies to extinguish unwanted behaviour and reinforce desirable behaviour through the identification and management of contingencies (i.e., antecedents and consequences) that are directly related to the behaviour. In addition these programmes involve reflective and distinctively cognitive interventions such as reframing and behavioural contracting. Parent Management Training (PMT) is shown to have a strong evidential base. Many other parenting programmes take their lead from this programme. However, it was, and always has been, a clinic-based programme, usually delivered by therapists. One example of a development from PMT is the Incredible Years programme (IY). This programme has built on the evidence produced by PMT to create a universal intervention, which is now available, in some formats, as a home-based intervention, with a very strong evidential base for enabling parents to manage behavioural problems in their children. IY has developed a community-based format which has been directed at hard-to-reach, socially-deprived families. School-based parent training, involving both parents and teachers as equal status trainees is likely to be a very promising model. A third development from PMT is the Triple P programme. This is a well-evidenced and well-supported parent-training programme, but has not, as yet, been shown to have any particular efficacy in educational contexts.

8

Multi-Agency Intervention

Overview

Throughout this book we have noted the enormous complexity of SEBD which is reflected in the bio-psycho-social approach which we have adopted in order to produce a comprehensive understanding of this phenomenon. One of the consequences of this complexity is the fact that different disciplines and agencies are confronted with SEBD, each of whom will have their own distinctive contribution to make to the prevention or remediation of SEBD. In this chapter of we address multi-agency intervention for SEBD, highlighting the evidence which shows how different disciplines and agencies can combine their efforts.

The challenges of multi-disciplinary interaction and cooperation are almost as serious as those of SEBD itself. They also reflect differences in perspective which are a source of enormous disagreement and ideological dispute for some commentators (see Chapter 1). However, it is not necessary to appeal to ideological issues in order to expose some of the major difficulties encountered by participants in multi-disciplinary situations. Different professions use different terms of reference, have difference ways of construing issues, and may have sometimes conflicting expectations about one another's roles or what can be achieved in an intervention (Atkinson and Hornby, 2002). This can be confusing and frustrating for professionals, and worse for clients, such as students and their carers who may find this bewildering and distressing. On the other hand, when professionals adopt a 'trans-disciplinary approach' (Hernandez and Blazer, 2006) which incorporates clients and is characterized by an openness of perspective and a shared willingness to respect, listen to and learn from others' viewpoints then the chances of positive outcomes are optimized. In these circumstances stakeholders not only learn to listen to one another they are enabled to incorporate new insights into their existing ways of thinking which can lead to modifications in outlook and understanding (Hughes and Cooper, 2007). These fundamental issues should be

From Inclusion to Engagement: Helping Students Engage with Schooling through Policy and Practice
By Paul Cooper and Barbara Jacobs   © 2011 John Wiley & Sons, Ltd

borne in mind in relation to the following sections of this chapter, which deal with empirically validated examples of multi-disciplinary working.

Longitudinal Studies of Preventive Programmes

Some of the earliest longitudinal prevention studies targeting children at the highest risk of developing conduct problems were set up in Montreal (Vitaro and Tremblay, 1994), Seattle (Hawkins *et al.*, 1991), and Chicago (Huesmann *et al.*, 1996), and used interventions which were partially school-based, and partially home/clinic based. In a study by Carbonneau *et al.* (2001), kindergarten boys (n = 1034) from the lower socioeconomic groups in Montreal were first screened in 1984. Those who scored above the 70th percentile in disruptive behaviour were randomly assigned to one of three groups: an intervention group, a control group, and an 'observational' group which was to be systematically observed by professionals. The observational group was created to act as a placebo group, for the purposes of discovering how children reacted to professional interest, whether or not those professionals intervened. As results showed no difference between this group and the control group, the two groups were later merged. The intervention began in the second year of the boys' schooling. It was made up of two components, one a form of parent training, the other a cognitive behavioural programme in which the boys were taught social skills in small-group sessions during school lunchtimes. These groups also involved peers with good prosocial skills at the ratio of three such children to one 'at risk' child, and ran for two years of the child's schooling, twice each week during the winter terms.

The short-term effects of this intervention were a marked decrease in aggressive behaviour. At the age of 12, these children had remained less aggressive than the control group. After two years the boys ranked slightly better on academic achievement, but the following year they were markedly better, despite the intervention having discontinued, and by the end of their elementary schooling 60% of these children were in an age-appropriate regular classroom, compared with 46% of the control group. By the age of 12, the boys were tested for engagement with education. Of the boys in the intervention group 29% were classed as 'well-adapted' compared to 19% of the control group. In the control group 44% had developed serious difficulties, but only 22% of the intervention group. A later study, when the boys were 16, showed significant differences between the groups for such anti-social behaviour as alcohol abuse (20% intervention/47% control) and drug use (15% intervention/35% control). These figures remained stable over time in later follow-ups. Another positive finding was that only half as many of the boys in the intervention group dropped out of school by the age of 17, as those in the control group. The study appeared to show that an early preventative intervention was far more successful at managing conduct and delinquency problems, than treatment programmes targeted at delinquent adolescents.

A RCT on a similar intervention, the Seattle Social Development Project, was begun in 1981 when, over the next three years, 1st grade children were randomly assigned to an intervention group, or a control group in eight elementary schools. In 1985 the scheme was expanded to include all 5th grade students in 10 additional Seattle elementary schools, for a further two years. Therefore, the research project consisted of three groups: those assigned to control (220), those initially assigned to intervention, both of which maintained their status for five years (156), and the late intervention group which received the intervention for only the last two years of elementary school (267). There were a total of 643 students taking part in this study by the beginning of 5th grade.

This study concentrated on teacher-training in the school-based part of the intervention, in the use of proactive classroom management, a form of Mastery Learning, and employed cooperative learning methods in which groups of children with different abilities and backgrounds learned together in small groups. In addition to this there was a curricular addition in the 1st grade, 'Interpersonal Problem Solving', a social skills training intervention, and in the 6th grade they were trained in 'refusal skills', how to say no to substances and social practices which may be regarded as dangerous. Parent-training was also offered, although in a limited way. Parents of children in the first two grades were offered seven sessions of workshops, in the 3rd grade parents received four sessions on enabling their child to succeed, and in the 5th and 6th grades a five session drug abuse prevention workshop was held.

Outcomes at the end of the first year (Hawkins *et al.*, 1991) showed a reduction in boys' aggressive behaviours in the intervention group compared to the control group, although there was no difference in those with internalizing (anxious and depressive symptomology). For girls, controls were found to be more self-destructive. After four years Hawkins *et al.* (1992) found that 21% of intervention students but 27% of control students had drunk alcohol and 42% interventions as opposed to 52% controls had committed some offence. A study in 1995 of low-income students found that intervention group boys were rated more socially competent by their teachers and had significantly higher grades, although they were as likely as controls to have run away from home, and tried marijuana, cigarettes and alcohol. For girls, only 7% of the intervention group against 36% of control group, had tried cigarettes and there were encouraging results for alcohol (19% against 39%), and marijuana (4% against 17%). However, they, like boys, were no less likely to have run away from home than controls (O'Donnell *et al.*, 1995).

At the end of 6th grade, Abbott *et al.* (1998) reported that students in the intervention classrooms had significantly higher California Achievement Test scores than controls. In analyzing the students' results at 18, a follow-up study (Hawkins *et al.*, 1999) found the intervention students had a marginally significant higher grade point average, were significantly less likely to have had to repeat a grade, were marginally less likely to have had a disciplinary action report, were significantly less likely to have reported school misbehaviour, been involved in violence, been involved with drugs, become pregnant or caused a pregnancy, or engaged in sexual activity, although there were no significant differences in other anti-social acts. For the late-intervention group, results were less positive with only school misbehaviour and sexual activity found to be lower than that of controls (Hawkins *et al.*, 1999).

One very interesting finding of the later study (Hawkins et al., 2005) was that the intervention group appeared to maintain, in adulthood, the gains made from an intervention programme delivered to them when they were between the ages of 5 and 11, a finding echoing that of the Montreal intervention group. There was, in Hawkins' 2005 analysis, some evidence that those who had the complete intervention fared better than those with the late intervention, whose life trajectory was not significantly improved compared to controls, but full intervention students compared to controls had far fewer mental health problems, a higher high-school graduation level, and significantly less likelihood of risky sexual practices, drug-dealing or criminality. Intervention students were marginally less likely to indulge in substance abuse, although those on the shortened course had as little protection as controls for these practices.

The further significance of these findings is that they appear to verify the value of an early intervention, as opposed to one later in a child's school career. The researchers were keen to emphasize that one of the important factors in preventative science research is the establishment of 'school bonding', which might be alternatively described as 'attachment to school' (see Chapter 2). The Seattle Social Development Project is now renamed as Skills, Opportunities and Recognition, (SOAR).

Among other multi-modal long-term preventative studies is the Metropolitan Area Child Study (MACS) (Tolan, 2004) which was investigated in Chicago and the outlying districts from the grade 1 school cohort in 1990–1991, until the 1996–1997 school year (Huesmann *et al.*, 1996; Tolan *et al.*, 1995a, 1995b). The study incorporated elements from other projects already trialled within the Chicago Metropolitan area, such as the GREAT families project (Smith *et al.*, 2004; Tolan and McKay, 1996), and small group training (Eargle *et al.*, 1994). The aim of this intervention was to prevent aggression and to enhance social competence, and results continue to be gathered and analyzed.

Initially, students (n = 2181) classified as high risk were selected from schools (n = 16) in inner city Chicago and areas of urban deprivation in Aurora, Illinois. The sample was 61% male and multiethnic (made up of 48% African Americans, 37% Hispanics and 16% non-Hispanic white). The 16 schools were blocked by community location and ethnicity. Blocks of four schools, one of each demographic, were then randomly assigned to control or intervention, with one school in each block of four designated the control school. The intervention, like most whole-school interventions, was tiered into three different measures. Level 1 was a universal delivery named 'Yes I Can', which consisted of a classroom-based intervention based on cognitive behavioural theories, and involved enhancing problem-solving skills, empathy skills, and skills designed to reduce aggressive response (Guerra *et al.*, 2007). This was delivered throughout 1st and 2nd grade to all students. Level 2 consisted of that intervention, and also small peer-group skills training for those students with greater SEBD risk and need. These students met with mentor instructors of graduate level for 22 sessions each year (Letendre *et al.*, 2003). The third level of intervention, of 22 sessions, involved parent participation, in a scheme which met in group workshops, but, if necessary, parents were offered additional support to discuss family problems with counsellors.

Outcomes from this programme (Eron *et al.*, 2002) indicated that the First Level programme was the most cost-effective, and that those who received it had greater academic success than control groups through the first four years of intervention, although no effect on achievement was recorded by students in the second and third levels. As for aggression, the intervention in grades one to six had little effect, throughout. Participants on the Level 2 programme, surprisingly, had higher levels of aggression than controls by the end of elementary school. The Level 3 programme, however, had significant effects on aggression for children living in a community protected by community resources, in Aurora, although the Chicago cohort at Level 3 were again rated more aggressive at outcome than their matched controls. Results showed that there was a positive impact on teacher behaviour towards this cohort, and especially to the high risk students (Gregory *et al.*, 2007). Data from this RCT are still being analyzed (Simon *et al.*, 2008).

Gatehouse

Gatehouse is another whole-school systemic multi-modal scheme, although on a much smaller scale, operated in Victoria, Australia (Patton *et al.*, 2000, 2003; Bond *et al.*, 2001, 2004a; 2004b). It is based on attachment theory and cognitive-behavioural approaches rather than on behaviourism, and on identifying risk and supporting resilience (see Chapter 2). The Gatehouse Project was specifically aimed at mental health promotion in secondary schools, and, unusually perhaps, was driven by adolescent mental health teams rather than by educators. Again, the scheme was data-driven, having identified the risk and protection factors in the social and learning environment of schools (n = 26). The study focused on year 8 students (n = 2678) in a Type 1 cluster randomized controlled trial, devised and delivered over a five-year period: 1997–2001.

The approach incorporated curriculum elements aimed at encouraging healthy practices, but took note of the character of each school as a community, their ethos and environment, incorporating this with partnership with community health services (Bond *et al.*, 2001). This had been the purpose of an earlier Health Promoting Schools initiative. However, although this was a framework for change, what had been noted was that schools seemed unable to implement the initiative effectively. The limitations were that many educational interventions were taken on with little regard to their sustainability, and were also specific to mental health promotions, in that communities and schools tended to see the role of health professionals only in their capacity to identify and assess health problems, rather than in a prevention role. This project, therefore, instead of regarding schools as being simply supportive of health initiatives, reframed the issue and viewed the schools as ecosystems which themselves were integral to the intervention. In this way, the schools chosen to take part in the Gatehouse Project incorporated the programme systemically, and the implementation issues became not an element which confounded the measurement of individual change but was regarded as an outcome of the project itself. The essential factor was systemic change, in addition to individual change. The specific focus was capacity building: changing infrastructure, building partnerships, and problem-solving.

The researchers hoped to reduce the risk factors for emotional health and well-being by building a sense of security, enhancing communication skills, and building a sense of positive regard. In this way they believed they might implement positive change in the mental and emotional health of children at risk. A school-based adolescent health team was established within the schools which derived its baseline information from instrumentation designed to establish that school's social climate, following which semi-structured interviews were conducted annually with key personnel in each school by the school's 'critical friend', a member of the health intervention team. It was this reliance on data gathering and monitoring which ensured that staff members of the schools were fully aware of what the problems may be and develop means to address them, providing a sense of shared ownership of the project.

The project incorporated interventions at classroom level, for instance, changing the seating and including more discussion in lesson time and displaying students' work, to whole school interventions like peer support and teacher-as-mentor training and teacher inductions, and finally whole school and community interventions which encouraged parental links and links with local media.

Outcome results were mixed. Although there were immediate positive effects on smoking, for instance, with far fewer of the Year 8 students starting to smoke or take drugs (Bond *et al.*, 2004b), the longitudinal effects on substance use had only a weak effect size (Bond *et al.*, 2004a). There appeared to be no effects on the students' social relationships or on their depressive symptoms, but there was a consistent 3%–5% risk difference between those in the intervention group for drinking and smoking and for mixing with friends who indulged in substance abuse, and controls. It should be remembered that this programme, although moderately effective, was small scale and independent, rather than a state-wide or national programme (Midford, 2007).

Fast Track

The 10-year Fast Track programme (Bierman, 1996, 1997, 2000, 2002a, 2002b, 2006; CPPRG, 1999a, 1999b; Slough, 2008) undertaken by the Conduct Problems Prevention Research group, has drawn significantly on the findings of these two earlier interventions in designing their implementation strategy. The researchers also took prevention as its aim and goal, attempting to reduce anti-social, aggressive adolescent behaviour in children at high risk of developing conduct problems. It is a large, multi-component, long-term trial originally envisaged in 1990 which aimed to retain both fidelity and flexibility in the operation of the programme and is an intervention strategy embedded within a longitudinal study of high risk and not at risk youth.

Fast Track draws on research from prevention science, but is also informed by a developmental model, not merely targeting individual competencies, but recognizing the effects which can be produced by the protection of contextual supports within school, home and the community. To that end the programme was implemented in a variety of settings across the United States and included children at the highest risk of developing later problems. These sites were selected on the basis of their crime and poverty statistics. The schools were then matched, demographically, with one set of schools selected to take part in the intervention, and the matched set acting as the control group in a Type 1 study. The purpose of setting up the scheme was to build up community and neighbourhood backing for it, after the research was completed, so that its effects would be long-term. The cohort studied comprised of three consecutive intakes of children who entered school in 1991, 1992 and 1993.

Of the 9000 children who were screened in kindergarten, 831 over the three years were identified as those who would benefit from this intervention. In their first year at school six different intervention strategies were put in place, some of which were later faded if there seemed no need for them. One part of the scheme was universal and this was the PATHS curriculum (Greenberg *et al.*, 1995), which was in place for all, throughout the project. This is essentially a cognitive behavioural curriculum, which includes four components:

- skills for emotional understanding;
- self-control and inhibitory skills;
- friendship skills; and
- social problem-solving skills.

It was taught, on average, for two to three sessions each week. In addition to this classroom-based intervention, were five additional components, for two hours each week, either after school, or on Saturday, on school premises, involving a parent-training group, while at the same time the children had social-skills training in small 'friendship groups' and if necessary, academic tutoring in reading. Home visits by Family Coordinators who played a support role to parents were also included, as was peer-pairing, which offered each child the opportunity to play and socialize with one other in a pairing scheme which was rotated throughout the year.

One interesting and important innovation in this intervention is that parental consent was sought before the start of the scheme, which meant that non-attendance rates were considerably lower in this study than in others which have involved parents. Another educational innovation was that in addition to the PATHS curriculum, this study, apart from the home visits, was school-based almost in its entirety and therefore placed the school, rather than the clinic or laboratory, at its centre. This is an important symbolic innovation, placing the school at the heart of the community as a whole. It is also important in forging a link between parents and school which may help those parents who may have had negative experiences of school to find schools more approachable.

The findings of the various studies which were carried out throughout the programme can be found in Table 8.1. At the end of the first year (CPPRG, 1999) many of the hypotheses made by the research team in the light of previous findings from earlier studies were validated, as the combination of elements produced moderate positive results on the children's social competencies in all

Table 8.1 Fast track evaluations

Author(s)	Focus	Findings	Comments
CPPG, United States 1999(a, b)	Longitudinal (10 year) evaluation of Multimodal Universal Intervention for prevention of conduct problems involving 1. Classroom programme PATHS (Cognitive Behavioural Programme) 2. Social Skills training 3. Academic tutoring 4. Parent Training 5. Peer pairing 6. Home visiting Longitudinal (1'0 year) evaluation of Initial screening of Kindergarten students (n = 9,000) at 4 sites in 3 cohorts identified students at high risk of developing serious conduct problems (n = 891).	1. Moderate positive effects on children's social, emotional and academic skills, academic skills, peer interactions, social status and conduct problems. 2. Parents reported less physical discipline, greater parenting satisfaction, ease of parenting. Engaged in more appropriate and consistent discipline and warmth. 3. Positive involvement with school (1999b) Significant + effects on peer ratings of aggression and hyperactive/disruptive acts.	Type 1 RCT. High power.
Bierman *et al.* (2002a, b, c)	Longitudinal (3 year) evaluation of Multimodal Universal Intervention for prevention of conduct problems. As above.	1. 37% free of serious conduct problems compared with 27% of control group 2. Peer relations did not improve after 1st Grade	Type1 RCT. Weakness of the study is that it was based on parent and teacher ratings only. They were not blind to the intervention. Mpoderate to low power.

Table 8.1 (*Continued*)

Author(s)	Focus	Findings	Comments
Bierman *et al.* (2004) United States	5 year follow up study. A above.	Significant but modest effect on social competence, social cognition, problems with deviant peers and conduct problems in the home and community. No evidence of impact on serious conduct problems in school, nor on academic attainment. Parental reports (not blind to intervention) could be responsible for discrepancies in outcome measures, or may be due to a slow down in improvement rate.	Type 1 RCT. As above.
Sharp and Davids (2003) Scotland	Evaluation of Multimodal Universal Intervention for prevention of conduct problems: 1. Classroom programme PATHS (Cognitive Behavioural Programme) 2. Social Skills training 3. Parent Training 4. Peer pairing 5. Home visiting (no academic tutoring/reading scheme). Target population:1st grade students (n = 246). Attrition reduced this to n = 144.	Patterns of difference were not as expected. Control schools had more satisfactory results than one of the experimental schools. This was in all probability caused by mobility within school populations and teaching staff.	Type 2 RCT. High attrition rate undermines the value of this study. Low power.

Table 8.1 (*Continued*)

Author(s)	Focus	Findings	Comments
Levallee *et al.* (2005), Bierman *et al.* (2004) United States	Evaluation of peer-pairing and coaching component of a Multimodal Universal Intervention for prevention of conduct problems in very aggressive mixed gender 3rd- 7th grade students (n = 266) 1. Classroom programme PATHS (Cognitive Behavioural Programme) 2. Social Skills training 3. Parent Training 4. Peer pairing 5. Home visiting Intervention	Although peers did escalate the disruptive in-session behaviour of some children, these effects were minimised in groups in which: 1. The most aggressive children are placed together, 2. Girls are integrated with boys, 3. Group processes are monitored	Type 3 study. Moderate power.
Bierman *et al.* (2007), United States	Follow up with above cohort at 5th to 9th grades.	Among the highest risk group the intervention by 9th grade had remained robust from 3rd grade and reduced: 1. the risk of CD cases by 75%, 2. the risk of ADHD behavioural symptomology by 53%, 3. 43% of all externalizing psychiatric disorder cases. For the moderate risk group there appeared to be little effect on externalizing disorders.	As above.

settings: school, home and social community. Parents who had been included throughout in implementing the scheme were showing less harsh discipline and a warmer and more understanding parenting style, while in the classroom there was far less aggression and disruption. Of the 40 outcome measures 18 showed significant intervention effects. By the end of 3rd grade (Bierman *et al.*, 2002b) 37% of the high risk cohort were free of serious conduct problems, compared to 27% in the control group, and on analysis of data at the end of elementary school, modest gains had been made in social competence, but there was little evidence on the impact on serious conduct problems or on academic attainment.

The final outcome measures (Bierman *et al.*, 2007) showed gains for the 3% of all children most at risk of conduct disorders, with the risk of conduct disorder reduced by 75% in the intervention group, and the risk of externalizing psychiatric disorders reduced by 43%. Also, the risk of ADHD was classed as being reduced by 53%. However, the researchers added that it was the risk of serious behavioural manifestations connected with ADHD which was reduced, rather than the incidence and prevalence of ADHD itself. On those at moderate risk of conduct disorder, the intervention showed little effect. The research team explained that as the scheme progressed it was those at the highest risk who were given the additional interventions, and that perhaps these should have been continued with all children.

An additional study, without the reading scheme, was carried out in four schools in Scotland (Sharp and Davids, 2003), with unexpected results. While in the two control schools and one of the intervention schools some positive results were obtained, in the other intervention school the results were negative. A complication of this study was that 'volunteer' schools were also involved, without full support or full engagement in the scheme. It is very unusual to see improvements in control cohorts, and even more unusual to see an intervention producing negligible or few improvements. The authors explain that the results were perhaps unreliable as the poorly-performing school had lost many of the original cohort through the three years of the intervention, and that these children had been replaced by many with serious problems. The result could be accounted for by the mobility of the school population, including: teachers and leaders moving on to other jobs; school staff having long absences; and 'supply' (temporary) staff being employed. Perhaps the unsatisfactory outcome of this study demonstrates that in order for complex interventions such as this to be evaluated accurately potentially confounding variables relating to the stability of the target population must be adequately controlled for.

One of the strengths of the Fast Track programme is its robust evidence driven theoretical underpinning. The CPPRG is driven by an imperative which seeks a preventative outcome, an imperative which has been in part justified by the demonstrated effects on predictions for anti-social behaviour. It has taken a number of elements related to SEBD which have been separately investigated and found to be crucial. One of these is early intervention through kindergarten screening. Another is the often negative effect on social behaviour of peer-group activity, an issue further studied within this research base (Levallee *et al.*, 2005). Yet another is parental training, for which there is very robust research support.

Further, there is the issue of language skills, particularly the ability to read, in predicting academic competence, which has been adequately addressed in this intervention by additional tutoring practices in phonemic pedagogy.

Although the research and data generated by Fast Track may take several years to validate in their entirety, the papers this project has produced are scrupulous in detail and critical acumen. The argument they produce is careful and considered, and is that when addressing the needs of children with SEBD, a developmental and multimodal approach, with some similarities in concept to Henggeler's Multi-systemic Therapy (MST) (Henggeler *et al.*, 1996) may be the most effective route to take. Since it may then be difficult to unpick the discrete effects of each interventionary element, this unpicking is not entirely necessary in a developmental context where bio-psycho-social effects interplay in an organic and holistic manner, and also in a temporal and contextual, situated, manner. The papers produced by this CPPRG affiliation have addressed the issue of SEBD through a reflexive and complex methodology.

Conclusion

As we noted at the beginning of this chapter multi-agency working faces many challenges. When it is successful, however, the outcomes are impressive in terms of their scope and long-term maintenance. In a complex area such as SEBD it is clearly well worth the effort of professionals to develop the skills for working in a multi-agency team. Such skills can be fostered through problem-based learning activities, where trainees and/or qualified professionals work together on simulation tasks (Hughes and Cooper, 2007). They will be further developed and enhanced through the practice of working in trans-disciplinary ways, which involve, by definition, the sharing of insights and expertise. Once again, we conclude a chapter with an emphasis on the importance of the development of new knowledge and skills.

Summary

In this chapter we have examined some examples of multi-agency approaches to SEBD. We have given particular attention to substantial and rigorously-evaluated programmes, most of them involving RCTs, incorporating health, social, and educational components. The most effective multi-agency programmes combine the following features:

- early identification through wide scale screening;
- support and training for parents delivered in the community;
- in-school curriculum adjustments targeted at improving basic skills, particularly in relation to language skills;

- behavioural and cognitive behavioural training to enable at risk students to improve emotional coping and self self-regulation; and
- interventions directed at peer groups.

Key projects which have been found to produce significant positive outcomes in terms of reducing high risk behaviours and improving behaviour as well as social and emotional functioning and promoting general social/emotional resilience include the Gatehouse and Fast Track programmes.

The chapter concluded with an emphasis on the importance of the development of new knowledge and skills among professionals.

9

A Summary of the Research Evidence

Overview

In this chapter we provide a brief summary of the findings from our review of the relevant research literature.

Main Findings of the Review

In each of the following sub-sections we summarize the main findings from the review regarding effective educational intervention for students with SEBD. We give particular emphasis to findings derived from the most rigorously empirical studies.

The teacher student-interface: Teachers' positive qualities and attributes and the power of the student peer group

In Chapter 3 we examined the kinds of understandings and skills that individual teachers possess who are effective in supporting and managing students with SEBD.

Personal warmth as a professional quality

Table 9.1 refers to studies which support the argument that teachers who demonstrate emotional warmth make a positive contribution to the well-being of students in terms of engagement with school and academic achievement. As the reader will note many of the studies cited are of relatively low power, when taken

Table 9.1 Studies showing the effects of personal warmth as positive teacher quality.

Author(s)	Focus	Findings	Comments
Buyse *et al.* (2008)	Two studies of kindergarten teachers in Belgium ([1] n = 3798; [2] n 237).	a teacher is associated with development of pro social behaviour in children with both externalizing and internalizing SEBD	Type 3 study; Observational data; moderately generalizable.
La Russo *et al.* (2008)	Questionnaire study of representative sample 14–18 year old students n = 476) in the United States.	Positive statistical relationship between student reports of their teachers' levels of emotional; healthy school climate and lower drug use; greater social belonging and lower levels of depression.	Type 5 study; No triangulation; good generalizability, but questions remain about the reliability and validity of the questionnaire.
Cooper and McIntyre (1996)	A qualitative study of students (n = 288) and teachers (n = 13) in English secondary schools (n = 5).	Strong relationship between students' self-declared sense of emotional security, which they attributed to teacher influence and their levels of academic engagement. Social constructivist pedagogy was strongly implicated.	This is a type 8 study. Low generalizability, but revealing of the kinds of interpersonal and pedagogical mechanism pertinent to the settings studied.
Gillies and Boyle (2008)	Case study of Australian teachers (n = 7).	Teacher ability to communicate, ask meta-cognitive questions, and to mediate learning in a social-constructivist manner were most successful in promoting student reflective thinking.	This is a type 8 study. Low generalizability, but revealing of the kinds of interpersonal and pedagogical mechanism pertinent to the settings studied.
Kremenitzer (2005), Flem *et al.* (2004), Poulou, 2005)	Small scale qualitative studies of the relationship between social interaction and learning/ behavioural outcomes.	Findings point to the value of personal warmth and communication skills as teacher qualities associated with positive student engagement.	Type 8 studies with low generalizability.

together the commonality of the findings shared among the studies adds up to a more persuasive conclusion than can be claimed by any individual study.

The importance of in-service training

There are a number of research studies which show that in-service training about the nature of SEBD is of considerable assistance to classroom teachers. The evidence for this claim is summarized in Table 9.2.

Management of the physical environment of the classroom

Effective approaches to managing the physical environment of the classroom in relation to SEBD are supported by a limited number of studies which tend to be very small scale and of Type 4 or 5 (prospective or retrospective case studies). There is only very low power evidence to indicate that poor quality educational environments inhibit the effective performance of both students and teachers (see Chapter 4). The main problem common across these studies (which is a major drawback of this study type) is the failure to control for potentially confounding variables (See Table 9.3).

Utilizing the power of the student peer group

Strategies for utilizing student peer influence are supported by promising empirical evidence, although there is a relative lack of convincing Type 1 or Type 2 studies.

Interventions for enhancing teachers' skills

In Chapter 4 we explored some of the ways in which teachers' skills can be nurtured and developed in order to improve their ability to promote the engagement of their students. We identified behaviour and cognitive behavioural strategies as being well supported by the research literature. We found instructional strategies based on cognitive behavioural principles to have relatively weak evidential support.

We noted that Behavioural Strategies receive support from a large body of research evidence including from well-conducted Type 1 studies (RCTs).

It was found that the Good Behaviour Game (GBG) is a well-studied and adaptable intervention that can be employed in a wide variety of educational settings to significant positive effect. General behavioural strategies, in the form of 'kernels', are likely to contribute to the effective management of students with SEBD. Functional Behavioural Analysis is a powerful and assessment and intervention tool, gaining support from a number of small-scale studies, though the complexities of this approach indicate the need for expert support in its use in schools (see Tables 9.5–9.7).

Table 9.2 Key studies showing the value of in-service training on SEBD.

Author(s)	Focus	Findings	Comments
Frölich *et al.* (2002)	Case study of an intensive three-month teacher in-service training programme on ADHD de.ivered in Cologne Primary School.	The programme had a positive impact on teachers' effectiveness in managing difficulties that they encountered in relation to ADHD.	Type 8 low power case study.
Schiff and BarGil, (2004)	Case study of effects of two workshops for elementary school teachers in Israel (n = 42) on the understanding and management of children with SEBD.	Intervention was followed by improvements in teachers' confidence in coping with SEBD.	Type 8 low power case study. No measures of effects on actual performance were taken.
Marzocchi *et al.* (2004)	Case study of effects of a7 month training programme in behaviour modification strategies in an Italian elementary school.	Statistically significant improvements in the students' attention, levels of hyperactivity and oppositional behaviours, and improved teacher-student relationships.	Type 8 low power case study. However, valid behavioural measures were employed in the study of the effects of the programme.
Rossbach and Probst (2005)	Case study of training programme where by advisory teachers (n = 18) in Hamburg school were trained in ADHD theory, contingency management and antecedent training, together with the structured learning intervention (TEACCH). The advisory teachers then trained 2 groups of teachers in schools for different lengths of time.	ADHD symptoms were significantly improved, in both treatment groups, with more maintenance in the group of those teachers who had received additional training.	Type 8 low power case study. However, this study is strengthened by the use of comparison groups.
Zentall and Javorsky (2007)	A prospective study of an in-service training intervention for teachers (n = 49) and students with ADHD (n = 796) in the United States.	Significant improvements in ADHD symptoms were found.	Type 3 study. Moderately powerful in its generalizability.

Table 9.3 Studies on the management of the physical environment of the classroom.

Author(s)	Focus	Findings	Comments
Kaser (2007)	Large scale retrospective, comparative study which controlled for socio-economic status.	School environments with dysfunctional toilets, poorly-maintained buildings and poor control of ambient conditions were associated with significantly lower standardized achievement scores than schools with better standards.	Type 5 study. Moderately generalizable owing to use of control measures.
Weinstein, (1992), Savage (1999), Cooper (1993), Cooper and Tiknaz, (2005, 2007)	By and large these are small scale qualitative case studies often of single educational settings focusing on students' perceptions. The larger study cited (Cooper and Tiknaz, 2006) treats the concern with environmental factors is incidental to the main foci of the studies.	the choices teachers make which affect the quality of the classroom environment can sometimes be interpreted to reflect to students and others what teachers value in behaviour and learning; as well as the extent to which the students themselves are valued as persons by the teacher.	Type 8, low power studies, for the most part, individually, the cumulative impact of which suggests a noteworthy effect.
MacAulay (1990), Fullan (1992), Rinehart 1991) Shores *et al.* (1993), Walker and Walker (1991), Walker *et al.* (1995), Wolfgang (1996), Stewart and Evans (1997), Bettenhausen (1998), Quinn *et al.* (2000), Wannarka and Ruhl (2008)	Studies of the spatial structure of the classroom focusing on such issues as patterns of student seating, the physical proximity of students to teachers, patterns of physical circulation in the classroom, and the overall sense of atmosphere and order.	These studies show that patterns of student seating, the physical proximity of students to teachers, patterns of physical circulation in the classroom, and the overall sense of atmosphere and order can have implications for student behaviour and educational engagement.	Mainly type 8 studies which are of low power. The findings reported in these studies, however, tend to suggest a high level of context specificity.

Table 9.4 Strategies for utilizing student peer influence.

Author(s)	Focus	Findings	Comments
Greenwood *et al.* (1987)	Two year prospective study of class-wide peer tutoring with 2nd Grade students (n = 211) in inner-city schools (n = 4) in United States.	Achievement gains were highest for students undergoing CWPT when compared to those under direct teacher instruction.	Type 3 study. Moderately powerful.
Greenwood *et al.* (1989)	Four year prospective study of class-wide peer tutoring in relation to SES with students (n = 416) in inner-city schools in United States.	Post hoc tests indicated that the low SES experimental group showed higher levels of educational engagement and achieved significantly greater gains in academic achievement than the equivalent low SES control group. Though SES status was a more powerful predictor of performance overall.	Type 3 study. Moderately powerful, though high attrition rate in experimental group.

Cognitive Behavioural (CB) strategies receive support from a large body of research evidence including Type 1 studies (see Tables 9.8–9.11).

The CB strategies most applicable to schools and supported by Type 1 studies are *self-evaluation* and *self-regulation* interventions. Many of these interventions can be employed by teachers, but they tend to be mainly directed at acting-out problems (Table 9.8).

There are effective CB strategies for *self-regulation for anxiety disorders* which have Type 1 evidential support but the most persuasive studies of this are either clinic-based or involve clinicians rather than school-based personnel in their implementation (Table 9.9).

There is significant empirical support for CB approaches to *social problem-solving* (Table 9.10).and *anger management* in schools (Table 9.11), including Type 1 studies.

Instructional strategies are pedagogical techniques employed by teachers in order to promote students' academic engagement. Unfortunately, when we examined the research literature in search of evidence of the efficacy of such approaches for students with SEBD, we find an array of only small-scale low-power studies which produce relatively weak findings (see Chapter 4).

Table 9.5 Behavioural strategies: The Good Behaviour Game.

Author(s)	Focus	Findings	Comments
Dolan *et al.* (1993), Kellam, (1994), Kellam and Anthony (1998), Poduska *et al.* (2008)	Longitudinal RCT of to two successive year groups of entrants (n = 2,311) to inner city middle schools in Baltimore, United States, who were exposed to the Good Behaviour Game (between 1985, 1988). Annual interviews with this cohort were conducted over 11 years, up to the age of 19/20.	After 6 months: significantly lower levels of aggression; greatest reductions for those who had exhibited the most aggression and disruption. In adolescence, most GBG participants maintained initial gains. GBG was more effective than parental-training. The CBG was protective against the development of conduct disorder, suspension from school, smoking and use of mental health services.	Type 1 study. High power. Highly generalizable.
van Lier *et al.* (2004)	RCT of pupils (n = 744; mean age: 6.9) in the Netherlands.	Significant improvements in student behaviour, including presentation of ADHD symptoms in classrooms.	Type 1 study. High power. Highly generalizable.

Whole school approaches and support systems

In Chapter 5 we examined 'whole-school' or 'universal' intervention programmes. These share many common features with interventions discussed in the previous chapter, and in some cases incorporate identical strategies. In particular these approaches rely on the same skills that were discussed previously.

Whole school academic interventions address those strategies which can be adopted by management teams, which can enhance the academic potential of students with SEBD.

The Success for All (SFA) programme was singled out as a well-evidenced approach to raising attainment in literacy that has a number of specific components that address directly some of the key barriers to educational engagement experienced by students with SEBD (see Table 9.12).

Table 9.6 Behavioural strategies (kernels).

Author(s)	Focus	Findings	Comments
Embry (2004), Embry and Biglan (2008)	In a review of a wide range of studies the authors identify and evaluate a number of behavioural 'kernels', 13 of which have particular relevance to educational settings.	The reviews reveal that kernels can produce significant and lasting behavioural change.	Type 7 study. Relatively low power as empirical studies, but the range of sources drawn on point to the construct of 'kernels' as being of promising value.

Table 9.7 Behavioural strategies: Functional Behavioural Analysis (FBA).

Author(s)	Focus	Findings	Comments
Umbreit *et al.* (2004), Lewis and Sugai (1996), Sutherland *et al.* (2000), Kamps *et al.* (2006), Chandler *et al.* (1999)	Case studies of small scale applications of FBA with small sample sizes (n = <10).	FBA effective in promoting positive behavioural change.	Type 8 low power studies.
Scott *et al.* (2005), van Acker *et al.* (2005), Blood and Neel (2007), Cook *et al.* (2007), Benazzi *et al.* (2006)	Case studies of FBA teams in United States.	Efficacy of FBA limited by local conditions in schools. Limitations of FBA training for teachers. Value of FBA specialists.	Type 8, low power study.
Martin *et al.* (2006)	Observational study of IEP meetings (n = 109); post-meeting survey, United States.	Low participation levels of students.	Type 4 study. No control group. Relatively low power.

Table 9.8 Cognitive behavioural strategies: Self-evaluation and self-regulation.

Author(s)	Focus	Findings	Comments
Shapiro and Cole (1995), Altepeter and Korger (1999), Kearney and Wadiak, (1999), Kazdin (2002), Fonagy *et al.* (2002), Fonagy and Kurtz, (2002), Schoenfeld and Janney (2008)	Previous reviews of empirical literature examining the effects of CB strategies on pupils with a range of SEBD.	CB has been found to be effective in improving the core symptoms of ADHD; ODD; CD; anxiety and depressive disorders.	Type 7 studies. These studies reflect (1) the extent of the literature on CB and (2) a consensus in the literature about the efficacy of CB.
Elias and Berk (2002)	Naturalistic observational study of children (n = 51) in a US kindergarten to examine effect of socio-dramatic play involving imaginative role-play on the development of self-regulation.	Children who engaged in complex socio-dramatic (CSD) play with others exercised higher levels of self-regulation in clean-up and circle time sessions than students who were not trained in CSD play. The effect was strongest for impulsive children.	Type 4 study. Moderate generalizability.
Davies and Witte (2000)	Prospective evaluation of an intervention in a grade 3 US mainstream classroom (n = 30) in which a teacher employed an 'interdependent group contingency' technique aimed at reducing the 'talking out of turn' behaviour of four students with ADHD.	The intervention had a dramatic and positive effect on the talking out of turn behaviour of the students with ADHD.	Type 3 study. Generalizability limited by small sample size.
Amato-Zech, *et al.* (2006), Gureasko-Moore *et al.* (2007), Rhode *et al.* (1983)	Small scale experimental studies (n = <10) of CB interventions.	Findings support the efficacy of CB interventions for acting out SEBD.	Type 3 studies limited by their very small sample sizes.

From Inclusion to Engagement

Table 9.9   Cognitive behavioural strategies: Self-regulation for anxiety disorders.

Author(s)	Focus	Findings	Comments
Kendall (1994)	RCT study on the application of a CB self regulation intervention for anxiety disorders on children aged 9-13 (n = 47). Systematic observation data were gathered by therapists, and parents and teachers completed standardized measures of students social, emotional and behavioural functioning in classroom and home settings.	Children who underwent the intervention showed significantly better performance than controls on children's' self-reported depressive symptoms, negative affectivity, and ability to cope with stressful situations. Parent and teacher perceptions supported these findings. These improvements were found to be maintained at follow-up after one year.	Type 1 study. This is a study of the highest calibre. Its generalizability is affected by the relatively small sample size.

Whole-school interventions for *social-emotional learning* can promote an increase in social-emotional literacy for SEBD students. Several of these interventions were examined.

Circle Time although widely used throughout the world, was found to have little by way of firm empirical support. Concerns were raised about the quality of its implementation and potential problems relating to inadequate training of staff employing the approach.

Social and Emotional Aspects of Learning (SEAL) is a social and emotional learning programme, intended to enable students to develop self regulatory and social problem solving skills, Although implemented on a large-scale in England and Wales, it has achieved relatively poor outcomes and appears to suffer from implementation problems.

Second Step is, in principle, very similar to the SEAL programme in terms of its emphasis on developing students' self-management and social engagement skills. However, it differs in important respects, particularly in its implementation design which has the programme embedded in the formal curriculum and delivered by teachers. Like SEAL the evaluation evidence is disappointing. Again, this may be due in part to implementation problems.

Table 9.10   Cognitive behavioural strategies: Social problem-solving.

Author(s)	Focus	Findings	Comments
Battistich *et al.* (1989)	Prospective study of the effects of a classroom-based social problem-solving programme on students (n = 342) from kindergarten to fourth grade in US elementary schools (n = 3) over five years. Students from similar schools (n = 3) where the programme was not followed were used as comparators.	The treatment group achieved significant gains in cognitive problem-solving skills and the use of resolution strategies. Findings were replicated in further study.	Type 3 study. The power of this study is moderate to high owing to the successful replication.
Kazdin *et al.* (1989)	RCT comparing the effects of person-centred relationship therapy (RT) and CB training in problem-solving skills (PSS) on the levels of anti-social behaviour among students (aged 7–13) with severe anti-social behavioural disorders (n = 112). A PSS + parent training condition was also included.	Treatment group showed significantly greater reductions in antisocial behaviour and overall behaviour problems, and greater increases in prosocial behaviour. Improvements maintained at 1 year follow up. Parent training enhanced the initial effects, but the enhancement faded at follow up.	Type 1 study. High power study; highly generalizable.
De Castro *et al.* (2003)	RCT of 3 CB 'stop and think' strategy on severely aggressive boys (n = 32) in a primary special school.	The strategy involving self monitoring of feelings was found to be highly effective in reducing aggressive behaviour. A strategy involving consider the feelings of others and delaying response in provocative situations were found to have a negative effect.	Type 1 study. This is only moderately powerful owing to the absence of in vivo observational data.

Table 9.10   (*Continued*)

Author(s)	Focus	Findings	Comments
Bloomquist et al. (1991)	RCT study of two school-based CB interventions for students with behavioural disorders (ADHD). (1) multi-component training for parents, teachers, and children; (2) training for teachers only.	Although the multi-component CBT condition was found to be significantly more effective than the teacher-only condition initially, differences between these two conditions faded after 6 weeks.	Type 2 RCT. This is rendered a Moderate to low power study by limitations created by the relatively short duration of the intervention and the lack of data in the comparability of the control group to the experimental group. Moderate to low power study.
Jordan and Métais (1997)	case study of 10-12 year olds (n = 26) on a 10-week cooperative learning programme.	The programme was effective in promoting pro-social behaviour.	Type 8 study. Short duration; small sample; low generalizability. Low power.

Whole-school behavioural management programmes can act as a universal programme for all students, but can also enhance the abilities of students with SEBD to engage with learning in a safe environment.

School-Wide Positive Behavioural Support (SWPBS) is a behaviourally-orientated programme which involves the development of a whole-school approach to devising and reinforcing rules for positive behaviour. There is strong evidence for its efficacy when implemented correctly. There is evidence from the research base to support the premise that school-based social-development interventions (such as SWPBS) that address specific risk factors are likely to improve not only in-school behaviour, but also school engagement and academic achievement (see Table 9.13).

Restorative Practices represent a set of approaches to conflict resolution that are based on the principles of restorative justice involving students in an active engagement with problems within the context of the school community. This approach has many positive features, including a model of social engagement which emphasizes mutual respect and tolerance of difference. However, to date, the programme has not undergone significant evaluation and, therefore, there is little evidence of its efficacy in relation to SEBD in schools.

Table 9.11   Cognitive behavioural strategies: Anger management.

Author(s)	Focus	Findings	Comments
Kellner *et al.* (2001)	Repeated measures design control group study in a US day special school with a single class of early adolescents with serious emotional or behavioural problems. Experimental group were taught self-monitoring and self-regulatory techniques relating to anger over 10 sessions. A sub group received booster sessions.	Target students were less likely to engage in fighting with peers, more likely to engage in increase in talking problem situations through with a counsellor when angry, and more likely to use anger logs. At the 4-month follow-up, students who received booster sessions continued to make more use of the log than controls.	Type 3 study. Moderate to low power, severely limited by sample size.
Feindler *et al.* (1984)	RCT of anger management programme for severely aggressive boys (n = 100) in a junior high school (United States).	Members of the treatment groups showed significant gains in relation to problem-solving ability and self-control, and were less likely to incur fines or be expelled for disruptive behaviour and for severe aggression after engaging in the programme.	Type 1 study. High power; high generalizability, limited only by the moderate sample size.

Cognitive Behavioural programmes can be universal and whole-school in their approach in supporting all students, but may be particularly effective for students with SEBD.

The *FRIENDS* programme is one of the most robustly-supported programmes for internalizing disorders, and has the backing of the World Health Organization. A number of large-scale Type 1 RCTs have been carried out in several countries showing that this 10-session CB programme (often delivered by teachers) is a highly effective *curriculum-embedded* intervention that is particularly successful

Table 9.12 The Success for All (SFA) programme.

Author(s)	Focus	Findings	Comments
Borman *et al.* (2007), Borman *et al.* (2005a, 2005b)	Cluster RCT involving 41 schools across 11 states which were randomised into SFA 'treatment' schools and used the scheme through kindergarten and first grades, and 'control' schools where the SFA programme would be used in Grades 3–5. A second sample of the longitudinal group (n = 3290) students, and in-movers (n = 890) who had joined treatment, or intent-to-treat control group schools, after baseline assessments, were also used in the study at the time of Year 2 post-tests.	Effect sizes for the intervention were, as hypothesized by the researchers, significantly improved from the outcomes at the end of Year One.	type 1. Power of this study is diminished by variations in implementation and some control group contamination.
Hopkins *et al.* (1998) (study in 1997 although variations due to implementation differences).	Two-year SFA pilot scheme evaluation in deprived area of UK, in primary (n = 5) and one secondary school.	In years 1-3 SFA students performed considerably better than expected, although there were less impressive gains in each of the following three years. Teachers reported that they had more confidence in and understanding of, the teaching of reading, and there were noted behavioural improvements in the intervention schools.	Type 3 study. Moderate to low power. Power of this study is diminished by variations in im-plementation.

Table 9.13 School-wide behavioural support.

Author(s)	Focus	Findings	Comments
Lassen *et al.* (2006)	Single case longitudinal (3 years) evaluation using web-based school-wide information system (SWIS) in an urban school in the Midwest (United States).	Improvements in school behaviour were reflected in academic performance, with specific reductions in office referrals and significantly-related increases in mathematics and reading scores.	Type 8 study. Low power and generalizability. Impressive demonstration of SWIS in action.
McIntosh *et al.* (2006) Luiselli *et al.* (2005)	Single case longitudinal evaluations using web-based school-wide information system (SWIS) in a kindergarten (Canada) and urban Elementary school (United States).	Findings concur with Lassen *et al.* 2006 (above).	Type 8 study. Low generalizability. Power enhanced by concurrence between small scale studies.
Sørlie and Ogden (2007)	A quasi-experimental study of PALS in Norway with pupils (n = 735) in grades three to seven in four elementary schools. There was an intervention group. (n = 363) and a control group (n = 72) composed of pupils in four similar elementary schools. A cognitive-behavioural element, the 'Stop Now And Plan' (SNAP) intervention, was added.	Teacher-observed and -reported reductions in disruptive classroom behaviour after two years ranged from moderate to large, and while teacher efficacy was significantly related to the better outcomes, student ratings of social competence and on classroom climate were insignificant. However, those schools with the highest levels of disruptive student behaviour at baseline were those which reported greatest decreases.	Type 3 study. Moderately powerful.

Table 9.14   Universal cognitive behavioural approach: FRIENDS.

Author(s)	Focus	Findings	Comments
Barrett *et al.* (2006)	Type 1 RCT of FRIENDS with Grade six and grade nine students (n = 669) in Australia.	Significant reductions in anxiety symptoms were maintained at 12, 24 and 36 month follow ups. Initial, more positive, effects on girls disappeared after 36 months.	Type 1 study. Schools are randomly allocated. High power.
Lowrey-Webster *et al.* (2001)	Type 1 RCT carried out on students (aged 10–13; n = 594) attending seven secondary schools in Brisbane, Australia.	Children in the FRIENDS condition reported significantly fewer anxiety symptoms, regardless of their risk status.	Type 1 study. Students are randomly allocated. High power.
Bernstein *et al.* (2005)	Type 1 RCT carried out with 7–11 year old students (n = 453) from three schools in the United States.	Students who had undergone the FRIENDS intervention programme showed significantly decreased anxiety levels. Students who underwent FRIENDS + parent training showed the best outcomes.	Type 1 study. Students are randomly allocated. High power.
Stallard *et al.* (2007)	Type 2 study of the application of the FRIENDS programme in three primary schools, with children aged between nine and 10 (n = 106) in the United Kingdom.	At the three month follow-up, anxiety levels had significantly decreased and self-esteem increased.	Type 2 study. No non-intervention group. Moderately powerful.

in helping all students, regardless of risk status, to develop strategies for managing anxiety (see Table 9.14).

Coping Power (CP) is a CB intervention that addresses aggressive/acting-out behaviour. Like *FRIENDS* it has strong empirical support based on Type 1 RCTs (see Table 9.15).

Table 9.15 Universal cognitive behavioural approach: Coping Power.

Author(s)	Focus	Findings	Comments
Lochman and Wells (2002a, 2002b, 2003, 2004)	Type 1 RCT of fifth and sixth grade boys (n = 1,578) in North Carolina, United States, with one tear follow up.	The Coping Power programme had significant impact on covert delinquency; parent-reported substance abuse, and school behaviour. Effects were enhanced by incorporation of parent training. Improvement in school behaviour was maintained at one year follow-up.	Type 1 RCT. High power, though limited by all male focus.

Small-scale provision for students with SEBD

Chapter 6 focused on small scale provision for students with SEBD. Evidence was reviewed for the efficacy of a range of small scale provisions for students with SEBD which are often created on the basis of strong evidence of a relationship between low levels of anti-social behaviour and small-scale settings. Unfortunately, there is a dearth of evaluation evidence on these interventions

Outreach Schools are a form of provision for students who have been excluded from mainstream schools prevalent in Canada. They operate on student-centred lines and emphasize student choice and voluntary attendance. The limited qualitative and quantitative evidence that exists indicates that they are popular with students and contribute to improvements in educational engagement.

Career Academies are small-scale vocationally-oriented programmes in some US high schools. There is good evidence that they achieve positive social and academic outcomes for at risk students (see Table 9.16).

Nurture Groups are a form of transitional provision pioneered in the United Kingdom. Although no RCT evidence has yet been gathered there is correlational evidence from a number of sources supporting their efficacy, especially for primary-aged students with SEBD, in promoting significant social, emotional and academic improvement (see Table 9.17).

The use of *special units and classrooms/PRUs* are supported through some limited evidence though the nature and diversity of this range of provision is such that it is difficult to make meaningful generalizations about its overall effectiveness. Where useful Type 8 (case study) evidence exists, this has not been followed up by further Type 1–4 larger scale studies.

Residential provision for SEBD is long established feature of the educational landscape, but one that is under-researched. Limited small-scale evidence indicates the effectiveness of residential provision in giving students respite from

Table 9.16 Career academies.

Author(s)	Focus	Findings	Comments
Kemple and Rock (1996), Kemple and Snipes, 2000)	Type 1 RCT involving students (n = 1953) across nine sites.	Drop-out rates were significantly reduced for students at high risk of school failure. Increased attendance rates, But no significant reduction in risk-taking behaviour. Benefits for students at low risk of school failure included: greater likelihood of graduating on time; increase in career-related courses in addition to completing academic courses.	Type 1 RCT. High power.

stress and helping them develop coping skills and improved social skills. However, maintenance effects are weak.

Working with parents

Chapter 7 explored the vital issue of *parent training* and has identified three empirically validated programmes. All three programmes are based primarily on behavioural principles (see previous chapters) whereby parents are taught strategies to extinguish unwanted behaviour and reinforce desirable behaviour through the identification and management of contingencies (i.e., Antecedents and consequences) that are directly related to the behaviour. In addition these programmes involve reflective and distinctively cognitive interventions such as reframing and behavioural contracting:

Parent Management Training (PMT) has a strong evidential base. Most of the parent-management programmes take their lead from this programme. However, it is a clinic-based programme, usually delivered by therapists (see Table 9.18).

The *Incredible Years* programme (IY) has built on the evidence produced by PMT to create a universal intervention, which is now available, in some formats, as a home-based intervention, with a very strong evidential base in enabling parents to manage behavioural problems in their children, and some growing evidence which points to parents and teachers enabled to brainstorm SEBD problems. It has developed a community-based format which has been directed at hard-to-reach, socially-deprived families. School-based parent training, involving both parents and teachers as equal status trainees, seems to be a very promising model (see Table 9.19).

Table 9.17   Nurture groups.

Author(s)	Focus	Findings	Comments
Iszatt and Wasilewska (1997)	Longitudinal study of children (n = 308) placed in NGs between 1984 and 1998 in London.	87% were able to return to the mainstream after a placement duration of less than one year. Longitudinal data indicate that three vast majority of these students required no further SEN support.	Type 5 study. No adequate control group. Low power study.
Cooper and White-bread (2007)	Two year longitudinal prospective study of the effects of Nurture Groups on children (n = 356) enrolled in nurture groups (n = 27) compared to four groups of children matched to members of the enrolled groups on various dimensions but who were not enrolled in nurture groups (n = 190).	Groups which had been in existence for two years or more achieved statistically significant improvements in pupils' social, emotional and behavioural functioning after two terms, when compared with the progress of pupils with SEBD in mainstream classrooms. Parents of NG pupils reported positive perceptions, and offered the possibility that NGs could have a positive effect of parent-child relationships.	Type 3 study. Study makes good use of matched comparison groups, though numbers in these groups are relatively small. Moderately powerful.
Reynolds et al. (2009)	A naturalistic prospective control group study focused on pupils (n = 221) aged between 5 and 7 years with SEBD attending primary schools (n = 32) in Glasgow). The intervention group (n = 117) attended nurture groups in 16 schools, whilst the remainder (n = 104) attended matched schools (n = 16) without nurture groups.	NG pupils made significant improvements in self-esteem, self-image, emotional maturity and attainment in literacy when compared to the group of pupils attending the schools without NG provision.	Type 3 study This is the first NG study to measure academic effects. Moderately powerful.

Table 9.18   Parent training: Parent management training.

Author(s)	Focus	Findings	Comments
Kaminski et al. (2008)	Meta-analytic review of PMT studies with the aim of identifying the components of successful parent training schemes for children up to the age of 8 years.	The three most effective components for predicting successful parenting behaviour were instruction in positive interactions with their child. Encouragement of emotional communication, and practicing with their own child. The mean effect size for parenting outcomes was larger than that for child outcomes. Children with internalizing disorders benefitted more from the interventions than those with externalizing disorders.	Type 6 study. Moderate power.
Lundahl et al. (2006).	Meta analysis of moderators and follow up effects in relation to PMT.	Follow-up effects were small in magnitude for behaviourally-based programmes, and parenting programmes were least effective with economically-disadvantaged families.	Type 6 study. Moderate power.

Triple P is a well-evidenced and well-supported parent-training programme, but has not, as yet, been developed for use in educational establishments.

Multi-agency approaches to SEBD

In Chapter 8 we examined some examples of multi-agency approaches to SEBD. We have given particular attention to substantial and rigorously-evaluated

Table 9.19 Parent training: Incredible Years programme.

Author(s)	Focus	Findings	Comments
Clondalkin Partnership (2006)	Mixed methods survey of effects of Incredible Years on parents (n = 32) and children (n = 28).	Improvements in children's conduct, relations with peers and emotional status were found.	Type 5 pilot study. Small sample; no control group. Low generalizability; power.
Mørch *et al.* 2004	An evaluation of a 2-year pilot scheme carried out in Norway.	65% of children with conduct problems were helped by the programme.	Type 3 study. Relatively small scale low to moderate power.
Eyberg *et al.* (2008), Weisz *et al.*(2004), Nixon *et al.* (2002)	Research reviews of Incredible Years without secondary data analyses,	These reviews report consistently positive effects of IY on children with SEBD.	Type 7 studies. The value of these relatively low powered studies is enhanced by the convergence of their findings.

programmes, most of them involving Type 1 studies, incorporating health, social, and educational components.

The most effective multi-agency programmes combined the following features:

- early identification through wide-scale screening;
- support and training for parents delivered in the community;
- in-school curriculum adjustments targeted at improving basic skills, particularly in relation to language skills;
- behavioural and cognitive behavioural training to enable at risk students to improve emotional coping and self-regulation; and
- interventions directed at peer groups.

Key projects which have been found to produce significant positive outcomes in terms of reducing high risk behaviours and improving behaviour as well as social and emotional functioning and promoting general social/emotional resilience include the *Gatehouse* and *Fast Track* programmes. Of these two Fast Track has the more impressive empirical support (see Table 9.20).

Conclusion: Hierarchical Summary of Main Interventions

In this section we present in tabular form a brief summary of the main intervention types in relation to the power of the evidence bases supporting the. Table 9.21 distils judgments made on the basis of our analysis of the evidence that

Table 9.20   Fast Track evaluations.

Author(s)	Focus	Findings	Comments
CPPG (1999a, b)	Longitudinal (10 year) evaluation of Multimodal Universal Intervention for prevention of conduct problems in students, initially in kindergarten (n = 891).	Moderate improvements in children's social, emotional and academic skills, academic skills, peer interactions, social status and conduct problems. Parents reported less physical discipline, greater parenting satisfaction, ease of parenting. Engaged in more appropriate and consistent discipline and warmth. Positive involvement with school (1999b) Significant + effects on peer ratings of aggression and hyperactive/disruptive acts.	Type 1 RCT. High power.
Bierman et al. (2002a, b, c)	Longitudinal (3 year) evaluation of Multimodal Universal Intervention for prevention of conduct problems. As above.	1. 37% free of serious conduct problems compared with 27% of control group. 2. Peer relations did not improve after 1st Grade	Type1 RCT. Weakness of the study is that it was based on parent and teacher ratings only. They were not blind to the intervention. Moderate to low power.
Bierman et al. (2004)	5 year follow up study. A above.	Significant but modest effect on social competence, social cognition, problems with deviant peers and conduct problems in the home and community. No evidence of impact on serious conduct problems in school, nor on academic attainment.	Type 1 RCT. As above.

Table 9.20 (*Continued*)

Author(s)	Focus	Findings	Comments
Sharp and Davids Scotland (2003)	Evaluation of Multimodal Universal Intervention for prevention of conduct problems. Target population:1st grade students (n = 246). Attrition reduced this to n = 144.	Control schools had more satisfactory results than one of the experimental schools. This was in all probability caused by mobility within school populations and teaching staff.	Type 2 RCT. High attrition rate undermines the value of this study. Low power.
Levallee *et al.* (2005) Bierman *et al.* (2004)	Evaluation of peer-pairing and coaching component of a Multimodal Universal Intervention for prevention of conduct problems in very aggressive mixed gender 3rd to7th grade students (n = 266).	Although peers did escalate the disruptive in-session behaviour of some children, these effects were minimized in groups in which: 1. The most aggressive children are placed together; 2. Girls are integrated with boys; or 3. Group processes are monitored.	Type 3 study. Moderate power.
Bierman *et al.* (2007)	Follow up with above cohort at 5th to 9th grades.	Among the highest risk group the intervention by 9th grade had remained robust from 3rd grade and reduced: 1. the risk of CD cases by 75%, 2. the risk of ADHD behavioural symptoms by 53%, 3. 43% of all externalizing psychiatric disorder cases. For the moderate risk group there appeared to be little effect on externalizing disorders.	As above.

From Inclusion to Engagement

Table 9.21   Hierarchical summary of main interventions.

	Teachers' qualities and skills	Whole school approaches	Small scale provision	Parental support	Multi-agency working
High level of empirical support	The Good Behaviour Game	FRIENDS	Career Academies		
Moderate level of empirical support	Kernels Student Peer Support Cognitive Behavioural Approaches	Success For All School-wide Positive Behavioural Support Coping Power	Nurture Groups	Parent Management Training	Fast Track
Low level of empirical support	Personal Warmth In Service Training (SEBD) The Management of the Physical Environment of the Classroom Applied Behavioural Analysis (ABA) Instructional Strategies	Circle Time SEAL Second Step Restorative Practices	Outreach Schools Residential Provision	Incredible Years Triple P	Gatehouse

we have examined. A number of important points need to be considered when interpreting the table. First, the review has taken a distinctively educational focus, and because of this we have focused in the main on studies that deal with interventions that take place within educational settings or have particular educational implications. Second, because we have endeavoured to be systematic in both our selection of the studies to be considered and in our evaluation of studies, we have given prominence to approaches which have been the subject of the most attention from researchers. Third, (see Chapter 1), we have given greatest weight to those approaches which have empirical evidence of their generalizability. The last point is of particular importance because it draws attention to the fact that most of the interventions which have been rated as having a low level of empirical support have not been subjected to the most rigorous forms of evaluation. It would be wrong, therefore, to dismiss these low-rated interventions on this basis. On the other hand, this draws attention to the need for such interventions, some of which are subject to considerable interest among educators (e.g., Circle Time and restorative practices), to be rigorously evaluated in order to establish their efficacy.

With these points in mind we must conclude that behavioural and cognitive behavioural interventions stand out as being the most strongly supported interventions at the high and moderate levels. Of particular interest here is the fact that many of these interventions are available in the form of manualized programmes or short training courses which make them suitable for and accessible to educational professionals, such as teachers, who work directly with young people who present with SEBD, but who do not necessarily have training or experience in the delivery of psycho-social interventions.

10

Conclusions

Overview

In this final chapter we highlight some of the main issues that have emerged from the preceding discussion and their implications for promoting the educational engagement of students with SEBD. Particular attention is given to the knowledge and skills required by staff in schools.

At the heart of this book is a commitment to the need to see Social, Emotional and Behavioural Difficulties in school students as posing a unique set of challenges to individuals, schools and the wider society. We note that schools and educators are well placed to help address these problems, and that the evidence suggests that some of the measures discussed in this book are being adopted in some schools. The problem remains, however, that in spite of the extensive evidence base that points to a variety of extremely promising approaches and strategies, there is still a widespread sense shared by many that by and large our schools are ill-equipped to deal with the challenges posed by SEBD.

As we have shown, the diversity of special educational need can only be fully met within a context that contains a diversity of provision. This is partly due to the inevitable unevenness in the quality of mainstream provision combined with the skills, knowledge and expertise of staff working in specialist provision.

The Importance of Education and Health Services Working Together: Towards Trans-Professionalism

As we noted in Chapter 2, an informed understanding of SEBD depends to a great extent on psycho-medical understandings. It is also important to note that the research evidence that we have reviewed on effective interventions (in Chapters

From Inclusion to Engagement: Helping Students Engage with Schooling through Policy and Practice
By Paul Cooper and Barbara Jacobs © 2011 John Wiley & Sons, Ltd

3, 4, 5, 6 and 7) for SEBD have at times emphasized psycho-social (particularly psychological) interventions (such as Cognitive Behavioural Approaches) which are sometimes associated with a bio-medical paradigm (e.g., Skidmore, 2004). As we have also shown, however, the educational sphere is a major site frequently implicated in the development, remediation and prevention of SEBD. Academic success is an important protective factor and the effectiveness of psycho-social interventions is often enhanced when they are delivered in schools, rather than clinics, and when they are, embedded in the curriculum where it is appropriate to do so. We have also shown that certain psychological interventions are most effective when they are delivered by teachers rather than other professionals (e.g., FRIENDS). Having said this, there is a limit to the level of knowledge and expertise that teachers in general can be expected to have. Psychologists and medical professionals, therefore, have two important roles in relation to intervention in schools. The first is a training role and the second is as a provider of intervention, both as a consultant to school staff and in direct intervention with students.

It is very important for both educational and health professionals to reflect on the ways in which they can combine their efforts and go beyond multi-professional approaches in order to embrace trans-professionalism (see Chapter 8). SEBD in school students is, arguably, one of the most fruitful targets for such an approach. Trans-professional approaches require professionals to step outside their professional silos in order to absorb, rather than simply engage with, some of the knowledge and understandings of representatives from other professions. As it stands, the evidence base shows that some members of the teaching profession have demonstrated conspicuous success in adopting and applying psychological approaches to SEBD that are informed by understandings of the underpinnings of social, emotional and behavioural dysfunction. These successes need to be built on. This aspiration will be advanced if medical professionals learn more about the potential that educational approaches have for remediating and preventing SEBD and contribute to the development of these approaches.

A Bio-Psycho-Social Approach

We argue very strongly in Chapter 2 for a bio-psycho-social approach. This approach integrates the individual biological and intrapsychic dimensions with the interpersonal and social dimensions. This makes the approach truly holistic and lends itself well to understandings of the complexities of SEBD and its concomitant interventions. The bio-psycho-social approach is, therefore, a valuable theoretical framework within which to locate a fully trans-disciplinary approach to SEBD. The importance of this approach is that it emphasizes a contextualized view of SEBD which suggests that the perceived problem may well be amenable to social and educational accommodations that go well beyond simplistic disciplinary procedures to embrace psycho-pedagogical interventions.

This discussion relates to the broader issue of problems that can arise from different disciplinary cultures and languages. We have noted in our review the importance attached by some commentators to 'the rejection of the medical model' in the historical development of inclusive education policies and practices. A potentially negative consequence of this might be to create problems in the all-important area of interdisciplinary working. Our suggested solution to this potential problem is the adoption of a bio-psycho-social framework that will incorporate and give equal respect to the contributions of different disciplines.

The Importance of the Skills of Teachers and other School Personnel

The cumulative evidence points overwhelmingly to the conclusion that the educational engagement of students with SEBD improves significantly when staff are trained in the use of behavioural and cognitive behavioural strategies. On the other hand, the absence of such skills among front line staff has been shown to be associated with poor outcomes, not only for students with SEN, but for all students (Blatchford *et al.*, 2009; MacBeath *et al.*, 2006).

Throughout this book we have devoted considerable attention to the central importance of the teacher–student relationship in effective teaching in general and its vital importance in the promotion of the educational engagement of students with SEBD. Research evidence supports the view that the quality of this relationship has a profound influence on the development, remediation and prevention of SEBD. We have also reviewed studies which indicate something of the range of technical skills and competencies of teachers who are effective in promoting the social and educational engagement of students with SEBD. These include behavioural and cognitive behavioural strategies in particular.

This emphasis on the knowledge and competencies of 'front line', school-based educators has important implications for the ways in which the various services work with staffing schools. At the present time in many countries a great deal of the specialist expertise for dealing with SEBD appears to reside outside schools, in the form of Educational Psychology Services, Behaviour Support specialists and other support agencies. We argue that the work of these groups in relation to SEBD in schools will be most effective if they are successful in supporting skills-development among school personnel.

At the policy level this requires a commitment to idea that SEBD is the extreme expression of the range of social and emotional needs shared by all human beings. Such an understanding forms the bedrock of effective prevention in this area and it highlights the importance of whole school (or 'universal') approaches through which shared values, understandings and approaches to the promotion of social and emotional well-being are emphasized.

It follows that the training functions of specialist services need to be prioritized, and that other sources of training and support (such as those provided by teacher training institutions) be promoted to staff in schools in a concerted way. The consequences of not making a priority of raising skill levels in schools are likely to be negative in a number of ways. Without an understanding and ownership of SEBD issues, mainstream staff may well become overly dependent on external support services. If the necessary skills are not an integral part of the repertoire of school staff, not only will preventable problems develop (thereby putting unnecessary pressure on external services), but they will also be likely to spread throughout schools to affect the broader school population. Such a situation, as MacBeath *et al.* (2006) show (See Chapter 1), severely undermines the inclusive education agenda.

There is always likely to be a need for centralized specialist support services, but it is essential that these services are understood to be and act as a means of supplementing and extending core skill bases in schools and not be seen as an alternative firm of provision.

Teaching assistants

An important issue here is the role and function of teaching assistants (TA) in schools. As Blatchford *et al.* (2009) show, untrained teaching assistants can in certain circumstances have a negative impact on student progress. On the other hand (as the Blatchford study also shows) it seems that appropriately skilled support staff can assist the work of teachers in important ways. A key issue here is the need for greater clarification about the roles and functions of teaching assistants. It is hard to escape the conclusion that, given the fact that teaching assistants are often employed to work with students who present with the most complex and challenging difficulties, that they should have a level of skill that matches the magnitude of this challenge. This suggests that teaching assistants, if they are to be employed in ways which require them to have significant responsibility for promoting the social and educational of students with complex needs, need to be appropriately qualified. In the United Kingdom there are currently a number of undergraduate programmes provided by universities which are designed to prepare TAs for their roles. The content of these programmes includes modules on child development, teaching and learning, as well as instruction in school curriculum subjects.

It is difficult to escape the conclusion, therefore, that TAs, like teachers, need to be given the professional status that comes with university level professional training. The taking on of such professional status brings with it responsibilities and expectations of people who occupy such roles. On the other hand, such responsibilities and expectations are likely to produce a second set of expectations in the form of a requirement by professionally trained TAs to be remunerated in a way that is consonant with their professional status.

Special Provision

As we have noted, one consequence of the inclusive education agenda may sometimes be to denigrate special school and other specialist provision for students with SEN as being exclusionary and outdated, or to be simply ignored in the mistaken belief that inclusive education can only take place within mainstream schools. We argue, however, that in a properly functioning integrated education system, special schools can make a significant contribution to educational social inclusion. It follows from this that good special schools are a valuable resource in terms of what they can offer to individual students and in their potential to share their expertise with staff in mainstream schools (O'Keefe, 2004).

A clear implication of this view is the need for the strengths and best practice in special schools and other non-mainstream provision to be identified and celebrated, and for close collaboration between special and mainstream schools to be encouraged. This sharing of expertise and resources between special and mainstream provision will, it is argued, help maximize cooperation between staff in different settings, raise skill levels, reduce the burden on external specialist services, and, in so doing, promote social and educational inclusion. A further implication that flows from this is the need for members of the specialist services to become familiar with the roles and functions of special schools and other non-mainstream provision, and their contribution to the continuum of services.

The value of small scale provision for students with SEBD within mainstream schools was highlighted in an earlier chapter. This is a potentially controversial area, owing the understandable fear that such provision can be used for exclusionary purposes. It should be emphasized, however, that the employment of all education intervention should be informed by clear, educationally literate thinking. We argue that all educational provisions should be clearly defined in terms of their:

1. educational function;
2. target population;
3. pedagogic and pupil management methods;
4. the skills, expertise and functions of staff;
5. assessment and monitoring procedures; and
6. student referral and exit strategies.

It is vital that such facilities target students with specific needs for relatively short periods of time (i.e., ideally well short of an academic year) and do not become 'sin bins' for difficult students. Provisions that cannot be accounted for in these terms are not worthy of the term 'educational'.

The Importance of Whole SCHOOL support systems for students with SEBD

We have also shown that the effectiveness of teachers and other workers with school students is enhanced when they work within organizations which have universal policies and structures geared towards the promotion of prosocial

behaviour and emotional well-being. We have identified a number of empirically supported whole school support systems for students with SEBD.

Work with Families

Families often provide the crucible in which SEBD are forged. They can also be
vital players in the 'melting down' and 'remoulding' process. Many governments
espouse a commitment to protecting the rights of parents to choose the manner
of their child's education, and claim to encourage parental involvement in the
governance of schools. It is interesting to note, however, that the challenges posed
by securing parental participation in schooling are very similar to those involved
in securing parental cooperation with schools in the area of SEBD. The parents of
the most troubled and vulnerable students are very often, themselves, vulnerable
and troubled too. Their vulnerability both partly flows from, and exacerbates,
their lack of cultural capital (Hanafin and Lynch, 2002). Schools and teachers are
often perceived as threatening or, at least, mystifying. This lack of cultural capital
is handicapping for both parent and child, and places a serious obstacle in the
way of the development of cooperation between school and family.

There are no simple formulae for increasing the stock of cultural capital held
by the most vulnerable members of society. As we saw, however, in our discussion
of the Success for All programme, there are proactive things that schools can do to
facilitate parental involvement. The primary issue here is the need for schools (and
other services) to see the importance of the need to motivate parental involvement,
rather than simply to expect it. This implies the need to make schools welcoming
and parent-friendly places. School and specialist personnel need to find ways of
either going to meet vulnerable parents on their own ground, or of engaging with
them in 'neutral' spaces.

In Conclusion

This book began on a decidedly negative note. We make no apology for this. To
express any degree of contentment with the current state of so called 'inclusive'
education systems, and their consequences for the most vulnerable students they
purport to serve, would be for us an act of deep dishonesty. Fortunately, we are
not alone in this view. Where we differ from some commentators, however, is in
how we define this problem and where we go to seek solutions. While we hold
a strong commitment to the pursuit social justice in society (and education),
we are frustrated by what we see as the diversionary discourse which privileges
ideology over understanding, and rhetoric over action. This is the discourse that
justifies the placement of socially vulnerable and educationally failing students
in so-called 'mainstream' schools, no matter how bad they are, rather than offering them the opportunity to attend 'special' schools, no matter how good they

are. Some of the consequences of this incoherence are outlined by MacBeath *et al.* (2006). They show us teachers in 'mainstream' schools, who are committed to the idea that mainstream schools should cater for all students, but who express feelings of guilt because of their failure to achieve this ideal, owing to the fact that they lack the knowledge, skills and resources necessary to approach this task.

We could have devoted the entire book to a critique of the muddled rhetoric that condemns 'labelling' but only in favour of an alternative set of ideologically preferred labels. In such a book we would point out, for example, that what determines the meaning of a label is the meaning that lies behind it (Cooper, 1996). We would, for example, lament the ignorance of writers who condemn entire bodies of research literature because of categories (i.e., 'labels') that such writers have attributed them to (e.g., Skidmore, 2004). We would probably have pointed out that labels can be helpful, especially when they are construed as reflecting positive attributions (Cooper, 1993). We would have gone on to argue that discourses and labels evolve in interesting ways when people of different persuasions talk to each other. This is where the present book meets the unwritten one.

The question which motivated us to write this book was: what do we know about successful educational and therapeutic ways of preventing SEBD in schools and dealing with it when it arises? We did the simple thing of going to the library. What we found out as a result of this action was (and we hope you agree) instructive, at the very least.

We found that there are many things that schools (of all kinds) and their staff can do to help them overcome the problems that have been identified. Our study suggests that the skills of front line practitioners are crucial and can be enhanced often in fairly straightforward ways. We also found that these individual abilities will be enhanced when there is a consistent whole-school approach in place. In addition, we found that specialist expertise and provision beyond that which is routinely available in the majority of schools (including parental/carer engagement) can make a significant contribution to enabling the educational engagement of the most vulnerable and challenging students.

We are aware that some people might challenge us with the argument that by failing to endorse an absolute commitment to abolition of non-mainstream provision we are helping to sustain exclusionary practices in education. Our response to this is straightforward: every child and young person should have the right to access the best available educational environment that is most suited to their requirements. Managers and workers in mainstream educational environments should continue to strive towards making themselves less discriminatory and more inclusive, but students should not have to put up with environments which do not prioritize their social, emotional and educational needs. Diverse human beings require flexibility and diversity in education provision. It has been the intention of this book to examine the evidence base in relation to the kinds of interventions that are available to help meet the diverse needs of a wide range of students, particularly those who are deemed to exhibit or experience social, emotional and behavioural difficulties. Undoubtedly, some of the interventions reviewed will help promote inclusive education in mainstream schools, others highlight the value of alternative, non-mainstream forms of provision. Together, these different types of intervention will contribute to a genuinely inclusive education system, that is, one which optimizes the opportunities for educational engagement of all students, particularly those who are at greatest risk of exclusion.

Appendix I

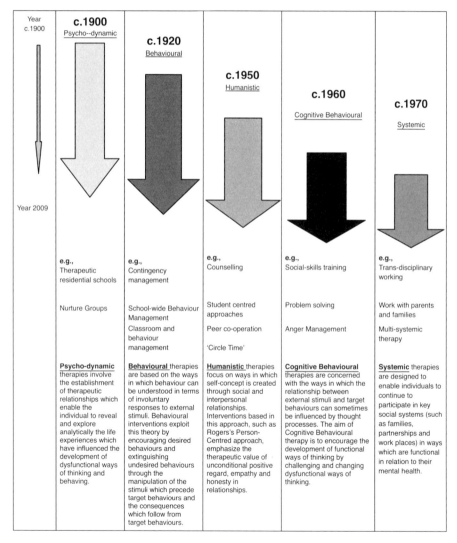

Year c.1900	**c.1900** Psycho--dynamic	**c.1920** Behavioural	**c.1950** Humanistic	**c.1960** Cognitive Behavioural	**c.1970** Systemic
Year 2009					
	e.g., Therapeutic residential schools	e.g., Contingency management	e.g., Counselling	e.g., Social-skills training	e.g., Trans-disciplinary working
	Nurture Groups	School-wide Behaviour Management Classroom and behaviour management	Student centred approaches Peer co-operation 'Circle Time'	Problem solving Anger Management	Work with parents and families Multi-systemic therapy
	Psycho-dynamic therapies involve the establishment of therapeutic relationships which enable the individual to reveal and explore analytically the life experiences which have influenced the development of dysfunctional ways of thinking and behaving.	**Behavioural** therapies are based on the ways in which behaviour can be understood in terms of involuntary responses to external stimuli. Behavioural interventions exploit this theory by encouraging desired behaviours and extinguishing undesired behaviours through the manipulation of the stimuli which precede target behaviours and the consequences which follow from target behaviours.	**Humanistic** therapies focus on ways in which self-concept is created through social and interpersonal relationships. Interventions based in this approach, such as Rogers's Person-Centred approach, emphasize the therapeutic value of unconditional positive regard, empathy and honesty in relationships.	**Cognitive Behavioural** therapies are concerned with the ways in which the relationship between external stimuli and target behaviours can sometimes be influenced by thought processes. The aim of Cognitive Behavioural therapy is to encourage the development of functional ways of thinking by challenging and changing dysfunctional ways of thinking.	**Systemic** therapies are designed to enable individuals to continue to participate in key social systems (such as families, partnerships and work places) in ways which are functional in relation to their mental health.

Figure AI.1 The evolution of interventions for SEBD in relation to major educational interventions.

From Inclusion to Engagement: Helping Students Engage with Schooling through Policy and Practice
By Paul Cooper and Barbara Jacobs © 2011 John Wiley & Sons, Ltd

Appendix II

Table AII.1 The pattern of provision for students with SEN in Europe and beyond.

SEN provision and support	Countries where this pattern of provision is to be found
Special schools	Austria, Belgium, Cyprus, England, Germany, Greece, Ireland, Liechtenstein, Lithuania, Malta, Netherlands, Switzerland, United States
Other off-site provision (e.g., PRUs, hospital schools/educational units, unspecified)	England, Ireland, Malta, United States
Specialist services from different disciplines (e.g., teachers, health professionals, social services, educational psychologists)	Australia, Austria, Belgium, Canada, Cyprus, Czech Republic, Denmark, England, Finland, France, Germany, Iceland, Ireland, Italy, Lithuania, Luxembourg, Malta, Norway, Poland,, Portugal, Spain, Sweden, United States
Remedial teachers	Belgium, Iceland, Ireland, Lithuania
External Special Educational Needs coordinator	Cyprus, Ireland
In-school Special Educational Needs coordinator	England
Pupil welfare team	Finland
Pupil support group	

(Source: *European Agency for Development of Special Needs Education. Special Needs Education in Europe: Thematic Publication, 2003*)

Table AII.2 Mainstream support for SEN in Europe and beyond.

Support for students with SEN in mainstream schools is provided by	Countries where this pattern of support is to be found
Special classes (e.g., nurture groups, learning support units)	Canada, England, Malta, United States, New Zealand
Specialist teachers from special schools	Austria, Belgium, Cyprus, England, Germany, Greece, Liechtenstein, Lithuania, Netherlands, Switzerland
Visiting professionals from specialist services, including peripatetic specialist teachers	Austria, Belgium, Cyprus, Czech Republic, Denmark, England, Finland, France, Germany, Iceland, Ireland, Italy, Lithuania, Luxembourg, Malta, Norway, Poland, Portugal, Spain, Sweden, United States
In-school specialist teachers	
Remedial teachers	Belgium, Iceland, Ireland, Lithuania
External SEN coordinators	Cyprus
SEN coordinator	England, Ireland
Pupil welfare teams	Finland
Pupil support groups	

References

Abbott, R.D., O'Donnell, J., Hawkins, J.D. *et al.* (1998) Changing teaching practices to promote achievement and bonding to school. *The American Journal of Orthopsychiatry*, 68, 542–552.

Abramowitz, A.J., O'Leary, S.G., and Rosén, L.A. (1987) Reducing off-task behavior in the classroom: A comparison of encouragement and reprimands. *Journal of Abnormal Child Psychology*, 15, 2, 153–163.

Acker, M.M., and O'Leary, S.G., (1987) Effects of reprimands and praise on appropriate behavior in the classroom. *Journal of Abnormal Child Psychology*, 15, 4, 549–557.

Adams, C.D., and Drabman, R.S. (1995) Improving morning interactions: Beat-the-Buzzer with a boy having multiple handicaps. *Child and Family Behavior Therapy*, 17, 3, 13–26.

Agathon, M., and Granjus, M., (1976) Behavior modification of a character disorder. *Perspectives Psychiatriques*, 27, 58, 1–274.

Ahmed, E., and Braithwaite, V., (2006) Forgiveness, reconciliation, and shame: Three key variables in reducing school bullying. *Journal of Social Issues*, 62, 2, 347–370.

Ali, D., Daud A., Best, C. *et al.* 1997. *Behaviour in Schools: A Framework for Intervention*, Birmingham Education Department, Birmingham, UK.

Allsopp, D.H. (1997) Using classwide peer tutoring to teach beginning algebra problem-solving skills in heterogeneous classrooms. *Remedial and Special Education*, 18, 6, 367–379.

Altepeter, T., and Korger, J. (1999) Disruptive behaviour: Oppositional defiance and conduct disorder, in *Child and Adolescent Psychological Disorders*, (eds S. Netherton, D. Holmes and E. Walker), New York: Oxford University Press, pp. 118–138.

Amato-Zech, N.A., Hoff, K.E., and Doepke, K.J. (2006) Increasing on-task behavior in the classroom: Extension of self-monitoring strategies. *Psychology in the Schools*, 43, 2, 211–221.

American Psychiatric Association (APA) (2007) *Diagnostic and Statistical Manual of Mental Disorders*, 4th edn, APA, Washington DC.

Amos, P.A. (2004) New considerations in the prevention of aversives, restraint, and seclusion: Incorporating the role of relationships into an ecological perspective. *Research and Practice for Persons with Severe Disabilities*, 29, 4, 263–272.

Ancess, J., and Allen, D. (2006) Implementing small theme high schools in New York City: Great intentions and great tensions. *Harvard Educational Review*, 76, 3, 401–416.

Anderson, C.M., and Kincaid, D. (2005) Applying behavior analysis to school violence and discipline problems: Schoolwide positive behavior support. *Behavior Analyst*, 28, 1, 49–63.

Andrews, H.B. (1970) The systematic use of the Premack principle in modifying classroom behaviors. *Child Study Journal*, 1, 2, 74–79.

Angelides, P., and Michailidou, A. (2007) Exploring the role of 'special units' in Cyprus schools: A case study. *International Journal of Special Education*, 22, 2, 87–95.

Artesani, A.J., and Mallar, L. (1998) Positive behavior supports in general education settings: Combining person-centered planning and functional analysis. *Intervention in School and Clinic*, 34, 1, 33–38.

Atkinson, M., and Hornby, G. (2002) *Mental Health Handbook for Schools*, Routledge-Falmer, London.

Babyak, A.E., Koorland, M., and Mathes, P.G. (2000) The effects of story mapping instruction on the reading comprehension of students with behavioral disorders. *Behavioral Disorders*, 25, 239–258.

Baer, D.M., Wolf, M.M., and Risley, T.R. 1968. Some current dimensions of applied Behavioral analysis. *Journal of Applied Behavioral Analysis*, 1, 1, 91–97.

Baker, S., Gersten, R., Dimino, J.A., and Griffiths, R. (2004) The Sustained use of research-based instructional practice: A case study of peer-assisted learning strategies in Mathematics. *Remedial and Special Education*, 25, 1, 5–24.

Ballard, J. (1982) *Circletime*, Irvington Publishers, New York.

Barkley, R. (1997) *AD/HD and the Nature of Self Control*, New York, Guilford.

Barnardo's (2006) *Failed By the System*, Barnardo's, London.

Barnhill, G.P. (2005) Functional behavioral assessment in schools. *Intervention in School and Clinic*, 40, 3, 131–143.

Baron-Cohen, S., Leslie, A.M., and Frith, U. 1985. Does the autistic child have a "theory of mind"? *Cognition*, 21, 1, 37–46.

Barrett, S.B., Bradshaw, C.P., and Lewis-Palmer, T. (2008) Maryland statewide PBIS initiative: Systems, evaluation, and next steps. *Journal of Positive Behavior Interventions*, 10, 2, 105–114.

Barrett, P.M., Farrell, L.J., Ollendick, T.H., and Dadds, M. (2006) Long-term outcomes of an Australian universal prevention trial of anxiety and depression symptoms in children and youth: An evaluation of the friends program. *Journal of Clinical Child and Adolescent Psychology*, 35, 3, 403–411.

Barrett, P.M., Lowry-Webster, H., and Turner, C.M. (1999) *FRIENDS for Children Group Leader Manual*, Australian Academic Press, Brisbane.

Barrett, P.M., and Turner, C.M. (2001) Prevention of anxiety symptoms in primary school children: Preliminary results from a universal school-based trial. *British Journal of Clinical Psychology*, 40, 399–410.

Barrish, H.H., Saunders, M., and Wolf, M.W. 1969. Good behavior game: Effects of individual contingencies for group consequences on disruptive behavior in a classroom. *Journal of Applied Behavior Analysis*, 2, 119–124.

Barth, J.M., Dunlap, S.T., Dane, H. *et al.* (2004) Classroom environment influences on aggression, peer relations, and academic focus. *Journal of School Psychology*, 42, 2, 115–133.

Barton, L. (2005) Response to Warnock M: Special needs: A new look. www.leeds.ac.uk/disability-studies/archiveuk/barton/Warnock.pdf (avvessed September 28, 2010).

Barton-Arwood, S.M., Wehby, J.H., and Falk, K.B. (2005) Reading instruction for elementary-age students with emotional and behavioral disorders: Academic and behavioral outcomes. *Exceptional Children*, 72, 1, 7–27.

Bateson, G., 1970. *Steps to an Ecology of Mind*, Aronson, New York.

Battistich, V., Solomon, D., Watson, M., *et al.* 1989. Effects of an elementary school program to enhance prosocial behavior on children's cognitive-social problem-solving skills and strategies. *Journal of Applied Developmental Psychology*, 10, 2, 147–169.

Baumann, J.F. (1984) Implications for reading instruction from research on teacher and school effectiveness. *Journal of Reading*, 28, 109–115.

Becker, B.J., Kennedy, M.M., and Hundersmarck, S. (2003) Communities of scholars, research, and debates about teacher quality. The Meeting of the American Educational Research Association, Chicago, April.

Beersma, B., Hollenbeck, J.R., Humphrey, S.E. *et al.* (2003) Cooperation, competition, and team performance: Toward a contingency approach. *Academy of Management Journal*, 46, 5, 572–590.

Benard, B. (1995) *Fostering Resilience in Children*, West Ed, Oakland, CA.

Benard, B. (2004) *Resiliency. What We Have Learned*, West Ed, Oakland, CA.

Benazzi, L., Horner, R.H., and Good, R.H. (2006) Effects of behavior support team composition on the technical adequacy and contextual fit of behavior support plans. *Journal of Special Education*, 40, 3, 160–170.

Bennathan, M., and Boxall, M. (1996) *Effective Intervention in Primary Schools: Nurture Groups*, Taylor and Francis, Bristol.

Bernstein, B. (1966) Education cannot compensate for society, *New Society*, 387, 344–347.

Bernstein, G.A., Layne, A.E., Egan, E.A., and Tennison, D.M. (2005) School-based interventions for anxious children. *Journal of the American Academy of Child and Adolescent Psychiatry*, 44, 11, 1118–1127.

Bettenhausen, S. (1998) Make proactive modifications to your classroom. *Intervention in School and Clinic*, 33, 3, 182–183.

Bierman, K.L., Coie, J.D., Dodge, K.A. *et al.* (1996) Integrating social-skills training interventions with parent training and family-focused support to prevent conduct disorder in high-risk populations. The Fast Track Multisite Demonstration Project, United States.

Bierman, K.L., Coie, J.D., Dodge, K.A. *et al.* (1997) Implementing a comprehensive program for the prevention of conduct problems in rural communities: The fast track experience. *American Journal of Community Psychology*, 25, 4, 493–514.

Bierman, K.L., Coie, J.D., Dodge, K.A. *et al.* (2000) Merging universal and indicated prevention programs: The fast track model. *Addictive Behaviors*, 25, 6, 913–927.

Bierman, K.L., Coie, J.D., Dodge, K.A. *et al.* (2002a) The implementation of the Fast Track program: An example of a large-scale prevention science efficacy trial. *Journal of Abnormal Child Psychology*, 30, 1, 1–17.

Bierman, K.L., Coie, J.D., Dodge, K.A. *et al.* (2002b) Evaluation of the first 3 years of the Fast Track prevention trial with children at high risk for adolescent conduct problems. *Journal of Abnormal Child Psychology*, 30, 1, 19–35.

Bierman, K.L., Coie, J.D., Dodge, K.A. *et al.* (2002c) Using the Fast Track randomized prevention trial to test the early-starter model of the development of serious conduct problems. *Development and Psychopathology*, 14, 4, 925–943.

Bierman, K.L., Coie, J.D., Dodge, K.A. *et al.* (2002d) Evaluation of the first 3 years of the Fast Track prevention trial with children at high risk for adolescent conduct problems. *Journal of Abnormal Child Psychology*, 30, 1, 19–35.

Bierman, K.L., Coie, J.D., Dodge, K.A. *et al.* (2004) The effects of the Fast Track program on serious problem outcomes at the end of elementary school. *Journal of Clinical Child and Adolescent Psychology*, 33, 4, 650–661.

Bierman, K.L., Coie, J.D., Dodge, K.A. *et al.* (2007) Fast track randomized controlled trial to prevent externalizing psychiatric disorders: Findings from grades 3 to 9. *Journal of the American Academy of Child and Adolescent Psychiatry*, 46, 10, 1250–1262.

Bierman, K.L., Nix, R.L., Maples, J.J. *et al.* (2006) Examining clinical judgment in an adaptive intervention design: The Fast Track program. *Journal of Consulting and Clinical Psychology*, 74, 3, 468–481.

Bifulco, R., Duncombe, W., and Yinger, J. (2005) Does whole-school reform boost student performance? The case of New York City. *Journal of Policy Analysis and Management*, 24, 1, 47–72.

Binnie, L.M., and Allen, K. (2008) Whole school support for vulnerable children: The evaluation of a part-time nurture group. *Emotional and Behavioural Difficulties*, 13, 3, 201–216.

Bishop, A., and Swain, J. (2000a) The bread, the jam and some coffee in the morning: Perceptions of a nurture group. *Emotional and Behavioural Difficulties*, 5, 3, 18–24.

Bishop, A., and Swain, J. (2000b) Early years education and children with behavioural and emotional difficulties: Nurturing parental involvement. *Emotional and Behavioural Difficulties*, 5, 4, 26–31.

Blatchford, P., Bassett, P., Brown, P. *et al.* (2009) *The Deployment and Impact of Support Staff in Schools*, DCSF, London.

Blood, E., and Neel, R.S. (2007) From FBA to implementation: A look at what is actually being delivered. *Education and Treatment of Children*, 30, 4, 67–80.

Bloomquist, M.L., August, G.J., and Ostrander, R. 1991. Effects of a school-based cognitive-behavioral intervention for ADHD children. *Journal of Abnormal Child Psychology*, 19, 5, 591–605.

Bond, L., Glover, S., Godfrey, C. *et al.* (2001) Building capacity for system-level change in schools: Lessons from the gatehouse project. *Health Education and Behavior*, 28, 3, 368–383.

Bond, L., Patton, G., Glover, S. *et al.* (2004b) The Gatehouse Project: Can a multilevel school intervention affect emotional wellbeing and health risk behaviours? *Journal of Epidemiology and Community Health*, 58, 12, 997–1003.

Bond, L., Thomas, L., Coffey, C. *et al.* (2004a) Long-term impact of the gatehouse project on cannabis use of 16-year-olds in Australia. *Journal of School Health*, 74, 1, 23–29.

Boorn, C. (2002) Locating a nurture group: Identifying and evaluating features within a school that would make a suitable host, unpublished MSc thesis, University of Sheffield.

Booth, T., and Ainscow, M. (1997) *From Them to Us*, Routledge, London.

Bor, W., Sanders, M.R., and Markie-Dadds, C. (2002) The effects of the triple P-positive parenting program on preschool children with co-occurring disruptive behavior and attentional/hyperactive difficulties. *Journal of Abnormal Child Psychology*, 30, 6, 571–587.

Boreham, N., Peers, I., Farrell, P., and Craven, D. (1995) Different perspectives of parents and educational psychologists when a child is referred for assessment, in *Children with EBD: Strategies for assessment and Intervention*, (ed. Farrell, P.) Falmer, Lewes, UK, pp. 17–33.

Borman, G.D., and Hewes, G.M. (2002) The long-term effects and cost-effectiveness of success for all. *Educational Evaluation and Policy Analysis*, 24, 4, 243–266.

Borman, G.D., Slavin, R.E., and Cheung, A.C.K. (2007) Final reading outcomes of the national randomized field trial of Success for All. *American Educational Research Journal*, 44, 3, 701–731.

Borman, G.D., Slavin, R.E., Cheung, A. *et al.* (2005a) Success for all: First-year results from the national randomized field trial. *Educational Evaluation and Policy Analysis*, 27, 1, 1–22.

Borman, G.D., Slavin, R.E., Cheung, A. *et al.* (2005b) The national randomized field trial of success for all: Second-year outcomes. *American Educational Research Journal*, 42, 4, 673–696.

Bowers, F.E., Woods, D.W., Carlyon, W.D., and Friman, P.C. (2000) Using positive peer reporting to improve the social interactions and acceptance of socially isolated adolescents in residential care: A systematic replication. *Journal of Applied Behavior Analysis*, 33, 2, 239–242.

Bowers, T. (2004) The forgotten 'E' in EBD, in (eds P. Clough, P. Garner, J. Pardeck and F. Yuen), *Handbook of Emotional and Behavioural Difficulties*, (eds P. Clough, P. Garner, J. Pardeck and F. Yuen), Sage, London, pp. 83–120.

Bowles, S., and Gintis, H. (1971) *Schooling in Capitalist America: Educational Reform and the Contradictions of Economic Life*, Basic Books, New York.

Bowman-Perrott, L.J., Greenwood, C.R., and Tapia, Y. (2007) The efficacy of CWPT used in secondary alternative school classrooms with small teacher/pupil ratios and students with emotional and behavioral disorders. *Education and Treatment of Children*, 30, 3, 65–87.

Boxmeyer, C.L., Lochman, J.E., Powell, N. *et al.* (2007) A case study of the coping power program for angry and aggressive youth. *Journal of Contemporary Psychotherapy*, 37, 3, 165–174.

BPS (British Psychological Society) (2000) *AD/HD: Guidelines and Principles for Successful Multi-Agency Working*, BPS, Leicester.

Brestan, E.V., and Eyberg, S.M. (1998) Effective psychosocial treatments of conduct-disordered children and adolescents: 29 years, 82 studies, and 5,272 kids. *Journal of Clinical Child Psychology*, 27, 2, 180–189.

Bridgeland, M. (1971) *Pioneer Work with Maladjusted Children*, Staples, London.

British Medical Association (2006) *Child and Adolescent Mental Health – A Guide for Healthcare Professionals*. BMA, London.

Bronfenbrenner, U. (1979) *The Ecology of Human Development*, Harvard University Press, Cambridge MA.

Browder, D.M., Hines, C., McCarthy, L.J., and Fees, J. (1984) A treatment package for increasing sight word recognition for use in daily living skills. *Education and Training of the Mentally Retarded*, 19, 3, 191–200.

Brown, N., and Redmon, W.K. (1989) The effects of a group reinforcement contingency on staff use of unscheduled sick leave. *Journal of Organizational Behavior Management*, 10, 3–17.

Burn, M. (1956) *Mr Lyward's Answer*, Hamish Hamilton, London.

Burssens, D., and Vettenburg, N. (2006) Restorative group conferencing at school: A constructive response to serious incidents. *Journal of School Violence*, 5, 2, 5–17.

Buyse, E., Verschueren, K., Doumen, S. *et al.* (2008) Classroom problem behavior and teacher-child relationships in kindergarten: The moderating role of classroom climate. *Journal of School Psychology*, 46, 4, 367–391.

Byrne, M., and Barry, M. (2003) *Lifeskills MindMatters Report on the Evaluation of a Mental Health Promotion Programme for Post-Primary Schools*, Centre for Health Promotion Studies, the National University of Ireland, Galway, Ireland.

Cajkler, W., Tennant, G., Tiknaz, Y. *et al.* (2007) A systematic literature review on the perceptions of ways in which teaching assistants work to support pupils' social and academic engagement in secondary classrooms (1988–2005). *Research Evidence in*

Education Library, EPPI-Centre, Social Science Research Unit, Institute of Education, University of London.

Callahan, K., Rademacher, J.A., and Hildreth, B.L. (1998) The effect of parent participation in strategies to improve the homework performance of students who are at risk. *Remedial and Special Education,* 19, 3, 131–141.

Canter, L., and Canter, M. (1976) *Assertive Discipline: A Take-Charge Approach for Today's Educator.* Canter and Associates, Los Angeles.

Carbonneau, R., Vitaro, F., and Tremblay, R.E. (2001) Prevention of anti-social behavior in high-risk boys: The Montreal longitudinal and experimental study. In Manuela Martinez, International Society for Research on Aggression World Meeting, Prevention and Control of Aggression and the Impact on its Victims: Proceedings of the XIV World Meeting for Research on Aggression, July 9–14 Valencia, Spain, Springer, New York, pp. 121–127.

Carter, I. N., and Shostak, D. A. (1980) Imitation in the treatment of the hyperkinetic behaviour syndrome, *Journal of Clinical Child & Adolescent Psychology,* 9, Issue 1, Spring, 63–66.

Carter, K., and Doyle, W. (2006) Classroom management in early childhood and elementary classrooms, in *Handbook of Classroom Management: Research Practice and Contemporary Issues,* (eds C. Everston and C. Weinstein), Lawrence Erlbaum Associates, London, pp. 373–406.

Casella, R. (2003) Zero tolerance policy in schools: Rationale, consequences, and alternatives. *Teachers College Record,* 105, 5, 872–892.

Cassidy, S. (2008) Education under fire: Fears over teaching standards push parents to private sector, *The Independent,* June 5, www.independent.co.uk/news/education/education-news/education-under-fire-fears-over-teaching-standards-push-parents-to-private-sector–840522.html (accessed September 28, 2010).

Cefai, C. (2007) Resilience for all: A study of classrooms as protective contexts. *Emotional and Behaviour Difficulties,* 12, 2, 119–134.

Cefai, C. (2008) *Promoting Resilience in the Classroom. A Guide to Developing Pupils' Emotional and Cognitive Skills,* Jessica Kingsley Publishers, London.

Cefai, C., Cooper, P., and Camillieri, L., (2008) *Engagement Time: A National Study of students with SEBD in Maltese Schools,* University of Malta, Malta.

Chambers, B., Cheung, A.C.K., Madden, N.A. *et al.* (2006) Achievement effects of embedded multimedia in a success for all reading program. *Journal of Educational Psychology,* 98, 1, 232–237.

Chambers, B., Slavin, R.E., Madden, N.A. *et al.* (2008) Technology infusion in success for all: Reading outcomes for first graders. *Elementary School Journal,* 109, 1, 1–15.

Chandler, L.K., Dahlquist, C.M., Repp, A.C., and Feltz, C. (1999) The effects of team-based functional assessment on the behavior of students in classroom settings. *Exceptional Children,* 66, 1, 101–122.

Charlton, T., and David, K. (1990) Towards a whole school approach, helping to ensure the schools are fit for the future. *Links,* 15, 3, 20–24.

Cheney, D., Flower, A., and Templeton, T. (2008) Applying response to intervention metrics in the social domain for students at risk of developing emotional or behavioral disorders. *Journal of Special Education,* 42, 2, 108–126.

Clarke, S., Dunlap, G., Foster-Johnson, L. *et al.* (1995) Improving the conduct of students with behavioral disorders by incorporating student interests into curricular activities. *Behavioral Disorders,* 20, 221–237.

Clondalkin Partnership (2006) *Incredible Years Basic Parenting Programme,* Clondalkin Partnership, Dublin.

Coard, B. (1971) *How the West Indian Child is Made Educationally Sub Normal by the British School System*, New Beacon Books, London.

Cole, T. (1986) *Residential Special Education*, Open University Press, Buckingham, UK.

Cole, T., Visser, J., and Daniels, H. (2000) *The Framework for Intervention: Identifying and Promoting Effective Practice*, Birmingham Education Department, Birmingham, UK.

Cole, T., Visser, J., and Upton, G. (1998) *Effective Schools for Pupils with EBD*, Fulton, London.

Cook, C.R., Crews, S.D., Wright, D.B. *et al.* (2007) Establishing and evaluating the substantive adequacy of positive behavioral support plans. *Journal of Behavioral Education*, 16, 3, 191–206.

Cooke, M.B., Ford, J., Levine, J. *et al.* (2007) The effects of city-wide implementation of "Second Step" on elementary school students' prosocial and aggressive behaviors. *Journal of Primary Prevention*, 28, 2, 93–115.

Cooper, J.O., Heron, T.E., and Hereward, W.L. (1987) *Applied Behavior Analysis*, Prentice Hall, New York.

Cooper, P. (1989) Respite, relationships and re-signification: The effects of residential schooling on students with emotional and behavioural difficulties. Unpublished PhD thesis, University of Birmingham, Birmingham, UK.

Cooper, P. (1993) *Effective Schools for Disaffected Students*, Routledge, London.

Cooper, P. (1996) Giving it a name: The value of descriptive categories in educational approaches to emotional and behavioural difficulties, Support for Learning, 11, 4, 146–150.

Cooper, P. (1997) Biology, behaviour and education: coming to terms with the challenge of Attention Deficit/Hyperactivity Disorder. *Education and Child Psychology*, 14, 1, 31–38.

Cooper, P. (2006) Supporting minority ethnic children and adolescents with social, emotional and behavioural difficulties in the United Kingdom. *Preventing School Failure*, 50, 2, 21–28.

Cooper, P., Arnold, R., and Boyd, E. (2001) Evaluation of nurture group provision in an English LEA. Unpublished research report, University of Leicester.

Cooper, P, Drummond, M, Hart, S, *et al.* (2000), *Positive Alternatives to Exclusion*, Routledge, London.

Cooper, P., and Ideus, K. (1996) *ADHD: a Practical Guide for Teachers*, Fulton, London.

Cooper, P., and Lovey, J. (1999) Early intervention in emotional and behavioural difficulties: The role of NGs. *European Journal of Special Needs Education*, 14, 2, 122–131.

Cooper, P., and Mcintyre, D. (1996) *Effective Teaching and Learning: Teachers' and Students' Perspectives*, Open University Press, Milton Keynes.

Cooper, P, and O'Regan, F. (2001) *ADHD: A Manual for Teachers*, Routledge, London.

Cooper, P., and Shea, T. (1999) AD/HD From the inside: An empirical study of young people's perceptions of the experience of AD/HD, in *ADHD: Research, Practice and Opinion*, (ed. P. Cooper and K. Bilton), Whurr, London, pp. 223–246.

Cooper, P., Smith, C., and Upton, G. (1994) *Emotional and Behavioural Difficulties – Theory to Practice*, Routledge, London.

Cooper, P., and Tiknaz, Y. (2005) Progress and challenge in nurture groups: Evidence from three case studies. *British Journal of Special Education*, 32, 4, 211–222.

Cooper, P., and Tiknaz, Y. (2007) *Nurture Groups at Home and in School: Connecting with Children with Social, Emotional and Behavioural Difficulties*, Jessica Kingsley Publishers, London.

Cooper, P., and Upton, G. 1990. An ecosystemic approach to emotional and behavioural difficulties in schools. *Educational Psychology*, 10, 4, 301–321.

Cooper, P., and Whitebread, D. (2007) The effectiveness of nurture groups on student progress: Evidence from a national research study. *Emotional and Behavioural Difficulties*, 12, 3, 171–190.

Corkum, P.V., Mullane, J.C., and Mckinnon, M.M. (2005) The effect of involving classroom teachers in a parent training program for families of children with ADHD. *Child & Family Behavior Therapy*, 27, 4, 29–49.

Correnti, R., and Rowan, B. (2007) Opening up the black box: Literacy instruction in schools participating in three comprehensive school reform programs. *American Educational Research Journal*, 44, 2, 298–338.

Cotton, K. (2001) New small learning communities: Findings from recent literature. www.smallschoolsproject.org/PDFS/kathleen_cotton_summary.pdf (accessed September 28, 2010).

Cowie, H., and Hutson, N. (2005) Peer support: A strategy to help bystanders challenge school bullying. *Pastoral Care in Education*, 23, 22, 40–44.

Cowie, H., Hutson, N., Jennifer, D., and Myers, C.A. (2008a) Taking stock of violence in U.K. schools: Risk, regulation, and responsibility. *Education and Urban Society*, 40, 4, 494–505.

Cowie, H., Hutson, N., Oztug, O., and Myers, C. (2008b) The impact of peer support schemes on pupils' perceptions of bullying, aggression and safety at school. *Emotional and Behavioural Difficulties*, 13, 1, 63–71.

Cowie, H., Naylor, P., Chauhan, L.T.P., and Smith, P.K. (2002) Knowledge, use of and attitudes towards peer support: A 2-year follow-up to the Prince's Trust survey. *Journal of Adolescence*, 25, 5, 453–467.

Cowie, H., and Olafsson, R. (2000) The role of peer support in helping the victims of bullying in a school with high levels of aggression. *School Psychology International*, 21, 1, 79–95.

CPPRG (1999a) Initial impact of the fast track prevention trial for conduct problems: I. The high-risk sample. *Journal of Consulting and Clinical Psychology*, 67, 5, 631–647.

CPPRG (1999b) Initial impact of the fast track prevention trial for conduct problems: II. Classroom effects. *Journal of Consulting and Clinical Psychology*, 67, 5, 648–657.

Cremin, H. (2002) Circle Time: Why it doesn't always work. *Journal of National Primary Trust*, 30, 23–29.

Criss, M.M., Pettit, G.S., Bates, J.E. *et al.* (2002) Family adversity, positive peer relationships, and children's externalizing behavior: a longitudinal perspective on risk and resilience. *Child Development*, 73, 4, 1220–1237.

Cronk, K. (1987) *Teacher-pupil Conflict in Secondary Schools*, Falmer, Lewes, UK.

Crosnoe, R., and Elder, G. (2004) Family dynamics, supportive relationships, and educational resilience during adolescence. *Journal of Family Issues*, 25, 5, 571–602.

Cunningham, C.C., and Davis, H. (1985) Working with Parents: Frameworks for Collaboration, Open University Press, Buckingham.

Cunningham, C.E., Bremner, R., and Boyle, M. 1995. Large group community-based parenting programs for families of preschoolers at risk for disruptive behaviour disorders: Utilization, cost effectiveness, and outcome. *Journal of Child Psychology and Psychiatry and Allied Disciplines*, 36, 7, 1141–1159.

Cunningham, H. (2006) *The Invention of Childhood*, BBC Books, London.

Curcic, S. (2009) Inclusion in the PK-12 and international perspective. *International Journal of Inclusive Education*, 13, 5, 517–538.

Dale, N. (1996) *Working with Families of Children with Special Educational Needs: Partnership and Practice*, Routledge, London.

Damon, W. (1984) Peer education: The untapped potential. *Journal of Applied Developmental Psychology*, 5, 4, 331–343.

Daniels, H., Cole, T., and Reykebill, N. (1999) *Emotional and Behavioural Difficulties in Mainstream Schools*, DfEE, London.

Darling-Hammond, L., Ancess, J., and Ort, S.W. (2002) Reinventing high school: Outcomes of the Coalition Campus Schools Project. *American Educational Research Journal*, 39, 3, 639–673.

Datnow, A., and Castellano, M. (2000) Teachers' responses to success for all: How beliefs, experiences, and adaptations shape implementation. *American Educational Research Journal*, 37, 3, 775–799.

Davies, S., and Witte, R. (2000) Self-management and peer-monitoring within a group contingency to decrease uncontrolled verbalizations of children with attention-deficit/hyperactivity disorder. *Psychology in the Schools*, 37, 2, 135–147.

Dawson, R. (1981) The place of four pioneer tenets in modern practice and opinion. *New Growth*, 1, 2, 44–47.

DCSF (2005) *Learning and Behaviour* (Steer Report), DCSF, London.

DCSF (2008) *Children in Mind: The Final Report of the National CAHMs Review*, Dscf, London.

De Castro, B., Bosch, J., Veerman, J., and Koops, W. (2003) The effects of emotion regulation, attribution and delay prompts on aggressive boys' social problem solving. *Cognitive Therapy and Research*, 27, 2, 153–166.

De Shazar, S. (1985) *Keys to Solution*, Norton, New York.

Degarmo, D.S., Patterson, G.R., and Forgatch, M.S. (2004) How do outcomes in a specified parent training intervention maintain or wane over time? *Prevention Science*, 5, 2, 73–89.

Delquadri, J., Greenwood, C.R., Whorton, D. *et al.* (1986) Classwide peer tutoring. *Exceptional Children*, 52, 6, 535–542.

DES (1989) *Discipline in Schools* (The Elton Report), DES, London.

DfES (2003) *Every Child Matters*, HMSO, London.

DfES (2004) Five Year Strategy for Children and Learners, DfES, London.

Dion, E., Fuchs, D., and Fuchs, L.S. (2005) Differential effects of peer-assisted learning strategies on students' social preference and friendship making. *Behavioral Disorders*, 30, 4, 421–429.

Dishion, T.J., McCord, J., and Poulin, F. (1999) When interventions harm: Peer groups and problem behavior. *American Psychologist*, 54, 9, 755–764.

Dolan, L.J., Kellam, S.G., Brown, C.H *et al.* 1993. The short-term impact of two classroom-based preventive interventions on aggressive and shy behaviors and poor achievement. *Journal of Applied Developmental Psychology*, 14, 3, 317–345.

Doolittle, J.H., Horner, R.H., Bradley, R. *et al.* (2007) Importance of student social behavior in the mission statements, personnel preparation standards, and innovation efforts of state departments of education. *Journal of Special Education*, 40, 4, 239–245.

Douglas, J. (1964) *Half Our Future*, Unwin, London.

Douglas, J., Ross, J., and Simpson, H. (1971) *All our Future*, Palmer, London.

Doyle, R. (2001) Using a readiness scale for reintegrating pupils with social, emotional and behavioural difficulties from a Nurture Group into their mainstream classroom: A pilot study. *British Journal of Special Education*, 28, 3, 126–132.

Drabman, R.S., and Creedon, D.L. (1979) Beat the buzzer. *Child Behavior Therapy*, 1, 295–296.

Drewery, W. (2004) Conferencing in schools: Punishment, restorative justice, and the productive importance of the process of conversation. *Journal of Community and Applied Social Psychology*, 14, 5, 332–344.

Dubey, D. R., and O'Leary, S. G. (1975) Increasing reading comprehension of two hyperactive children: preliminary investigation, *Perceptual and Motor Skills*, 41, 691–694.

Dukes, C., and Lamar-Dukes, P. (2007) Conceptualizing special education services in small learning communities. *Urban Education*, 42, 5, 412–431.

Dumas, J.E., and Wahler, R.G. (1983) Predictors of treatment outcome in parent training: mother insularity and socioeconomic disadvantage. *Behavioral Assessment*, 5, 4, 301–313.

Dunlap, G., Strain, P.S., Fox, L. *et al.* (2006) Prevention and intervention with young children's challenging behavior: Perspectives regarding current knowledge. *Behavioral Disorders*, 32, 1, 29–45.

DuPaul, G.J., and Henningson, P.N. (1993) Peer Tutoring effects on the classroom performance of children with Attention Deficit Hyperactivity Disorder. *School Psychology Review*, 22, 1, 134–143.

DuPaul, G., and Stoner, G. (1995) *ADHD in The Schools*, Guilford, New York.

EADSNE (European Agency for Development in Special Needs Education) (2003) *Special Education Across Europe in 2003: Trends in Provision in 18 European Countries*, EADSNE, Middelfart, Denmark.

Eargle, A.E., Guerra, N.G., and Tolan, P.H. (1994) Preventing aggression in inner-city children: Small group training to change cognitions, social skills, and behavior. *Journal of Child and Adolescent Group Therapy*, 4, 4, 229–242.

Educational Testing Service (ETS) (2005) Towards inequality: Disturbing trends in Higher Education, www.ets.org/research/policy_research_reports/pic-inequality (accessed September 28, 2010).

Elias, C.L., and Berk, L.E. (2002) Self-regulation in young children: Is there a role for sociodramatic play? *Early Childhood Research Quarterly*, 17, 2, 216–238.

Elias, M.J. (2004) The connection between social-emotional learning and learning disabilities: Implications for intervention. *Learning Disability Quarterly*, 27, 1, 53–63.

Elias, M.J., and Weissberg, R.P. (2000) Primary prevention: Educational approaches to enhance social and emotional learning. *Journal of School Health*, 70, 5, 186–190.

Elias, M.J., Zins, J.E., Graczyk, P.A., and Weissberg, R.P. (2003) Implementation, Sustainability, and Scaling up of Social-Emotional and Academic Innovations in Public Schools. *School Psychology Review*, 32, 3, 303–319.

Embry, D.D. (2002) The Good Behavior Game: A best practice candidate as a universal behavioral vaccine. *Clinical Child and Family Psychology Review*, 5, 4, 273–297.

Embry, D.D. (2004) Community-based prevention using simple, low-cost, evidence-based kernels and behavior vaccines. *Journal of Community Psychology*, 32, 5, 575–591.

Embry, D.D., and Biglan, A. (2008) Evidence-based kernels: Fundamental units of behavioral influence. *Clinical Child and Family Psychology Review*, 11, 75–113.

Embry, D.D., Flannery, D.J., Vazsonyi, A.T. *et al.* (1996) PeaceBuilders: A theoretically driven, school-based model for early violence prevention. *American Journal of Preventative Medicine*, 12, 91–91.

Epstein, J.L., and Sheldon, S.B. (2002) Present and accounted for: Improving student attendance through family and community involvement. *Journal of Educational Research*, 95, 5, 308–318.

Eron, L., Huesmann, R., Spindler, A., Guerra, N., Henry, D., Tolan, P., and Vanacker, R. (2002) A cognitive-ecological approach to preventing aggression in urban settings: Initial outcomes for high-risk children. *Journal of Consulting and Clinical Psychology*, 70, 1, 179–194.

Ervin, R.A., Miller, P.M., and Friman, P.C. (1996) Feed the hungry bee: Using positive peer reports to improve the social interactions and acceptance of a socially rejected girl in residential care. *Journal of Applied Behavior Analysis*, 29, 2, 251–253.

Eyberg, S.M., Edwards, D., Boggs, S.R., and Foote, R. (1998) Maintaining the treatment effects of parent training: The role of booster sessions and other maintenance strategies. *Clinical Psychology: Science and Practice*, 5, 4, 544–554.

Eyberg, S.M., Nelson, M.M., and Boggs, S.R. (2008) Evidence-based psychosocial treatments for children and adolescents with disruptive behavior. *Journal of Clinical Child and Adolescent Psychology*, 37, 1, 215–237.

Fabiano, G.A., Pelham, W.E., Manos, M.J. *et al.* (2004) An evaluation of three time-out procedures for children with attention deficit/hyperactivity disorder. *Behavior Therapy*, 35, 3, 449–469.

Falk, K.B., and Wehby, J.H. (2000) The effects of peer-assisted learning strategies on the beginning reading skills of young children with emotional or behavioral disorders. *Behavioral Disorders*, 26, 4, 344–359.

Farrell, P., and Ainscow, M. (2002) eds, *Making Special Education Inclusive*, David Fulton, London.

Farrell, P., and Polat, F. (2003) The long-term impact of residential provision for pupils with emotional and behavioural difficulties. *European Journal of Special Needs Education*, 18, 3, 277–292.

Farrington, D.P., and Welsh, B.C. (2003) Family-based prevention of offending: A meta-analysis. *Australian and New Zealand Journal of Criminology*, 36, 2, 127–151.

Feindler, E.L., Marriott, S.A., and Iwata, M. 1984. Group anger control training for junior high school delinquents. *Cognitive Therapy and Research*, 8, 3, 299–311.

Felner, R.D., Seitsinger, A.M., Brand, S. *et al.* (2007) Creating small learning communities: Lessons from the project on high-performing learning communities about "what works" in creating productive, developmentally enhancing, learning contexts. *Educational Psychologist*, 42, 4, 209–221.

Filter, K.J., Mckenna, M.K., Benedict, E.A. *et al.* (2007) Check in/ check out: A post-hoc evaluation of an efficient, secondary-level targeted intervention for reducing problem behaviors in schools. *Education and Treatment of Children*, 30, 1, 69–84.

Fishbein, J.E., and Wasik, B.H. 1981. Effect of the good behavior game on disruptive library behavior. *Journal of Applied Behavior Analysis*, 14, 89–93.

Fitzgerald, M., Bellgrove, M., and Gill, M. (eds) (2007) *Handbook of ADHD*, Wiley, Chichester.

Flem, A., Moen, T., and Gudmundsdottir, S. (2004) Towards inclusive schools: A study of inclusive education in practice. *European Journal of Special Needs Education*, 19, 1, 85–98.

Fleming, C.B., Haggerty, K.P., Catalano, R.F. *et al.* (2005) Do social and behavioral characteristics targeted by preventive interventions predict standardized test scores and grades? *Journal of School Health*, 75, 9, 342–349.

Florian, L. (2008) Special or inclusive education: Future trends. *British Journal of Special Education*, 35, 4, 202.

Foley, R.M., and Epstein, M.H. 1993. A structured instructional system for developing the school survival skills of adolescents with behavioral disorders. *Behavioral Disorders*, 18, 139–147.

Fonagy, P., and Kurtz, A. (2002) Disturbance of conduct, in *What Works for Whom?* (eds P. Fonagy, M. Target, D. Cottrell, J *et al.*), Guilford, New York, pp. 106–114.

Fonagy, P., Target, M., Cottrell, D. *et al.* (2002) *What Works for Whom? A Critical Review of Treatments for Children and Adolescents*, Guilford, New York.

Forehand, R., and Kotchick, B.A. (2002) Behavioral parent training: Current challenges and potential solutions. *Journal of Child and Family Studies*, 11, 4, 377–384.

Forehand, R., and Long, N. (1988) Outpatient treatment of the acting out child: Procedures, long term follow-up data, and clinical problems. *Advances in Behaviour Research and Therapy*, 10, 3, 129–177.

Foreman, S.G. (1980) A comparison of cognitive training and response cost procedures in modifying aggressive behavior of elementary school children. *Behavior Therapy*, 11, 594–600.

Foxx, R.M., and Schaeffer, M.H. (1981) A company-based lottery to reduce the personal driving of employees. *Journal of Applied Behavior Analysis*, 14, 273–285.

Frankham, J., Edwards-Kerr, D., Humphrey, N., and Roberts, L. (2007) *School Exclusions: Learning Partnerships Outside Mainstream Education*, Joseph Rowntree Foundation, Manchester.

Freeman, R., Eber, L., Anderson, C., Irvin, L. *et al.* (2006) Building inclusive school cultures using school-wide positive behavior support: Designing effective individual support systems for students with significant disabilities. *Research and Practice for Persons with Severe Disabilities*, 31, 1, 4–17.

Frith, U. (1992) Cognitive development and cognitive deficit. *The Psychologist*, 5, 13–19.

Frölich, J., Döpfner, M., Biegert, H., and Lehmkuhl, G. (2002) Teacher training in the management of children with Attention Deficit Hyperactivity Disorder. *Praxis der Kinderpsychologie und Kinderpsychiatrie*, 51, 6, 494–506.

Fuchs, L.S., Fuchs, D., and Karns, K. (2000a) Enhancing kindergartners' mathematical development: Effects of peer-assisted learning strategies. *Elementary School Journal*, 101, 5, 495–510.

Fuchs, L.S., Fuchs, D., and Kazdan, S. (1999) Effects of peer-assisted learning strategies on high school students with serious reading problems. *Remedial and Special Education*, 20, 5, 309–318.

Fuchs, L.S., Fuchs, D., Kazdan, S., and Allen, S. (2000b) Effects of peer-assisted learning strategies in reading with and without training in elaborated help giving. *Elementary School Journal*, 99, 3, 200–219.

Fuchs, L.S., Fuchs, D., Yazdian, L., and Powell, S.R. (2002) Enhancing first-grade children's mathematical development with peer-assisted learning strategies. *School Psychology Review*, 31, 4, 569–583.

Fullan, M. (1992) *Successful School Improvement*, Open University Press, Milton Keynes.

Gardner, F., Burton, J., and Klimes, I. (2006) Randomised controlled trial of a parenting intervention in the voluntary sector for reducing child conduct problems: Outcomes and mechanisms of change. *Journal of Child Psychology and Psychiatry and Allied Disciplines*, 47, 11, 1123–1132.

Garmezy, N., and Rutter, M. (1983) *Stress, Coping and Development in Children* McGraw-Hill, New York.

Garner, P. (1995) Schools by scoundrels: The views of 'disruptive' pupils in mainstream schools in England and the United States, in *On the Margins: The Educational Experience of 'Problem' Pupils*, (eds M. Lloyds-Smith and J. Davies), Trentham, London.

Ghosh, S., and Chattopadhyay, P.K. (1993) Application of behaviour modification techniques in treatment of attention deficit hyper-activity disorder: A case report. *Indian Journal of Clinical Psychology*, 20, 2, 124–129.

Gibbs, S., and Gardiner, M. (2008) The structure of primary and secondary teachers' attributions for pupils' misbehaviour: A preliminary cross-phase and cross-cultural investigation. *Journal of Research in Special Educational Needs*, 8, 2, 68–77.

Gibson-Klein, J. (1996) *Adolescence: From Crisis to Coping*, Oxford: Butterworth-Heinemann.

Gillies, R.M., and Boyle, M. (2008) Teachers' discourse during cooperative learning and their perceptions of this pedagogical practice. *Teaching and Teacher Education*, 24, 5, 1333–1348.

Ginsburg-Block, M.D., Rohrbeck, C.A., and Fantuzzo, J.W. (2006) A meta-analytic review of social, self-concept, and behavioral outcomes of peer-assisted learning. *Journal of Educational Psychology*, 98, 4, 732–749.

Gladden, R. (1998) The small school movement: A review of the literature, in *Small Schools, Big Imaginations: A Creative Look at Urban Public Schools*, (eds M. Fine and J.I. Somerville), Cross City Campaign for Urban School Reform, Chicago IL, pp. 113–133.

Glass, N. (1999) Sure Start: The development of an early intervention programme for young children in the United Kingdom. *Children & Society*, 13, 4, 257–264.

Gonzalez, M., and Ribes, E. (1975) Reversibility of the reinforcement-punishment function in children. *Revista Mexicana de Analisis de la Conducta*, 1, 1, 55–67.

Gottfredson, D.C. (1986) An empirical test of school-based environmental and individual interventions to reduce the risk of delinquent behavior. *Criminology*, 24, 705–731.

Gottfredson, G.D. (1987) Peer group interventions to reduce the risk of delinquent behavior: A selective review and a new evaluation. *Criminology*, 25, 3, 671–714.

Gray, R., and Francis, E. (2007) The implications of US experiences with early childhood interventions for the UK Sure Start Programme. *Child: Care, Health and Development*, 33, 6, 655–663.

Graziano, A.M., and Diament, D.M. (1992) Parent behavioral training: An examination of the paradigm. *Behavior Modification*, 16, 1, 3–38.

Greenbaum, P.E., Dedrick, R.F., Friedman, R.M. *et al.* (1996) National Adolescent and Child Treatment Study (NACTS): Outcomes for children with serious emotional and behavioral disturbance. *Journal of Emotional and Behavioral Disorders*, 4, 3, 130–146.

Greenberg, M.T., Kusche, C.A., Cook, E.T., and Quamma, J.P. (1995) Promoting emotional competence in school-aged children: The effects of the PATHS curriculum. *Development and Psychopathology*, 7, 117–136.

Greenberg, M.T., Weissberg, R.P., O'Brien, M.U. *et al.* (2003) Enhancing school-based prevention and youth development through coordinated social, emotional, and academic learning. *American Psychologist*, 58, 6/7, 466–474.

Greenhaulgh, P. (1994) *Emotional Growth and Learning*, Routledge, London.

Greenhill, L.L., and Ford, R.E. (2002) Childhood attention-deficit hyperactivity disorder: Pharmacological treatments, in *A Guide to Treatments that Work*, (eds P. Nathan and J. Gorman), Oxford University Press, New York, pp. 25–55.

Greenwood, C.R., Delquadri, J., and Hall, R.V. (1989) Longitudinal Effects of Classwide Peer Tutoring. *Journal of Educational Psychology*, 81, 371–383.

Greenwood, C.R., Dinwiddie, G., Bailey, V. *et al.* (1987) Field replication of classwide peer tutoring. *Journal of Applied Behavior Analysis*, 20, 2, 151–160.

Gregory, A., Henry, D.B., Schoeny, M.E. *et al.* (2007) School climate and implementation of a preventive intervention. *American Journal of Community Psychology*, 40, 3/4, 250–260.

Grey, I.M., Honan, R., McClean, B., and Daly, M. (2005) Evaluating the effectiveness of teacher training in Applied Behaviour Analysis. *Journal of Intellectual Disabilities*, 9, 3, 209–227.

Grimshaw, R., and Berridge, D. (1994) *Educating Disruptive Children*, NCB, London.

Grossman, D.C., Neckerman, H.J., Koepsell, T.D. (1997) Effectiveness of a violence pre-vention curriculum among children in elementary school: A randomized controlled trial. *Journal of the American Medical Association*, 277, 20, 1605–1611.

Guerra, N., Henry, D., Huesmann, L.R., and Tolan, P. (2007) Changing the way children "think" about aggression: Social-cognitive effects of a preventive intervention. *Journal of Consulting and Clinical Psychology*, 75, 1, 160–167.

Gullotta, T. (1996) *Adolescent Dysfunctional Behaviour*, Sage, London.

Gupta, R., Stringer, B., and Meakin, A. (1990) A study to access the effectiveness of home-based reinforcement in a secondary school: Some preliminary findings. *Association of Educational Psychologists Journal*, 5, 4, 197.

Gureasko-Moore, S., DuPaul, G., and White, G.P. (2007) Self-management of classroom preparedness and homework: Effects on school functioning of adolescents with At-tention Deficit Hyperactivity Disorder. *School Psychology Review*, 36, 4, 647–664.

Haft, W. (2000) More than zero: The cost of zero tolerance and the case for restorative justice in schools. *Denver University Law Review*, 77, 4, 795–812.

Hall, R.V., Delquadri, J., Greenwood, C.R., and Thurston, L. (1982) The importance of opportunity to respond to children's academic success, in *Serving Young Handicapped Children: Issues and Research*, (eds N. Edgar, N. Haring, J. Jenkins and C. Pious) University Park Press, Baltimore, MD, pp. 107–140.

Hallam, S., Rhamie, J., and Shaw, J. (2006) *Evaluation of the Primary Behaviour and Attendance Pilot*, DfES, London.

Hamblin, D.H. (1979) *Counselling in Schools*. Routledge, London.

Hamre, B.K., and Pianta, R.C. (2001) Early teacher-child relationships and the trajectory of children's school outcomes through eighth grade. *Child Development*, 72, 2, 625–638.

Hanafin, J., and Lynch, A. (2002) Peripheral voices: parental involvement, social class, and educational disadvantage. *British Journal of Sociology of Education*, 23, 1, 35–49.

Hargreaves, D. (1967) *Social Relations in a Secondary School*, Routledge, London.

Hargreaves, D., Hester, S., and Mellor, F. (1975) *Deviance in Classrooms*, Routledge, London.

Harris, J., Cook, M., and Upton, G. (1996) *Pupils with Severe Learning Disabilities who Present Challenging Behaviour*, BILD, Kidderminster, UK.

Harrison, R.G., and Schaeffer, R.W. (1975) Another test of the Premack principle. *Bulletin of the Psychonomic Society*, 6, 6, 565–568.

Harriss, L., Barlow, J., and Moli, P. (2008) Specialist residential education for children with severe emotional and behavioural difficulties: Pupil, parent and staff perspectives. *Emotional and Behavioural Difficulties*, 13, 1, 7–20.

Harvey, M.T., Lewis-Palmer, T., Horner, R.H., and Sugai, G. (2003) Trans-situational inter-ventions: Generalization of behavior support across school and home environments. *Behavioral Disorders*, 28, 3, 299–312.

Hawkins, J.D., Catalano, R.F., Kosterman, R. *et al.* (1999) Preventing adolescent health risk behaviors by strengthening protection during childhood. *Archives of Pediatrics and Adolescent Medicine*, 153, 226–234.

Hawkins, J.D., Catalano, R.F., Morrison, D.M. *et al.* (1992) SSDP: Effects of the first four years on protective factors and problem behaviors, in *The Prevention of Antisocial Behavior in Children*, (eds J. McCord and R. Tremblay), Guilford, New York, pp. 139–161.

Hawkins, J.D., Kosterman, R., Catalano, R.F. *et al.* (2005) Promoting positive adult func-tioning through social development intervention in childhood: Long-term effects from the Seattle Social Development Project. *Archives of Pediatrics and Adolescent Medicine*, 159, 1, 25–31.

Hawkins, J.D., Von Cleve, E., and Catalano, R.F. 1991. Reducing early childhood aggression: Results of a primary prevention program. *Journal of the American Academy of Child & Adolescent Psychiatry*, 30, 2, 208–217.

Hayden, C. (1997) Exclusion from primary school: Children in need and children with special educational needs. *Emotional and Behavioural Difficulties*, 2, 3, 36–44.

Henggeler, S.W. (1999) Multisystemic Therapy: An overview of clinical procedures, outcomes, and policy implications. *Child Psychology & Psychiatry Review*, 4, 2–10.

Henggeler, S.W., Cunningham, P.B., Pickrel, S.G., S *et al.* (1996) Multisystemic therapy: An effective violence prevention approach for serious juvenile offenders. *Journal of Adolescence*, 19, 1, 47–61.

Hernandez, L., and Blazer, D. (2006) *Genes, Behavior and the Social Environment*, NIH, Washington DC.

Herrnstein, R., and Murray, C. (1994) *The Bell Curve*, The Free Press, New York.

Heydenberk, R.A., and Heydenberk, W.R. (2005) Increasing meta-cognitive competence through conflict resolution. *Education and Urban Society*, 37, 4, 431–452.

Hinshaw, S., Henker, B., and Whelan, B., (1984) Self-control in hyperactive boys in anger-induced situations: Effects of cognitive-behavioral training and methylphenidate. *Journal of Abnormal Child Psychology*, 12, 55–77.

Hinshaw, S.P., Owens, E.B., Wells, K.C. *et al.* (2000) Family processes and treatment outcome in the MTA: Negative/ineffective parenting practices in relation to multimodal treatment. *Journal of Abnormal Child Psychology*, 28, 6, 555–568.

HMSO (1981) *Education Act*, HMSO, London.

Hoath, F.E., and Sanders, M.R. (2002) A feasibility study of Enhanced Group Triple P - Positive parenting program for parents of children with attention-deficit/hyperactivity disorder. *Behaviour Change*, 19, 4, 191–206.

Hoff, K.E., and DuPaul, G.J. (1998) Reducing disruptive behavior in general education classrooms: The use of self-management strategies. *School Psychology Review*, 27, 2, 290–303.

Hoigaard, R., Safvenbom, R., and Tonnessen, F.E. (2006) The relationship between group cohesion, group norms, and perceived social loafing in soccer teams. *Small Group Research*, 37, 3, 217–232.

Holsen, I., Smith, B.H., and Frey, K.S. (2008) Outcomes of the social competence program *Second Step* in Norwegian elementary schools. *School Psychology International*, 29, 1, 71–88.

Homme, L.E., Debaca, P.C., Devine, J.V. *et al.* (1963) Use of the Premack principle in controlling the behavior of nursery school children. *Journal of the Experimental Analysis of Behavior*, 6, 4, 544–544.

Hopkins, D., Harris, A., Youngman, M. *et al.* (1998) *An Evaluation of the Initial Effects of Success for All in Nottingham*, Centre for School and Teacher Development, Nottingham, UK.

Hornby, G., and Witte, C. (2008) Follow-up study of ex-students of a residential school for for children with emotional and behavioural difficulties in New Zealand. *Emotional and Behavioural Difficulties*, 31, 2, 79–94.

Horner, R.H., Todd, A.W., Lewis-Palmer, T. *et al.* (2004) The School-wide Evaluation Tool (SET): A research instrument for assessing school-wide positive behavior support. *Journal of Positive Behavior Interventions*, 6, 1, 3–12.

Hosie, T.W., Gentile, J.R., and Carroll, J.D. 1974. Pupil preferences and the Premack principle. *American Educational Research Journal*, 11, 3, 241–247.

Houghton, S., Wheldall, K., Jukes, R., and Sharpe, A. 1990. The effects of limited private reprimands and increased private praise on classroom behaviour in four British secondary school classes. *The British Journal of Educational Psychology*, 60, 3, 255–265.

Housego, B.E.J. (1999) Outreach schools: An educational innovation. *Alberta Journal of Educational Research*, 45, 1, 85–101.

Howard, S., Dryden, J., and Johnson, B. (1999) Childhood resilience: review and critique of literature. *Oxford Review of Education*, 25, 3, 307–323.

Howes, A., Emanuel, J., and Farrell, P. (2003) Can nurture groups facilitate inclusive practice in primary schools? in *Making Special Education Inclusive*, (eds P. Farrell and M. Ainscow), David Fulton, London.

Huesmann, L.R., Maxwell, C.D., Eron, L. *et al.* (1996) Evaluating a cognitive/ecological program for the prevention of aggression among urban children. *American Journal of Preventive Medicine*, 12(5 Suppl.), 120–128.

Hughes, L., and Cooper, P. (2007) *Understanding and Supporting Pupils with ADHD*, Paul Chapman, London.

Humphrey, N., Kalambouka, A., Bolton, J. *et al.* (2008) *Primary Social and Emotional Aspects of Learning (SEAL): Evaluation of Small Group Work*, DCSF, London.

Hurley, E.A., Chamberlain, A., Slavin, R.E., and Madden, N.A. (2001) Effects of success for all on TAAS reading scores: A Texas statewide evaluation. *Phi Delta Kappan*, 82, 10, 750–756.

Ialongo, N., Poduska, J., Werthamer, L., and Kellam, S. (2001) The distal impact of two first-grade preventive interventions on conduct problems and disorder in early adolescence. *Journal of Emotional and Behavioral Disorders*, 9, 3, 146–160.

IDEA Legislation (1987) Individuals with Disabilities EducationAct, 20 U.S.C. [ss] 1401–1485.

Irvin, L.K., Horner, R.H., Ingram, K., Todd, A.W. *et al.* (2006) Using office discipline referral data for decision making about student behavior in elementary and middle schools: An empirical evaluation of validity. *Journal of Positive Behavior Interventions*, 8, 1, 10–23.

Iszatt, J., and Wasilewska, T. (1997) NGs: An early intervention model enabling vulnerable children with emotional and behavioural difficulties to integrate successfully into school. *Educational and Child Psychology*, 14, 3, 121–139.

Jensen, A. (1969) How Much Can We Boost IQ and Scholastic Achievement? *Harvard Education Review*, 39, (Winter/Summer), 1–123, 449–483.

Joliffe, W. (2006) The National Literacy Strategy: Missing a crucial link? A comparative study of the National Literacy Strategy and Success For All. *Education 3–13*, 34, 1, 37–48.

Jones, E.M., Gottfredson, G.D., and Gottfredson, D.C. (1997) Success for some: An evaluation of a success for all program. *Evaluation Review*, 21, 6, 643–670.

Jones, K., Daley, D., Hutchings, J. *et al.* (2007) Efficacy of the Incredible Years Basic parent training programme as an early intervention for children with conduct problems and ADHD. *Child: Care, Health and Development*, 33, 6, 749–756.

Jones, K.M., Young, M.M., and Friman, P.C. (2000) Increasing peer praise of socially rejected delinquent youth: Effects on cooperation and acceptance. *School Psychology Quarterly*, 15, 1, 30–39.

Jones, R. (1995) *The Child School Interface*, Cassell, London.

Jordan, D.W., and Métais, J.L. (1997) Social skilling through cooperative learning. *Educational Research*, 39, 1, 3–21.

Kahne, J., and Bailey, K. (1999) The role of social capital in youth development: The case of "I Have a Dream" programs. *Educational Evaluation and Policy Analysis*, 21, 321–343.

Kahne, J.E., Sporte, S.E., De La Torre, M., and Easton, J.Q. (2008) Small high schools on a larger scale: The impact of school conversions in Chicago. *Educational Evaluation and Policy Analysis*, 30, 3, 281–315.

Kaminski, J.W., Valle, L.A., Filene, J.H., and Boyle, C.L. (2008) A meta analytic review of components associated with Program Training Progress Effectiveness. *Journal of Abnormal Child Psychology*, 36, 567–589.

Kamps, D., Abbott, M., Greenwood, C. *et al.* (2008a) Effects of small-group reading instruction and curriculum differences for students most at risk in kindergarten: Two-year results for secondary- and tertiary-level interventions. *Journal of Learning Disabilities*, 41, 2, 101–114.

Kamps, D., Wendland, M., and Culpepper, M. (2006) Active teacher participation in functional behavior assessment for students with emotional and behavioral disorders risks in general education classrooms. *Behavioral Disorders*, 31, 2, 128–146.

Kamps, D.M., Greenwood, C., Arreaga-Mayer, C. *et al.* (2008) The efficacy of class wide peer tutoring in middle schools. *Education and Treatment of Children*, 31, 2, 119–152.

Kane, J., Lloyd, G., Mccluskey, G. *et al.* (2008) Collaborative evaluation: Balancing rigour and relevance in a research study of restorative approaches in schools in Scotland. *International Journal of Research and Method in Education*, 31, 2, 99–111.

Karier, C. (1976) Business values and the educational state, in *Schooling and Capitalism*, (eds R. Dale, G. Esland and M. MacDonald), Open University Press, Milton Keynes.

Karp, D.R. (2001) Restorative justice in school communities. *Youth and Society*, 33, 2, 249–272.

Kaser, C.H. (2007) Series on Highly Effective Practices: Classroom Environment 1. http://education.odu.edu/esse/research/series/environments.shtml (accessed September 28, 2010).

Kauffman, J., Batz, J., and McCullough, J. (2002) Separate and better: a special public school class for students with emotional and behavioural disorders, *Exceptionality*, 10, 3, 149–170.

Kazdin, A.E. (1997) Parent management training: Evidence, outcomes, and issues. *Journal of the American Academy of Child and Adolescent Psychiatry*, 36, 10, 1349–1356.

Kazdin, A.E. (1980) Acceptability of alternative treatments for deviant child behavior. *Journal of Applied Behavior Analysis*, 13, 2, 259–273.

Kazdin, A.E. (2002) Psychosocial treatments for conduct disorder, in *A Guide to Treatments that Work*, 2nd edn, (eds P. Nathan and J. Gorman), Oxford University Press, Oxford, pp. 57–86.

Kazdin, A.E. (2008) Evidence-based treatment and practice – New opportunities to bridge clinical research and practice, enhance the knowledge base, and improve patient care. *American Psychologist*, 63, 3, 146–159.

Kazdin, A.E., Bass, D., Siegel, T., and Thomas, C. (1989) Cognitive-behavioral therapy and relationship therapy in the treatment of children referred for antisocial behavior. *Journal of Consulting and Clinical Psychology*, 57, 4, 522–535.

Kazdin, A.E., Esveldt-Dawson, K., French, N.H., and Unis, A.S. (1987) Effects of parent management training and problem-solving skills training combined in treatment of antisocial child behavior. *Journal of the American Academy of Child and Adolescent Psychiatry*, 26, 416–424.

Kearney, C., and Wadiak, D. (1999) Anxiety disorders, in *Child and Adolescent Psychological Disorders*, (eds S. Netherton, D. Holmes and E. Walker), Oxford University Press, Oxford, 282–303.

Kellam, S.G., and Anthony, J.C. (1998) Targeting early antecedents to prevent tobacco smoking: Findings from an epidemiologically based randomized field trial. *American Journal of Public Health*, 88, 10, 1490–1495.

Kellam, S.G., Rebok, G.W., Ialongo, N., and Mayer, L.S. (1994) The course and malleability of aggressive behavior from early first grade into middle school: Results of a developmental epidemiologically-based preventive trial. *Journal of Child Psychology and Psychiatry and Allied Disciplines*, 35, 2, 259–281.

Kelley, M. L., Carper, L. B., Witt, J. C., and Elliott, S. N. (1988) Home-based reinforcement procedures. In: *Handbook of Behavior Therapy in Education* (eds C. Witt, S. N. Elliott and F. M. Gresham) Plenum, New York, p. 419.

Kellner, M.H., Bry, B.H., and Colletti, L. (2001) Teaching anger management skills to students with severe emotional or behavioral disorders. *Behavioral Disorders*, 27, 4, 400–407.

Kelly, A., Carey, S., McCarthy, S., and Coyle, C. (2007) Principals' experience of stress and perception of the effects of challenging behaviour on staff in special schools in Ireland. *European Journal of Special Needs Education*, 22, 2, 161–181.

Kelshaw-Levering, K., Sterling-Turner, H.E., Henry, J.R., and Skinner, C.H. (2000) Randomized interdependent group contingencies: Group reinforcement with a twist. *Psychology in the Schools*, 37, 6, 523–533.

Kemple, J., and Rock, J.L. (1996) *Career Academies; Early Intervention Lessons from a 10-site Evaluation*, Manpower Demonstration Research Corporation, New York.

Kemple, J., and Scott-Clayton, J. (2004) *Career Academies: Impact on Labor Market Outcomes and Educational Attainment*, Manpower Demonstration Research Corporation, New York.

Kemple, J., and Snipes, J.C. (2000) *Career Academies: Impacts on Students' Engagement and Performance in High School*, Manpower Demonstration Research Corporation, New York.

Kemple, J., and Wilner, C.J. (2008) *Career Academies: Long-term impact on Labor Market outcomes, Educational Attainment and Transitions into Adulthood*, Manpower Demonstration Research Corporation, New York.

Kendall, P.C. (1994) Treating anxiety disorders in children: Results of a randomized clinical trial. *Journal of Consulting and Clinical Psychology*, 62, 1, 100–110.

Kendall, P.C., and Finch, A.J. (1976) A cognitive- behavioral treatment for impulse control: A case study. *Journal of Consulting & Clinical Psychology*, 44, 852–857.

Kern, L., Delaney, B., Clarke, S. *et al.* (2001) Improving the classroom behavior of students with emotional and behavioral disorders using individualized curricular modifications. *Journal of Emotional and Behavioral Disorders*, 9, 239–247.

Kivlighan, K. T., and Granger, D. A. (2006) Salivary a-amylase response to competition: Relation to gender, previous experience, and attitudes. *Psychoneuroendocrinology*, 31, 703–714.

Klein, R. (1999) *Defying Disaffection*, Trentham Books, Stoke on Trent, UK.

Knapp, T.J. (1976) The Premack principle in human experimental and applied settings. *Behaviour Research and Therapy*, 14, 2, 133–147.

Koffman, D.M., Lee, J.W., Hopp, J.W., and Emont, S.L. (1998) The impact of including incentives and competition in a workplace smoking cessation program on quit rates. *American Journal of Health Promotion*, 13, 2, 105–111.

Kohler, F.W., and Greenwood, C.R. (1990) Effects of collateral peer supportive behaviors within the classwide peer tutoring program. *Journal of Applied Behavior Analysis*, 23, 3, 307–322.

Kounin, J. (1970) *Discipline and Group Management in Classrooms*, Routledge, London.

Kozol, J. (2006) Success for all: Trying to make an end run around inequality and segregation. *Phi Delta Kappan*, 87, 8, 624–626.

Krantz, P.J., and Risley, T.R. (1977) Behavioral ecology in the classroom, in *Classroom Management: The Successful Use of Behavior Modification.* 2nd edn, (eds K.D. O'Leary and S.G. O'Leary), Pergamon, New York, pp. 349–367.

Kremenitzer, J.P. (2005) The emotionally intelligent early childhood educator: Self-reflective journaling. *Early Childhood Education Journal*, 33, 1, 3–9.

La Russo, M.D., Romer, D., and Selman, R.L. (2008) Teachers as builders of respectful school climates: Implications for adolescent drug use norms and depressive symptoms in high school. *Journal of Youth and Adolescence*, 37, 4, 386–398.

Laing, R. (1960) *The Divided Self*, Penguin, London.

Landrum, T.J., Tankersley, M., and Kauffman, J.M. (2003) What is special about special education for students with emotional or behavioral disorders? *Journal of Special Education*, 37, 3, 148–156.

Lane, K.L., Wehby, J.H., Little, M.A., and Cooley, C. (2005) Students educated in self-contained classrooms and self-contained schools: Part II – How do they progress over time? *Behavioral Disorders*, 30, 4, 363–374.

Laslett, R., Cooper, P., Maras, P. *et al.* (1997) *Changing Perceptions: Emotional and Behavioural Difficulties since 1945*, AWCEBD, East Sutton.

Lassen, S.R., Steele, M.M., and Sailor, W. (2006) The relationship of school-wide positive behavior support to academic achievement in an urban middle school. *Psychology in the Schools*, 43, 6, 701–712.

Lavallee, K.L., Bierman, K.L., Nix, R.L. *et al.* (2005) The impact of first-grade "friendship group" experiences on child social outcomes in the fast track program. *Journal of Abnormal Child Psychology*, 33, 3, 307–324.

Lawrence, J., Steed, D., and Young, P. (1984) *Disruptive Children – Disruptive Schools?* Croom Helm, Beckenham.

Layard, R., and Dunn, J. (2009) *A Good Childhood*, Penguin, London.

Leclerc, R., and Thurston, C. (2003) Applications of the Premack principle by the parents of an autistic child. *Revue Francophone de la Deficience Intellectuelle*, 14, 2, 139–150.

Lee, M., and Friedrich, T. (2007) The 'smaller' the school, the better? The Smaller Learning Communities (SLC) program in US high schools. *Improving Schools*, 10, 3, 261–282.

Lepkowska, D, (2005) Inclusion lottery exposed, *Times Educational Supplement*, July 29, http://tes.co.uk/article?storycode=2119630 (last accessed August 14, 2009).

Letendre, J., Henry, D., and Tolan, P.H. (2003) Leader and therapeutic influences on prosocial skill building in school-based groups to prevent aggression. *Research on Social Work Practice*, 13, 5, 569–587.

Leung, C., Sanders, M.R., Leung, S. *et al.* (2003) An outcome evaluation of the implementation of the Triple P-Positive Parenting Program in Hong Kong. *Family Process*, 42, 4, 531–544.

Levy, F., and Hay, D. (eds) (2001) *Attention, Genes and ADHD*, Brunner-Routledge, London.

Lewinsohn, P.M., and Clark, G.N. (1990) Cognitive-behavioral treatment for depressed adolescents. *Behavior Therapy*, 19, 385–401.

Lewis, A., and Norwich, B, (2005) *Special Teaching for Special Children?* Open University, Buckingham, UK.

Lewis, T.J., and Newcomer, L.L. (2002) Examining the efficacy of school-based consultation: Recommendations for improving outcomes. *Child and Family Behavior Therapy*, 24, 1/2, 165–181.

Lewis, T.J., and Sugai, G. (1996) Functional assessment of problem behavior: A pilot investigation of the comparative and interactive effects of teacher and peer social attention on students in general education settings. *School Psychology Quarterly*, 11, 1, 1–19.

Lipsey, M.W., and Wilson, D.B. (1993) The efficacy of psychological, educational, and behavioral treatment: Confirmation from meta-analysis. *American Psychologist*, 48, 12, 1181–1209.

Little, L.M., and Kelley, M.L. (1989) The efficacy of response cost procedures for reducing children's noncompliance to parental instructions. *Behavior Therapy*, 20, 525–534.

Lloyd, G., and Norris, C. (1999) Including ADHD?, *Disability and Society*, 14, 4, 505–517.

Lochman, J.E., Boxmeyer, C., Powell, N. *et al.* (2007) The use of the coping power program to treat a 10-year-old girl with disruptive behaviors. *Journal of Clinical Child and Adolescent Psychology*, 36, 4, 677–687.

Lochman, J.E., and Lampron, L.B. (1985). The usefulness of peer ratings of aggression and social acceptance in the identification of behavioral and subjective difficulties in aggressive boys. *Journal of Applied Developmental Psychology*, 6, 2/3, 187–198.

Lochman, J.E., and Wells, K.C. (2002a) The coping power program at the middle-school transition: Universal and indicated prevention effects. *Psychology of Addictive Behaviors*, 16, suppl. 14, 40–54.

Lochman, J.E., and Wells, K.C. (2002b) Contextual social-cognitive mediators and child outcome: A test of the theoretical model in the Coping Power program. *Development and Psychopathology*, 14, 4, 945–967.

Lochman, J.E., and Wells, K.C. (2003) Effectiveness of the Coping Power program and of classroom intervention with aggressive children: Outcomes at a 1-year follow-up. *Behavior Therapy*, 34, 4, 493–515.

Lochman, J.E., and Wells, K.C. (2004) The coping power program for preadolescent aggressive boys and their parents: Outcome effects at the 1-year follow-up. *Journal of Consulting and Clinical Psychology*, 72, 4, 571–578.

Lodge, A., and Lynch, K. (2003) Young people's concerns: The invisibility of diversity, in *Encouraging Voices*, (eds M. Shevlin and R. Rose), NDA, Dublin.

Long, P., Forehand, R., Wierson, M., and Morgan, A. (1994) Does parent training with young noncompliant children have long-term effects? *Behaviour Research and Therapy*, 32, 1, 101–107.

Lougy, R.A., Deruvo, S.L., and Rosenthal, D. (2007) *Teaching Young Children with ADHD: Successful Strategies and Practical Interventions for Prek-3*, Corwin Press, Thousand Oaks, CA.

Lowe, J. (1990) The interface between educational facilities and learning climate. PhD dissertation, Texas A&M University.

Lowe, T.O., and McLaughlin, E.C. (1974) The use of verbal reinforcement by paraprofessionals in the treatment of under- achieving elementary school students. *Journal of the Student Personnel Association for Teacher Education*, 12, 3, 95–95.

Lowry-Webster, H.M., Barrett, P.M., and Dadds, M.R. (2001) A universal prevention trial of anxiety and depressive symptomatology in childhood: Preliminary data from an Australian study. *Behaviour Change*, 18, 1, 36–50.

Luiselli, J.K., Putnam, R.F., Handler, M.W., and Feinberg, A.B. (2005) Whole-school positive behaviour support: Effects on student discipline problems and academic performance. *Educational Psychology*, 25, 2/3, 183–198.

Lundahl, B., Risser, H.J., and Lovejoy, M.C. (2006) A meta-analysis of parent training: Moderators and follow-up effects. *Clinical Psychology Review*, 26, 1, 86–104.

Luthar, S.S., Cicchetti, D., and Becker, B. (2000) The construct of resilience: A critical evaluation and guidelines for future work. *Child Development*, 71, 3, 543–562.

Maag, J.W., and Katsiyannis, A. (1998) Teacher preparation in E/BD: A national survey. *Behavioral Disorders*, 24, 3, 189–196.

MaCauley, D. (1990) Classroom environment: A literature review. *Educational Psychology*, 10, 3, 239–253.

MacBeath, J., Galton, M., Steward, S. *et al.* (2006) *The Costs of Inclusion*, University of Cambridge Faculty of Education, Cambridge, UK.

MacDonald, R. (ed.) (1997) *Youth, the Underclass, and Social Exclusion*, Routledge, London.

MacMillan, L. (2009) *Social Mobility and the Professions*, Centre for Market and Public Organisation – Social Mobility, University of Bristol www.bristol.ac.uk/cmpo/publications/other/socialmobility.pdf (accessed September 28, 2010).

Malik, K. (2000) *Man, Beast and Zombie*, Weidenfeld and Nicolson, London.

Maras, P., and Cooper, P. (2000) *AD/HD: Guidelines and Principles for Successful Multi-Agency Working*, British Psychological Society, Leicester.

Marchant, M., and Young, K.R. (2001) The effects of a parent coach on parents' acquisition and implementation of parenting skills. *Education and Treatment of Children*, 24, 3, 351–373.

Marchant, M., Young, K.R., and West, R.P. (2004) The effects of parental teaching on compliance behavior of children. *Psychology in the Schools*, 41, 3, 337–350.

Marsh, P., Rosser, E., and Harre, R. (1978) *The Rules of Disorder*, Routledge, London.

Martens, B.K., Hiralall, A.S., and Bradley, T.A. (1997) A note to teacher: Improving student behavior through goal setting and feedback. *School Psychology Quarterly*, 12, 1, 33–41.

Martin, D., and Martin, M. (2007) Implementing a family/school partnership in an urban elementary school to reduce negative behavior and increase academic achievement. *Family Therapy*, 34, 3, 141–152.

Martin, J.E., Van Dycke, J.L., Greene, B.A. *et al.* (2006) Direct observation of teacher-directed IEP meetings: Establishing the need for student IEP meeting instruction. *Exceptional Children*, 72, 2, 187–200.

Marzocchi, G.M., DI Pietro, M., Vio, C. *et al.* (2004) Management of classroom hyperactivity and opposition behavior: A teacher training study. *Psicoterapia Cognitiva e Comportamentale*, 10, 2, 83–96.

Mathes, P.G., Howard, J.K., Allen, S.H., and Fuchs, D. (1998) Peer-assisted learning strategies for first-grade readers: Responding to the needs of diverse learners. *Reading Research Quarterly*, 33, 1, 62–94.

Matheson, A.S., and Shriver, M.D. (2005) Training teachers to give effective commands: Effects on student compliance and academic behaviors. *School Psychology Review*, 34, 202–219.

McArdle, P. (2007) ADHD and co-morbid oppositional defiant and conduct disorders, in (eds M. Fitzgerald, M. Bellgrove and M. Gill), *Handbook of ADHD*. John Wiley and Sons, Chichester, pp. 53–68.

McCain, A.P., and Kelley, M.L. (1993) Managing the classroom behavior of an ADHD preschooler: The efficacy of a school-home note intervention. *Child and Family Behavior Therapy*, 15, 33–44.

McCluskey, G., Lloyd, G., Stead, J. *et al.* (2008) "I was dead restorative today": From restorative justice to restorative approaches in school. *Cambridge Journal of Education*, 38, 2, 199–216.

McConaughy, S.H., Kay, P.J., and Fitzgerald, M. (2000) How long is long enough? Outcomes for a school-based prevention program. *Exceptional Children*, 67, 1, 21–34.

McCraty, R., Atkinson, M., Tomasino, D., Goelitz, J., and Mayrovitz, H.N. (1999) The impact of an emotional self-management skills course on psychosocial functioning and autonomic recovery to stress in middle school children. *Integrative Physiological and Behavioral Science*, 34, 4, 246–268.

McDonald Connor, C., Son, S., Hindman, A.H., and Morrison, F.J. (2005) Teacher qualifications, classroom practices, family characteristics, and preschool experience: Complex effects on first graders' vocabulary and early reading outcomes. *Journal of School Psychology*, 43, 4, 343–375.

McGarrigle, M. (2006) *Pilot Implementation of Restorative Practices in Post-Primary Schools in the Northwest Region*, National University of Ireland, Galway/Health Service Executive, Ireland.

McIntosh, K., Brigid Flannery, K., Sugai, G., Braun, D.H., and Cochrane, K.L. (2008) Relationships between academics and problem behavior in the transition from middle school to high school. *Journal of Positive Behavior Interventions*, 10, 4, 243–255.

McIntosh, K., Horner, R.H., Chard, D.J. *et al.* (2006) The use of reading and behavior screening measures to predict non response to school-wide positive behavior support: A longitudinal analysis. *School Psychology Review*, 35, 2, 275–291.

McLaughlin, T.F. (1991) Use of a personalized system of instruction with and without a same-day retake contingency on spelling performance of behaviorally disordered children. *Behavioral Disorders*, 16, 137–162.

Medland, M.B., and Stachnik, T.J. (1972) Good-behavior game: A replication and systematic analysis. *Journal of Applied Behavior Analysis*, 5, 1, 45–51.

Meichenbaum, D. (1977) *Cognitive Behavioural Modification: an Integrative Approach*. Plenum, New York.

Merrett, F., and Tang, W.M. (1994) The attitudes of British primary school pupils to praise, reward, punishments and reprimands. *The British Journal of Educational Psychology*, 64, 91–103.

Metzger, S., and Jia Wu, M. (2008) Commercial teacher selection instruments: the validity of selecting teachers through beliefs, attitudes, and values. *Review of Educaional Research*, 78, 4, 921–940.

Midford, R. (2007) Is Australia 'fair dinkum' about drug education in schools? *Drug and Alcohol Review*, 26, 4, 421–427.

Ministry of Education (1955) *Report of the Committee on Maladjusted Children* (The Underwood Report), HMSO, London.

Ministry of Health (1945) *Handicapped Pupils and School Health Service Regulations*, HMSO, London.

Minuchin, S. (1973) *Families and Family Therapy*, Harvard University Press, Cambridge MA.

Molnar, A., and Lindquist, B. (1989) *Changing Problem Behavior in School*, Jossey-Bass, San Francisco, CA.

Mooij, T., and Smeets, E. (2006) Design, development and implementation of inclusive education. *European Educational Research Journal*, 5, 2, 94–109.

Mooij, T., and Smeets, E. (2008) Towards systemic support of pupils with emotional and behavioural disorders. *International Journal of Inclusive Education*, 13, 6, 597–616.

Moore, L.A., Waguespack, A.M., Wickstrom, K.F. *et al.* (1994) Mystery motivator: An effective and time efficient intervention. *School Psychology Review*, 23, 106–117.

Mørch, W., Clifford, G., Larsson, B. *et al* (2004) *The Incredible Years – The Norwegian Webster-Stratton Programme 1998–2004*, Norwegian Research Council, NTNU, Trondheim, Norway.

Moroz, K.B., and Jones, K.M. (2002) The effects of positive peer reporting on children's social involvement. *School Psychology Review*, 31, 2, 235–245.

Morrison, B., Blood, P., and Thorsborne, M. (2005) Practicing restorative justice in school communities: The challenge of culture change. *Public Organization Review*, 5, 4, 335–357.

Mortimore, P. 1997, *The Road to Improvement*, Taylor & Francis, London.

Mortimore, P., Sammons, L., Stoll, C., and Ecob, R. (1988) *School Matters*, Open Books, London.

Mortweet, S.L., Utley, C.A., Walker, D. *et al* (1999) Classwide peer tutoring: Teaching students with mild mental retardation in inclusive classrooms. *Exceptional Children*, 65, 4, 524–536.

Mosley, J. (1993) *Turn Your School Round*, LDA, Wisbech, UK.

Murray, D.W., Rabiner, D., Schulte, A., and Newitt, K. (2008) Feasibility and integrity of a parent-teacher consultation intervention for ADHD students. *Child and Youth Care Forum*, 37, 3, 111–126.

Myers, S.S., and Pianta, R.C. (2008) Developmental commentary: Individual and contextual influences on student-teacher relationships and children's early problem behaviors. *Journal of Clinical Child and Adolescent Psychology*, 37, 3, 600–608.

Nathan, P., and Gorham, J. (2002) *A Guide to Treatments that Work*, 2nd edn, Oxford University Press, Oxford.

National Institute for Health and Clinical Excellence (NICE) (2008) *Guidance on the Use of Methylphenidate for AD/HD*, NICE, London.

Neill, A.S. (1968) *Summerhill*, Penguin, Harmondsworth.

NESS Research Team (2005) *Early Impacts of Sure Start Local Programmes for Children and Families: Report 13*, DfES, London.

NESS Research Team (2008) *The Impact of Sure Start Local Programmes on Three Year Olds and Their Families*, DfES, London.

Nixon, R.D.V. (2002) Treatment of behavior problems in preschoolers: A review of parent training programs. *Clinical Psychology Review*, 22, 4, 525–546.

Nolan, B., and Whelan, C.T. (2000) Urban housing and the role of 'underclass' processes: the case of Ireland. *Journal of European Social Policy*, 10, 1, 5–21.

Norwich, B. (1990) *Reappraising Special Needs Education*, Cassell, London.

O'Connor, T., and Colwell, J. (2003) Understanding nurturing practices – a comparison of the use of strategies likely to enhance self-esteem in nurture groups and normal classrooms. *British Journal of Special Education*, 30, 3, 119–124.

O'Donnell, J.J., Hawkins, D., Catalano, R.F. *et al.* (1995) Preventing school failure, drug use, and delinquency among low-income children: Long-term intervention in elementary schools. *American Journal of Orthopsychiatry*, 65, 1, 87–100.

Ostrower, C., and Ziv, A. (1982) Soft reprimands and self-control as ways of behavior modification in the classroom. *Israeli Journal of Psychology and Counseling in Education*, 15, 21–28.

Oswald, K., Safran, S., and Johanson, G. (2005) Preventing trouble: Making schools safer places using positive behavior supports. *Education and Treatment of Children*, 28, 3, 265–278.

Palincsar, A.S., and Brown, A.L. (1984) Reciprocal teaching of comprehension – fostering and comprehension – monitoring activities. *Cognition and Instruction*, 1, 2, 117–175.

Palmer, E., and Finger, S. (2001), An early description of ADHD: Dr Alexander Crichton and "mental restlessness" (1798). *Child Psychology and Psychiatry Review*, 6, 66–73.

Panacek, L.J., and Dunlap, G. (2003) The social lives of children with emotional and behavioral disorders in self-contained classrooms: A descriptive analysis. *Exceptional Children*, 69, 3, 333–348.

Park, V., and Datnow, A. (2008) Collaborative assistance in a highly prescribed school reform model: The case of success for all. *Peabody Journal of Education*, 83, 3, 400–422.

Patrick, C.A., Ward, P., and Crouch, D.W. (1998) Effects of holding students accountable for social behaviors during volleyball games in elementary physical education. *Journal of Teaching in Physical Education*, 17, 2, 143–156.

Patterson, G., Reid, J., and Dishion, T. (1992) *Antisocial Boys*, vol. 4, Castalia, Eugene OR.

Patterson, G.R., Debaryshe, B.D., and Ramsey, E. 1989. A developmental perspective on antisocial behavior. *The American Psychologist*, 44, 2, 329–335.

Patterson, G.R., Forgatch, M.S., Yoerger, K.L., and Stoolmiller, M. (1998) Variables that initiate and maintain an early-onset trajectory for juvenile offending. *Development and Psychopathology*, 10, 3, 531–547.

Patterson, G.R., and Stouthamer-Loeber, M. (1984) The correlation of family management practices and delinquency. *Child Development*, 55, 4, 1299–1307.

Patton, G., Bond, L., Butler, H., and Glover, S. (2003) Changing schools, changing health? Design and implementation of the Gatehouse Project. *Journal of Adolescent Health*, 33, 4, 231–239.

Patton, G.C., Glover, S., Bond, L. *et al.* (2000) The Gatehouse Project: A systematic approach to mental health promotion in secondary schools. *Australian and New Zealand Journal of Psychiatry*, 34, 4, 586–593.

Pavlov, I. (1927) *Conditioned Reflexes*, Oxford University Press, Oxford.

Pellegrini, A., and Horvat, M. (1995) A developmental contextualist critique of AD/HD. *Educational Researcher*, 24, 1, 13–20.

Pfiffner, L.J., O'Leary, S.G., Rosen, L.A., and Sanderson, W.C. (1985) A comparison of the effects of continuous and intermittent response cost and reprimands in the classroom. *Journal of Clinical Child Psychology*, 14, 4, 348–352.

Pianta, R.C., and Walsh, D.J. (1998) Applying the construct of resilience in schools: Cautions from a developmental systems perspective. *School Psychology Review*, 27, 3, 407–417.

Piazza, C.C., Bowman, L.G., Contrucci, S.A. *et al.* (1999) An evaluation of the properties of attention as reinforcement for destructive and appropriate behavior. *Journal of Applied Behavior Analysis*, 32, 4, 437–449.

Pierce, C.D., Reid, R., and Epstein, M.H. (2004) Teacher-Mediated interventions for children with EBD and their academic outcomes. *Remedial and Special Education*, 25, 3, 175–188.

Pigott, H.E., Fantuzzo, J.W., and Clement, P.W. (1986) The effects of reciprocal peer tutoring and group contingencies on the academic performance of elementary school children. *Journal of Applied Behavior Analysis*, 19, 1, 93–98.

Plomin, R. (1990) *Nature and Nurture: An Introduction to Human Behavioral Genetics*, Brooks/Cole, Pacific Grove CA.

Poduska, J.M., Kellam, S.G., Wang, W. *et al.* (2008) Impact of the Good Behavior Game, a universal classroom-based behavior intervention, on young adult service use for problems with emotions, behavior, or drugs or alcohol. *Drug and Alcohol Dependence*, 95, Suppl. 1, 29–44.

Pogrow, S. (2000a) Success for all does not produce success for students. *Phi Delta Kappan*, 82, 1, 67–80.

Pogrow, S. (2000b) The unsubstantiated "success" of success for all: Implications for policy, practice, and the soul of our profession. *Phi Delta Kappan*, 81, 8, 596–600.

Pogrow, S. (2002) Success for all is a failure. *Phi Delta Kappan*, 83, 6, 463–468.

Pomeroy, E. (2000) *Experiencing Exclusion*, Trentham Books, Stoke on Trent, UK.

Poulou, M. (2005) The prevention of emotional and behavioural difficulties in schools: teachers' suggestions. *Educational Psychology in Practice*, 21, 1, 37–52.

Purdie, N., Hattie, J., and Carroll, A. (2002) A review of the research on interventions for attention deficit hyperactivity disorder: What works best? *Review of Educational Research*, 72, 1, 61–99.

Purkey, S., and Smith, M. (1984) Effective schools: A review. *Elementary School Journal*, 83, 4, 427–453.

Quinn, M., Osher, D., Warger, C. *et al.* (2000) *Teaching and Working with Children who have Emotional and Behavioral Challenges*, Sopris West, Longmont CO.

Raywid, M.A., and Oshiyama, L. (2000) Musings in the wake of Columbine: What can schools do? *Phi Delta Kappan*, 81, 6, 444–449.

Rees, P., and Bailey, K. (2003) Positive exceptions: Learning from students who "beat the odds," *Educational and Child Psychology*, 20, 4, 41–59.

Reeves, C. (2001) Minding the child: The legacy of Barbara Dockar-Drysdale. *Emotional and Behavioural Difficulties*, 6, 4, 213–235.

Reid, M.J., and Webster-Stratton, C. (2001) The Incredible Years parent, teacher, and child intervention: Targeting multiple areas of risk for a young child with pervasive conduct problems using a flexible, manualized treatment program. *Cognitive and Behavioral Practice*, 8, 4, 377–386.

Reid, M.J., Webster-Stratton, C., and Baydar, N. (2004) Halting the development of conduct problems in head start children: The effects of parent training. *Journal of Clinical Child and Adolescent Psychology*, 33, 2, 279–291.

Reid, M.J., Webster-Stratton, C., and Beauchaine, T. (2002) Parent training in Head Start: A comparison of program response among African American, Asian American, Caucasian, and Hispanic mothers. *Prevention Science*, 2, 209–226.

Reid, M.J., Webster-Stratton, C., and Hammond, M. (2003) Follow-up of children who received the Incredible Years intervention for oppositional-defiant disorder: Maintenance and prediction of 2-year outcome. *Behavior Therapy*, 34, 4, 471–491.

Reid, R., Gonzalez, J.E., Nordness, P.D *et al.* (2004) A meta-analysis of the academic status of students with emotional/behavioral disturbance. *Journal of Special Education*, 38, 3, 130–143.

Resnick, M.D., Bearman, P.S., Blum, R.W. *et al.* (1997) Protecting adolescents from harm: Findings from the national longitudinal study on adolescent health. *Journal of the American Medical Association*, 278, 823–832.

Reynolds, D., and Sullivan, M. (1979) Bringing schools back, in *Schools, Pupils and Deviance*, (eds L. Barton and R. Meighan), Nafferton, Driffield, UK.

Reynolds, S., MacKay, T., and Kearney, M. (2009) Nurture groups: A large scale, controlled study of effects on development and academic attainment. *British Journal of Special Education*, 36, 4, 204–212.

Rhode, G., Morgan, D.P., and Young, K.R. (1983) Generalization and maintenance of treatment gains of behaviorally handicapped students from resource rooms to regular classrooms using self-evaluation procedures. *Journal of applied Behavior Analysis*, 16, 2, 171–188.

Rief, S.F. (2003) Educating the child with Attention-Deficit/Hyperactivity Disorder. *Primary Psychiatry*, 10, 4, 61–65.

Rinehart, J. (1991) Organization of the environment, in *Interventions for Students with Emotional Disorders*, (eds S. Morgan and J. Rinehart), Pro-Ed, Austin TX.

Robinson, C.M., and Robinson, L.W. (1979) Involving parents in the treatment of behaviorally disordered children. *Clinical Social Work Journal,* 7, 3, 182–193.

Rogers, C. (1951) *Client Centered Therapy,* Houghton Mifflin, Boston MA.

Rogers, C. (1980) *A Way of Being,* Houghton Mifflin, Boston MA.

Rohrbeck, C.A., Ginsburg-Block, M.D., Fantuzzo, J.W., and Miller, T.R. (2003) Peer-assisted learning interventions with elementary school students: A meta-analytic review. *Journal of Educational Psychology,* 95, 2, 240–257.

Rose, S (2004) The new brain sciences, in *The New Brain Sciences: Perils and Promises,* (eds D. Rees and S. Rose), Cambridge University Press, Cambridge, UK, pp. 3–15.

Rose, T.L. (1984) Effects of previewing on the oral reading of main-streamed behaviorally disordered students. *Behavioral Disorders,* 10, 33–39.

Rosenkoetter, S.E., and Fowler, S.A. (1986) Teaching mainstreamed children to manage daily transitions. *Teaching Exceptional Children,* 19, 1, 20–23.

Rosenthal, R., and Jacobson, L. (1968) *Pygmalion in the Classroom,* Holt, Reinhart and Winston, New York.

Roseth, C.J., Johnson, D.W., and Johnson, R.T. (2008) Promoting early adolescents' achievement and peer relationships: The Effects of cooperative, competitive, and individualistic goal structures. *Psychological Bulletin,* 134, 2, 223–246.

Ross, S.M., Smith, L.J., and Casey, J.P. (1999) "Bridging the gap": The effects of the success for all program on elementary school reading achievement as a function of student ethnicity and ability level. *School Effectiveness and School Improvement,* 10, 2, 129–150.

Ross, S.M., Smith, L.J., Slavin, R.E., and Madden, N.A. (1997) Improving the academic success of disadvantaged children: An examination of success for all. *Psychology in the Schools,* 34, 2, 171–180.

Rossbach, M., and Probst, P. (2005) Development and evaluation of an ADHD teacher group training – A pilot study. *Praxis der Kinderpsychologie und Kinderpsychiatrie,* 54, 8, 645–663.

Rosser, D., and Harre, R. (1976) The meaning of "trouble," in *The Process of Schooling,* (eds M. Hammersley and P. Woods) Open University Press, Milton Keynes, pp. 171–178.

Rothi, D.M., Leavey, G., and Best, R. (2008) On the front-line: Teachers as active observers of pupils' mental health. *Teaching and Teacher Education,* 24, 5, 1217–1231.

Royer, E. (1999) Cognitive approaches to the education and training of children with ADHD, in *ADHD: Research, Practice and Opinion,* (eds P. Cooper and K. Bilton), Whurr, London, pp. 158–169.

Runswick-Cole K.A., and Hodge N. (2008) Needs or Right? A challenge to the discourse of special education. Erasmus Mundus Special Educational Needs International Conference, The University of Prague. Prague, Czech Republic.

Russ, J., and Harris, A. (2005) *Success for All: An Evaluation Summary.* Leadership, Policy and Development Unit, Warwick: University of Warwick.

Rutter, M. (1983) School effects on pupil progress: Research findings and policy implications. *Child Development,* 54, 1–29.

Rutter, M. (1991) Childhood experiences and adult psychosocial functioning, in *The Childhood Environment and Adult Disease. Ciba Foundation Symposium no. 156,* (eds G.R. Bock and J. Whelan), Wiley, Chichester, 189–208.

Rutter, M., Maughan, B., Mortimore, P., and Ouston, J. (1979) *Fifteen Thousand Hours: Secondary Schools and Their Effects on Children,* Open Books, London.

Rutter, M., and Smith, D. (eds) (1995) *Psychosocial Disorders in Young People,* Wiley, Chichester.

Rutter, M., Tizard, J., and Whitemore, K. (1971) *Education, Health and Behavior.* Wiley, New York.

Sage, R. (2002) Start talking and stop misbehaving: teaching pupils to communicate, think and act appropriately. *Emotional and Behavioral Difficulties*, 7, 2, 85–96.

Saigh, P.A., and Umar, A.M. (1983) The effects of a good behavior game on the disruptive behavior of Sundanese elementary school students. *Journal of Applied Behavior Analysis*, 16, 3, 339–344.

Sailor, W., Stowe, M.J., Rutherford Turnbull III, H., and Kleinhammer-Tramill, J.P. (2007) A case for adding a social-behavioral standard to standards-based education with schoolwide positive behavior support as its basis. *Remedial and Special Education*, 28, 6, 366–376.

Sanders, M.R. (1999) Triple P-positive parenting program: Towards an empirically validated multilevel parenting and family support strategy for the prevention of behavior and emotional problems in children. *Clinical Child and Family Psychology Review*, 2, 2, 71–90.

Savage, T. (1999) Teaching Self-control through Management and Discipline, Allyn and Bacon, Boston MA.

Schick, A., and Cierpka, M. (2005) Faustlos – Promotion of social-emotional competences in elementary schools and kindergartens. *Psychotherapie Psychosomatik Medizinische Psychologie*, 55, 11, 462–468.

Schick, A., and Cierpka, M. (2006) Evaluation of the Faustlos-curriculum for kindergartens. *Praxis der Kinderpsychologie und Kinderpsychiatrie*, 55, 6, 459–474.

Schiff, M., and Bargil, B. (2004) Children with Behavior Problems: Improving Elementary School Teachers' Skills to Keep These Children in Class. *Children and Youth Services Review*, 26, 2, 207–234.

Schloss, P.J., Harriman, N.E., and Pfefier, K. (1985) Application of a sequential prompt reduction technique to the independent composition performance of behaviorally disordered youth. *Behavioral Disorders*, 11, 17–23.

Schoenfeld, N.A., and Janney, D.M. (2008) Identification and treatment of anxiety in students with emotional or behavioral disorders: A review of the literature. *Education and Treatment of Children*, 31, 4, 583–610.

Schopler, E., Brehm, S.S., Kinsbourne, M., and Reichler, R.J. (1971) Effect of treatment structure on development in autistic children. *Archives of General Psychiatry*, 24, 5, 415–421.

Schostak, J. (1982) *Maladjusted Schooling*, Falmer Press, Lewes, UK.

Scott, S., Spender, Q., Doolan, M. *et al.* (2001) Multicentre controlled trial of parenting groups for childhood antisocial behaviour in clinical practice. *British Medical Journal*, 323, 194–194.

Scott, T.M., McIntyre, J., Liaupsin, C. *et al.* (2005) An examination of the relation between functional behavior assessment and selected intervention strategies with school-based teams. *Journal of Positive Behavior Interventions*, 7, 4, 205–215.

Scruggs, T.E., and Marsing, L. (1987) Teaching test-taking skills to behaviorally disordered students. *Behavioral Disorders*, 13, 240–244.

Sebba, J., and Sachdev, D. (1997) *What Works in Inclusive Education?*, Barnado's, London.

Selvini-Palazzoli, M., Boscolo, L., Ceccin, G., and Prata, G. (1973) *Paradox and Counter Paradox*, Aronson, New York.

Shapiro, E., and Cole, C. (1999) Self-monitoring in assessing children's problems. *Psychological Assessment*, 11, 448–457.

Sharkey, L., and Fitzgerald, M. (2007) Diagnosis and Classification of ADHD in Childhood, in *Handbook of ADHD*, (eds M. Fitzgerald, M. Bellgrove and M. Gill), John Wiley and Sons, Ltd, Chichester, 13–36.

Sharp, R., and Green, A. (1975) *Education and Social Control*, Routledge, London.

Sharp, S., and Davids, E. (2003) Early intervention in behaviour: A study of the Fast-Track programme. *Emotional and Behavioural Difficulties*, 8, 3, 173–188.

Shaw, G. (2007) Restorative practices in Australian schools: Changing relationships, changing culture. *Conflict Resolution Quarterly*, 25, 1, 127–135.

Shaw, O. (1965) *Maladjusted Boys*, Allen and Unwin, London.

Sherman, L.W., and Strang, H. (2007) *Restorative Justice: The Evidence*, Smith Institute, London.

Shevlin, M., Kenny, M., and Loxley, A. (2008) A time of transition: Exploring special educational provision in the Republic of Ireland, *Journal of Research in Special Educational Needs*, 8, 3, 141–152.

Shneiders, J., Drukker, M., Van Der Ende, J. *et al.* (2003) Neighbourhood socio-economic disadvantage and behavioural problems from late childhood into early adolescence, *Journal of Epidemiology and Community Health*, 57, 699–703.

Shores, R., Gunter, P., and Jack, S. (1993) Classroom management strategies: Are they setting events for coercion? *Behavioral Disorders*, 18, 2, 92–102.

Sideridis, G.D., Utley, C., Greenwood, C.R. (1997) Classwide peer tutoring: Effects on the spelling performance and social interactions of students with mild disabilities and their typical peers in an integrated instructional setting. *Journal of Behavioral Education*, 7, 4, 435–462.

Silberman, C. (1971) *Crisis in the Classroom*, Random House, New York.

Simon, T.R., Ikeda, R.M., Smith, E.P. *et al.* (2008) The multisite violence prevention project: Impact of a universal school-based violence prevention program on social-cognitive outcomes. *Prevention Science*, 9, 4, 231–244.

Skidmore, D. (2004) *Inclusion.* Open University Press, Milton Keynes, UK.

Skinner, B.F. (1971) *Beyond Freedom and Dignity.* Knopf, New York.

Skinner, C.H., Cashwell, C.S., and Dunn, M.S. (1996) Independent and interdependent group contingencies: Smoothing the rough waters. *Special Services in the Schools*, 12, 61–78.

Skinner, C.H., Neddenriep, C.E., Robinson, S.L. *et al.* (2002) Altering educational environments through positive peer reporting: Prevention and remediation of social problems associated with behavior disorders. *Psychology in the Schools*, 39, 2, 191–202.

Slavin, R.E. (2002) Mounting evidence supports the achievement effects of Success for All. *Phi Delta Kappan*, 83, 6, 469–480.

Slavin, R.E. (2004) Built to last: Long-term maintenance of Success for All. *Remedial and Special Education*, 25, 1, 61–67.

Slavin, R.E., Chamberlain, A., and Daniels, C. (2007) Preventing reading failure. *Educational Leadership*, 65, 2, 22–27.

Slavin, R.E., Cheung, A., Groff, C., and Lake, C. (2008) Effective reading programs for middle and high schools: A best-evidence synthesis. *Reading Research Quarterly*, 43, 3, 290–322.

Slavin, R.E., and Madden, N.A. (2001) Research on achievement outcomes of success for all: A summary and response to critics. *Phi Delta Kappan*, 82, 1, 38–66.

Slavin, R.E., and Madden, N.A. (2006) Reducing the gap: Success for All and the achievement of African American students. *Journal of Negro Education*, 75, 3, 389–400.

Slee, R. (1995) *Changing Theories and Practices of Discipline*, Falmer Press, London.

Slough, N.M., and McMahon, R.J. (2008) Preventing serious conduct problems in school-age youth: The Fast Track program. *Cognitive and Behavioral Practice*, 15, 1, 3–17.

Smith, D. (2006) *School Experience and Delinquency at Ages 13 to 16*, University of Edinburgh, Centre for Law and Society, Edinburgh.

Smith, D., and Tomlinson, S. (1989) *The School Effect: A Study of Multi-Racial Comprehensives*, Routledge, London.

Smith, E.P., Gorman-Smith, D., Quinn, W.H *et al.* (2004) Community-based multiple family groups to prevent and reduce violent and aggressive behavior: The GREAT Families Program. *American Journal of Preventive Medicine*, 26, suppl. 1, 39–47.

Snyder, J., Cramer, A., Afrank, J., and Patterson, G.R. (2005) The contributions of ineffective discipline and parental hostile attributions of child misbehavior to the development of conduct problems at home and school. *Developmental Psychology*, 41, 1, 30–41.

Solomon, D., Battistich, V., Il-Kim, D., and Watson, M. (1997b) Teacher practices associated with students' sense of the classroom as a community. *Social Psychology of Education*, 1, 235–267.

Solomon, D., Battistich, V., Watson, M. *et al.* (2000) A six district study of educational change: direct and mediated effects of the child development project. *Social Psychology of Education*, 4, 3–51.

Solomon, D., Watson, M., Battistisch, V., Schaps, E., and Delucchi, K. (1997a) Creating classrooms that students experience as communities. *American Journal of Community Psychology*, 24, 6, 719–748.

Solomon, Y., and Rogers, C. (2001) Motivational patterns in disaffected school students: Insights from pupil referral unit clients. *British Educational Research Journal*, 27, 3, 330–345.

Sonuga-Barke, E.J.S., Thompson, M., Daley, D., and Laver-Bradbury, C. (2004) Parent training for attention deficit/hyperactivity disorder: Is it as effective when delivered as routine rather than as specialist care? *British Journal of Clinical Psychology*, 43, 4, 449–457.

Sørlie, M.., and Ogden, T. (2007) Immediate impacts of PALS: A schoolwide multi-level programme targeting behaviour problems in elementary school. *Scandinavian Journal of Educational Research*, 51, 5, 471–492.

Stallard, P., Simpson, N., Anderson, S. *et al.* (2007) The FRIENDS emotional health programme: Initial findings from a school-based project. *Child and Adolescent Mental Health*, 12, 1, 32–37.

Stern, D., Raby, M., and Dayton, C. (1992) *Career Academies: Partnerships for Reconstructing American High Schools*, Jossey-Bass, San Francisco.

Stern, D., and Wing, J.Y. (2004) Is there Solid Evidence of Positive Effects for High School Students? *High School Reform: Using Evidence to Improve Policy and Practice*, January 22–23, 2004, Career Academies Support Network, University of California at Berkeley, pp. 1–36.

Stevenson, .P,(2001) *Billy*, Harper Collins, New York.

Stewart, S.C., and Evans, W.H. (1997) Setting the stage for success: Assessing the instructional environment. *Preventing School Failure*, 41, 2, 53–56.

Stinchcomb, J.B., Bazemore, G., and Riestenberg, N. (2006) Beyond zero tolerance: Restoring justice in secondary schools. *Youth Violence and Juvenile Justice*, 4, 2, 123–147.

Strayhorn, J.R. (2002a) Self-control: Theory and research. *Journal of the American Academy of Child and Adolescent Psychiatry*, 41, 1, 7–16.

Strayhorn, J.R. (2002b) Self-Control: Toward Systematic Training Programs. *Journal of the American Academy of Child and Adolescent Psychiatry*, 41, 1, 17–27.

Strayhorn, J.M., and Weidman, C.S. (1989) Reduction of attention deficit and internalizing symptoms in preschoolers through parent–child interaction training. *Journal of the American Academy of Child and Adolescent Psychiatry*, 28, 6, 888–896.

Sugai, G., and Horner, R.R. (2002) The evolution of discipline practices: School-wide positive behavior supports. *Child and Family Behavior Therapy*, 24, 1&2, 23–50.

Sugai, G., and Horner, R.R. (2006) A promising approach for expanding and sustaining school-wide positive behavior support. *School Psychology Review*, 35, 2, 245–259.

Sugai, G., Lewis-Palmer, T., Todd, A., and Horner, R.H. (2001) *School-wide Evaluation Tool*, University of Oregon, Eugene.

Sutherland, K.S., Alder, N., and Gunter, P.L. (2003) The effect of varying rates of opportunities to respond to academic requests on the classroom behavior of students with EBD. *Journal of Emotional and Behavioral Disorders*, 11, 4, 239–248.

Sutherland, K.S., Wehby, J.H., and Copeland, S.R. (2000) Effect of varying rates of behavior-specific praise on the on-task behavior of students with EBD. *Journal of Emotional and Behavioral Disorders*, 8, 1, 2–26.

Sutton Trust, (2008) *Social Mobility*, The Sutton Trust www.suttontrust.com/reports/social-mobility.pdf (no longer available).

Sutton Trust, (2010) *Education and Social Mobility in England*, London, The Sutton Trust http://www.suttontrust.com/reports/Education_mobility_in_england.pdf (accessed September 28, 2010).

Svedin, C.G., and Wadsby, M. (2000) Day school treatment in Sweden: A 4-year follow-up study of maladjusted pupils. *Children and Youth Services Review*, 22, 6, 465–486.

Szatz, T. (1960) *The Myth of Mental Illness*, Harper and Row, New York.

Tannock, R. (1998) AD/HD: Advances in cognitive, neurobiological and genetic research, *Journal of Child Psychology and Psychiatry*, 39, 1, 65–99.

Tattum, D. (1982) *Disruptive Pupils in Schools and Units*, John Wiley and Sons, Chichester, UK.

Taylor, M. (2003) *Going Round in Circles: Implementing and Learning from Circle Time*, NFER, Slough.

Taylor, V.L., Cornwell, D.D., and Riley, M.T. (1984) Home-based contingency management programs that teachers can use. *Psychology in the Schools*, 21, 3, 368.

T.E.S. (2005) Editorial, October 14.

Thomas, G., and Vaughan, M. (2006) *Inclusive Education: Readings and Reflections*, Open University Press, Buckingham.

Tingstrom, D.H., Sterling-Turner, H.E., and Wilczynski, S.M. (2006) The Good Behavior Game: 1969–2002, *Behavior Modification*, 30, 2, 225–253.

Todd, A.W., Campbell, A.L., Meyer, G.G., and Horner, R.H. (2008) The effects of a targeted intervention to reduce problem behaviors: Elementary school implementation of check in-check out. *Journal of Positive Behavior Interventions*, 10, 1, 46–55.

Tolan, P.H. (2004) Lessons learned in the Multisite Violence Prevention Project collaboration – Big questions require large efforts. *American Journal of Preventive Medicine*, 26(, suppl. 1, 62–71.

Tolan, P.H., Guerra, N.G., and Kendall, P.C. (1995a) Introduction to special section: Prediction and prevention of antisocial behavior in children and adolescents. *Journal of Consulting and Clinical Psychology*, 63, 4, 515–517.

Tolan, P.H., Guerra, N.G., and Kendall, P.C. (1995b) A developmental-ecological perspective on antisocial behavior in children and adolescents: Toward a unified risk and intervention framework. *Journal of Consulting and Clinical Psychology*, 63, 4, 579–584.

Tolan, P.H., and McKay, M.M. 1996. Preventing serious antisocial behavior in inner-city children: An empirically based family intervention program. *Family Relations*, 45, 2, 148–155.

Tomlinson, S. (1982) *A Sociology of Special Education*, Routledge, London.

Topping, K.J. (2005) Trends in peer learning. *Educational Psychology*, 25, 6, 631–645.

Travell, C., and Visser, J (2006) "ADHD does bad stuff to you": young people's and parents' experiences and perceptions of ADHD. *Emotional and Behavioural Difficulties*, 11, 3, 205–216.

Trout, A.L., Nordness, P.D., Pierce, C.D., and Epstein, M.H. (2003a) Research on the academic status of children with emotional and behavioral disorders: A review of the literature from 1961 to 2000. *Journal of Emotional and Behavioral Disorders*, 11, 4, 198–210.

Twemlow, S.W., and Fonagy, P. (2005) The prevalence of teachers who bully students in schools with differing levels of behavioral problems. *American Journal of Psychiatry*, 162, 12, 2387–2389.

Tymms, P., and Merrell, C. (2000) *Success for All Evaluation Report*. University of Durham, Durham.

Uline, C., and Tschannen-Moran, M. (2008) The walls speak: The interplay of quality facilities, school climate, and student achievement. *Journal of Educational Administration*, 46, 1, 55–73.

Umbreit, J., Lane, K.L., and Dejud, C. (2004) Improving classroom behavior by modifying task difficulty: Effects of increasing the difficulty of too-easy tasks. *Journal of Positive Behavior Interventions*, 6, 1, 13–20.

Valdez, C.R., Carlson, C., and Zanger, D. (2005) Evidence-based parent training and family interventions for school behavior change. *School Psychology Quarterly*, 20, 4, 403–433.

Van Acker, R., Boreson, L., Gable, R.A., and Potterton, T. (2005) Are we on the right course? Lessons learned about current FBA/BIP practices in schools. *Journal of Behavioral Education*, 14, 1, 35–56.

Van De Weil, N.M.H., Matthys, W., Cohen-Kettenis, P., and Van Engeland, H. (2003) Application of the Utrecht Coping Power Program and care as usual to children with disruptive behaviour disorders in out-patient clinics: A comparison study of cost and course of treatment. *Behavior Therapy*, 34, 4, 421–436.

Van Lier, P.A.C., Muthen, B.O., Van Der Sar, R.M., and Crijnens, A.A.M. (2004) Preventing disruptive behavior in elementary schoolchildren: Impact of a universal classroom-based intervention. *Journal of Consulting and Clinical Psychology*, 72, 3, 467–478.

Van Schoiack-Edstrom, L., Frey, K.S., and Beland, K. (2002) Changing adolescents' attitudes about relational and physical aggression: An early evaluation of a school-based intervention. *School Psychology Review*, 31, 2, 201–216.

Vaughn, B.J. (2006) The wave of SWPBS: Who is left behind? *Research and Practice for Persons with Severe Disabilities*, 31, 1, 66–69.

Veerkamp, M.B., Kamps, D.M., and Cooper, L. (2007) The effects of classwide peer tutoring on the reading achievement of urban middle school students. *Education and Treatment of Children*, 30, 2, 21–51.

Visser, J. (1997) Response to Cooper, P. The myth of the myth of attention deficit/hyperactivity disorder: Towards a constructive perspective, *British Psychological Society Education Section Review*, 21, 1, 15–16.

Vitaro, F., and Tremblay, R.E. (1994) Impact of a prevention program on aggressive children's friendships and social adjustment. *Journal of Abnormal Child Psychology*, 22, 4, 457–475.

Von Bertalannfy, L. (1968) *General Systems Theory: Foundations, Development, Applications*, Brazillier, New York.

Vygotsky, L. (1987–1999) *The Collected Works*, Plenum, London and New York.

Walberg, H.J., and Greenberg, R.C. (1999) Educators should require evidence. *Phi Delta Kappan*, 81, 2, 132–135.

Walker, H., Colvin, G., and Ramsey, E. (1995) *Antisocial Behavior in Schools: Strategies and Best Practices*, Brooks/Cole, Pacific Grove, CA.

Walker, H., Ramsey, E., and Gresham, F.M. (2004) *Antisocial Behavior in School: Evidence-based Practices*, 2nd edn, Wadsworth, Cengage Learning, Belmont, CA.

Walker, H.M., Horner, R.H., Sugai, G. *et al.* (1996) Integrated approaches to preventing antisocial behavior patterns among school-age children and youth. *Journal of Emotional and Behavioral Disorders*, 4, 4, 194–209.

Walker, H., and Walker, J. (1991) *Coping with Noncompliance in the Classroom: A Positive Approach for Teachers*, Pro-Ed, Austin TX.

Waller, R. (2006) *Fostering Child and Adolescent Mental Health in the Classroom*, Sage, Thousand Oaks, CA.

Wang, M.C., and Haertel, G.D. (1995) Educational resilience, in *Handbook of Special Education: Research and Practice*, (eds M.C. Wang, M.C. Reynolds and H.J. Walberg), Pergamon, New York.

Wang, M.C., Haertel, G.D., and Walberg, H.J. (1993) Synthesis of research: What helps students learn ? *Educational Leadership*, 51, 4, 74–79.

Wannarka, R., and Ruhl, R. (2008) Seating arrangements that promote positive academic and behavioural outcomes: a review of literature. *Support for Learning*, 23, 2, 89–93.

Ware, L. (1998) I kind of wonder if we're fooling ourselves, in *From Them to Us: an International Study of Inclusion in Education*, (eds T. Booth and M. Ainscow), Routledge, London, pp. 21–42.

Wassef, A., Mason, G., Collins, M.L. *et al.* (1996) In search of effective programs to address students' emotional distress and behavioral problems part III: Student assessment of school-based support groups. *Adolescence*, 31, 121, 1–16.

Wasserman, T.H. (1977) The utilization of a clock-light cueing device to signal group progress towards reinforcement in a classroom setting. *Psychology in the Schools*, 14, 4, 471–479.

Watson, J.B. (1924) *Behaviorism*, Norton, New York.

Waxman, H.C., Grey, G.P., and Padron, Y.N. (2004) *Review of Research on Educational Resilience. A Research Report*, Center for Research on Education, Diversity and Excellence, Santa Cruz, CA.

Weare, K., and Gray, C. (2003) *What Works in Developing Children's Emotional and Social Competence and Wellbeing?* DfES, London.

Wearmouth, J., McKinney, R., and Glynn, T. (2007) Restorative justice in schools: A New Zealand example. *Educational Research*, 49, 1, 37–49.

Webster-Stratton, C. (1984) Randomized trial of two parent-training programs for families with conduct-disordered children. *Journal of Consulting and Clinical Psychology*, 52, 4, 666–678.

Webster-Stratton, C. (1990) Long-term follow-up of families with young conduct problem children: From preschool to grade school. *Journal of Clinical Child Psychology*, 19, 2, 144–149.

Webster-Stratton, C. (1992) Individually administered videotape parent training: "who benefits?" *Cognitive Therapy and Research*, 16, 1, 31–52.

Webster-Stratton, C. (1994) Advancing videotape parent training: A comparison study. *Journal of Consulting and Clinical Psychology*, 62, 3, 583–593.

Webster-Stratton, C., Hollinsworth, T., and Kolpacoff, M. (1989) The long-term effectiveness and clinical significance of three cost-effective training programs for families with conduct-problem children. *Journal of Consulting and Clinical Psychology*, 57, 4, 550–553.

Webster-Stratton, C., Jamila Reid, M., and Stoolmiller, M. (2008) Preventing conduct problems and improving school readiness: Evaluation of the Incredible Years Teacher and Child Training Programs in high-risk schools. *Journal of Child Psychology and Psychiatry and Allied Disciplines*, 49, 5, 471–488.

Webster-Stratton, C., Kolpacoff, M., and Hollinsworth, T. (1988) Self-administered video-tape therapy for families with conduct-problem children: Comparison with two cost-effective treatments and a control group. *Journal of Consulting and Clinical Psychology*, 56, 4, 558–566.

Webster-Stratton, C., and Reid, M.J. (2003) Treating conduct problems and strengthening social and emotional competence in young children: The Dina Dinosaur treatment program. *Journal of Emotional and Behavioral Disorders*, 11, 3, 130–143.

Webster-Stratton, C., and Reid, M.J. (2004) Strengthening social and emotional competence in young children - The foundation for early school readiness and success: Incredible years classroom social skills and problem-solving curriculum. *Infants and Young Children*, 17, 2, 96–113.

Webster-Stratton, C., Reid, M.J., and Hammond, M. (2001) Preventing conduct problems, promoting social competence: A parent and teacher training partnership in Head Start. *Journal of Clinical Child and Adolescent Psychology*, 30, 3, 283–302.

Webster-Stratton, C., Reid, M.J., and Hammond, M. (2004) Treating Children with Early-Onset Conduct Problems: Intervention Outcomes for Parent, Child, and Teacher Training. *Journal of Clinical Child and Adolescent Psychology*, 33, 1, 105–124.

Wehby, J.H., Falk, K.B., Barton-Arwood, S. *et al.* (2003) The impact of comprehensive reading instruction on the academic and social behavior of students with emotional and behavioral disorders. *Journal of Emotional and Behavioral Disorders*, 11, 4, 225–238.

Wehlage, G.G., Rutter, R.A., Smith, G.A., Lesko, N., and Fernandez, R. (1989) *Reducing the Risk. Schools as Communities of Support*, Falmer Press, London.

Weinstein, C.S. (1992) Designing the instructional environment: Focus on seating. Proceedings of Selected Research and Development Presentations at the Convention of the Association for Educational Communications and Technology, Association for Educational Communications and Technology.

Weisz, J.R., Hawley, K.M., and Jensen Doss, A. (2004) Empirically tested psychotherapies for youth internalizing and externalizing problems and disorders. *Child and Adolescent Psychiatric Clinics of North America*, 13, 4, 729–815.

Werner, E., and Smith, R. (1988) *Vulnerable but Invincible: A Longitudinal Study of Resilient Children and Youth*, Adams, Bannister and Cox, New York.

Werner, E., and Smith, R. (1992) *Overcoming the Odds: High-Risk Children from Birth to Adulthood*, Cornell University Press, New York.

Wheldall, K. (ed.) (1987) *The Behaviourist in the Classroom*, Allen and Unwin, London.

Wheldall, K., and Merrett, F. (1984) *Positive Teaching: The Behavioural Approach*, Allen and Unwin, London.

Williams, D.D., Yanchar, S.C., Jensen, L.C., and Lewis, C. (2003) Character education in a public high school: A multi-year inquiry into unified studies. *Journal of Moral Education*, 32, 1, 3–33.

Williams, H., Bonathan, M., Daniels, A. (1997) *Conclusions of the Study. New Outlooks Project*, Birmingham Education Department, Birmingham, UK.

Willis, P. (1977) *Learning to Labour*, Saxon House, Farnborough.

Wills, D. (1960) *Throw Away Thy Rod*, Gollancz, London.

Wilson, S.J., Lipsey, M.W. (2006) The Effects of School-based Social Information Processing Interventions on Aggressive Behavior: Part 1 : Universal Programs. Nashville TN. *Center for Evaluation Research and Methodology*.

Wiltz, N.W., and Klein, E.L. (2001) What do you do in child care? Children's perceptions of high and low quality classrooms. *Early Childhood Research Quarterly*, 16, 2, 209–236.

Wolf, M., Risley, T.R., Johnston, M. *et al.* (1967) Application of operant conditioning procedures to the behavior problems of an autistic child: A follow-up and extension. *Behaviour Research and Therapy*, 5, 2, 103–112.

Wolfe, D.A., Kelly, J.A., and Drabman, R.S. (1981) "Beat the buzzer": A method for training an abusive mother to decrease recurrent child conflicts. *Journal of Clinical Child Psychology*, 10, 2, 114–116.

Wolfgang, C. (1996) *The Three Faces of Discipline for the Elementary School Teacher: Empowering the Teacher and Students*, Allyn and Bacon, Boston MA.

Wood, C., and Caulier-Grice, J. (2006) *Fade or Flourish: How Primary Schools can Build on Children's Early Progress*, The Social Market Foundation, London.

World Health Organization (WHO) (1990) International Classification of Diseases, 10th edn, WHO, Geneva.

Young, M. (1971) *Knowledge and Control*, Macmillan, London.

Youth Justice Board for England and Wales (2004) *National Evaluation of the Restorative Justice in Schools Programme*, Youth Justice Board for England and Wales, London.

Zellman, G.L., and Waterman, J.M. (1998) Understanding the impact of parent school involvement on children's educational outcomes. *Journal of Educational Research*, 91, 6, 370–380.

Zentall, S.S. (1995) Modifying classroom tasks and environments, in (ed. S. Goldstein), *Understanding and Managing Children's Classroom Behavior*. John Wiley and Sons, Inc, New York, pp. 356–374.

Zentall, S.S., and Javorsky, J. (2007) Professional development for teachers of students with ADHD and characteristics of ADHD. *Behavioral Disorders*, 32, 2, 78–93.

Zentall, S.S. and Meyer, M.J. (1987) Self-regulation of stimulation for ADD-H children during the reading and vigilance task performance, *Journal of Abnormal Child Psychology*, 15, 519–536.

Zentall, S.S., and Smith, Y.N. (1992) Assessment and validation of the learning and behavioral style preferences of hyperactive and comparison children. *Learning and Individual Differences*, 4, 25–41.

Zins, J.E., and Elias, M.J. (2007) Social and emotional learning: Promoting the development of all students. *Journal of Educational and Psychological Consultation*, 17, 2/3, 233–255.

Zonnevylle-Bender, M.J.S., Matthys, W., Van De Weil, N.M.H., and Lochman, J.E. (2007) Preventative effects of treatment of disruptive behavior disorder in middle childhood on substance use and delinquent behavior. *Journal of the American Academy of Child and Adolescent Psychiatry*, 46, 1, 33–39.

Index

Note: Page numbers in italics refer to tables.